The Sociolinguistics of Writing

Edinburgh Sociolinguistics

Series Editors:
Paul Kerswill (Lancaster University)
Joan Swann (Open University)

Volumes available in the series:
Paul Baker, *Sociolinguistics and Corpus Linguistics*
Scott F. Kiesling, *Linguistic Variation and Change*
Theresa Lillis, *The Sociolinguistics of Writing*

Forthcoming titles include:
Kevin Watson, *English Sociophonetics*

Visit the Edinburgh Sociolinguistics website at www.euppublishing.com/series/
edss

The Sociolinguistics of Writing

Theresa Lillis

EDINBURGH
University Press

© Theresa Lillis, 2013

Edinburgh University Press Ltd
22 George Square, Edinburgh EH8 9LF

www.euppublishing.com

Typeset in 10/12pt Adobe Garamond
by Servis Filmsetting Ltd, Stockport, Cheshire, and
printed and bound in the United States of America

A CIP record for this book is available from the British Library

ISBN 978 0 7486 3748 5 (hardback)
ISBN 978 0 7486 3750 8 (paperback)
ISBN 978 0 7486 3749 2 (webready PDF)
ISBN 978 0 7486 7751 1 (epub)
ISBN 978 0 7486 7750 4 (Amazon ebook)

Contents

Figures

Tables

Author's acknowledgements

Over the period of writing this book I have had many different kinds of support from many people.

` I would like to thank the ESCR (RES-063-27-0263), who awarded me a research fellowship which enabled me to spend an extended period of time on research and writing, and also my institution The Open University for enabling this period of leave. Thanks to all at the Open University for advice, encouragement and inspiration: colleagues in the Centre for Language and Communication, with particular thanks to Joan Swann, Janet Maybin and Barbara Mayor for always being willing to discuss ideas however large or small; and colleagues in the monthly Academic Literacies discussion forum- Sally Baker Corinne Boz, Marianne Cole, Lynn Coleman, Robin Goodfellow, Mary Lea, Maria Leedham, Jenny McMullan, Lucy Rai, Jackie Tuck- for so many rigorous, intense, funny and insightful discussions.

I would like to express my warmest appreciation to colleagues near and far who have shared their time, their thinking and their academic friendship with me over the years; in particular, Manoel Correa, Mary Jane Curry, Isabelle Delchambre, Tiane Donohue, Bruce Horner, Roz Ivanič, Mary Ellan Kerans, Min Zhan Lu, Carolyn McKinney, Ana Moreno, Mary Scott, Brian Street, Lucia Thesen, Joan Turner.

My heartfelt gratitude goes to Carol Johns-Mackenzie for helping to prepare the manuscript and for her endless cheerfulness and patience.

And. My love to Mum, Fin, Dee and Jim.

Y como siempre a Guillermo, Liam y Carmen – juntos vamos inventando familia y vida. . . .

Publisher's acknowledgements

The author and publishers would like to thank the following for kind permission to use copyright material:

Figure 2.2: Wilson, A. (2003), 'Researching in the third space: locating, claiming and valuing the research domain', in S. Goodman et al. (eds), *Language, Literacy and Education: A Reader*, Stoke on Trent: Trentham Books, pp. 293–307.

Figure 2.6 (a, b, c, d): Scollon, R. and S. Scollon (2003), *Discourses in Place. Language in the Material World*, London: Routledge.

Figure 3.1: Herring, S. C., I. Kouper, L. A. Scheidt and E. Wright, E. (2004), 'Women and children last: The discursive construction of weblogs', in L. J. Gurak, S. Antonijevic, L. Johnson, C. Ratcliff and J. Reyman (eds), *Into the Blogosphere: Rhetoric, Community, and Culture of Weblogs*, available at http://blog.lib.umn.edu/blogosphere/women and children.html (accessed 30 June 2011).

Figure 3.2: Swales, J. (2004), *Research Genres: Explorations and Applications*, Cambridge: Cambridge University Press, p. 230.

Figure 3.5: Moore, T. (2010), 'The "processes" of learning: on the use of Halliday's transitivity in academic skills advising', in C. Coffin, T. Lillis and K. O'Halloran (eds), *Applied Linguistics Methods. A Reader*, London: Routledge, pp. 52–71.

Figure 3.6: Pietikäinen, S. and H. Kelly-Holmes (2011), 'The local political economy of languages in a Sámi tourism destination: authenticity and mobility in the labelling of souvenirs', *Journal of Sociolinguistics*, 15: 3, 323–46.

Figure 3.10: Chouliaraki, L. and N. Fairclough (1999), *Discourse in Late Modernity. Rethinking Critical Discourse Analysis*, Edinburgh: Edinburgh University Press, p. 11.

Figure 3.11: Baker, C. (2010), *Sociolinguistics and Corpus Linguistics*, Edinburgh: Edinburgh University Press.

Figure 4.3: Ivanič, R., R. Edwards, D. Barton, M. Martin-Jones, Z. Fowler, B. Hughes, G. Mannion, K. Miller, C. Satchwell and J. Smith (2009), *Improving Learning in College. Rethinking Literacies across the Curriculum*, London: Routledge.

Figure 4.5: Pelli, D. G. and C. Bigelow (2009a), 'A writing revolution', available at http://seedmagazine.com/content/article/a_writing_revolution/ (accessed 20 Nov. 2011).

Figure 5.1: Bell, A. (1991), *The Language of News Media*, Oxford: Blackwell.

Figure 5.2: Pontille, D. (2010), 'Updating a biomedical database: writing, reading and invisible contribution', in D. Barton and U. Papen (eds), *The Anthropology of Writing*, London: Continuum, pp. 47–66.

Figure 5.11: Berkenkotter, B. and C. Hanganu-Bresch (2011), 'Lunatic asylum occult genres and the certification of madness in the 19th century', *Written Communication*, 28: 220–50.

Figure 6.3: Lillis, T. (2001), *Student Writing: Access, Regulation, Desire*, London: Routledge.

Figure 7.4e: Fairclough, N. (2001), *Language and Power*, 2nd edn, Harlow: Pearson.

Table 3.1: Pratt, C. and C. Pratt (1995), 'Comparative content analysis of food and nutrition advertisements, *Ebony*, *Essence* and *Ladies' Home Journal*, *Journal of Nutrition Education*, 27: 1, 11–18.

Table 3.2: Hyland, K. (2002), 'Authority and invisibility: authorial identity in academic writing', *Journal of Pragmatics*, 34: 1091–112.

Every effort has been made to trace copyright holders but this may not have been possible in all cases.

In loving memory of Noel Lillis 1925–2011, *'Lonely I wander . . .'*

Chapter 1

Writing in sociolinguistics

INTRODUCTION

Whilst the primary concern of sociolinguistics is the relationship between language and society, 'language' has to a large extent, either implicitly or by design, been understood as spoken language. In this book I question this emphasis with particular reference to *writing*. I seek to illustrate how the study of writing not only merits a place within sociolinguistics but serves to throw into critical relief core notions within sociolinguistics which continue to need careful re-examination; these include the continued *binary framing* of spoken and written language that casts a shadow over approaches to all modes, materialities and technologies of communication; the normative approach towards *functions* of language use; tensions surrounding the stated sociolinguistic goal of description, rather than prescription, which is much discussed but takes on a particular – and perhaps more hidden – significance when exploring writing.

The chapter summarises the key principles driving sociolinguistics and argues that, whilst these principles are commonly used to justify the study of spoken language, they apply equally to the study of writing. Writing, in short, is a sociolinguistic issue. This chapter:

- outlines core principles of sociolinguistics
- discusses the different ways in which writing has been, and continues to be, positioned in 'mainstream' sociolinguistics – as of limited interest, as secondary to spoken language and as an acceptable site for a strongly normative stance on writing, or to use Cameron's phrase, 'closet prescriptivism' (Cameron 2012: 9)
- argues for the legitimacy of the study of writing within sociolinguistics both as a disciplinary goal and as the means by which sociolinguistics can contribute to wider debates about writing
- introduces the rest of the chapters and outlines how my specific interests in writing have shaped the contents of this book.

SPOKEN LANGUAGE AS THE OBJECT OF THE
SOCIOLINGUISTIC GAZE

There are always dangers in characterising what a particular field of study is, what it does or doesn't do or what it holds as its legitimate objects of inquiry. Fields are dynamic and are constantly changing at the level of objects of inquiry, methodologies and epistemologies. But it is fair to say that spoken language has been and continues to be overwhelmingly the empirical object of gaze in sociolinguistics.[1]

This position is illustrated in the opening to a well-used introductory text which reflects a position running through sociolinguistic texts and overviews:

> Sociolinguists study the relationship between language and society. They are interested in explaining why we speak differently in different social contexts, and they are concerned with identifying the social functions of language and the ways it is used to convey social meaning.
>
> (Holmes 2001: 1)

As in other texts, the broad disciplinary interest is made clear, that of the study of the relationship between language and society. And whilst the explicit reference to speech could be construed as being used superordinately here to refer to *language use* in all its forms, a trawl through this and other texts indicates that the empirical object at the heart of this study of the relationship between language and society has been – and continues to be – spoken language. This centrality of speech to the sociolinguist's gaze has not fundamentally shifted in fifty years. In a recent introductory reader of thirty-two chapters (Meyerhoff and Schleef 2010), twenty-eight explicitly and centrally focus on spoken data, and whilst four acknowledge written data or written practices as part of the data analysed, no chapter concerns itself centrally with writing. Consider also the following comments from the Introduction to a recent edited collection by Coupland and Jaworski (2009: 5) where they state: 'we are assuming that speech rather than writing is sociolinguists' main concern'.

In justifying this focus on spoken language, Coupland and Jaworski use the 'primacy argument' – widespread in sociolinguistics – that is to say that speech has: 'primacy over writing in biological, cognitive, historical and developmental terms' (Coupland and Jaworski 2009: 5). The primacy argument – that speech comes first chronologically in individual lifespan, human development and the histories of societies – is further enhanced by a claim to the greater or more profound social significance of speech, particularly with regard to identity: 'Speech is central in socialising processes and important in the formulation and expression of people's social identities and relationships' (Coupland and Jaworski 2009: 5).

Whilst Coupland and Jaworksi do conclude their brief overview of the primacy argument by saying it would be a mistake to restrict the study of 'language' in sociolinguistics to the study of speech alone and point to the rise in multimodal frameworks which are sensitive to the interplay between visual and spoken communicative modes, the spoken is clearly claimed as the central legitimate object of study. In similar vein, in their introductory text on sociolinguistics, Mesthrie et al. (2009: 27) acknowledge that 'it is an oversight to exclude a focus on writing in exploring the "linguistic ecology" of modern societies' but admit that their book does not include a focus on writing.

In a field dedicated to exploring the relationship between language and society, the primacy argument continues to provide a strong justification for the emphasis on *spoken* language. In addition, several specific geo-historical warrants and drivers are often cited in the move to legitimise the focus on everyday speech as central to the establishment of sociolinguistics as a field of inquiry. These include:

1. The need to record fast disappearing languages (under threat for economic, political and cultural reasons) including North American languages at the turn of the twentieth century and rural languages/varieties in Europe which were threatened by changing demographics and urbanisation (see for examples, Boas 1911; Trudgill 1974).
2. The educational imperative in large urban areas to explore the relationship between everyday language use and schooled language and 'literacy', in particular in relation to the underachievement of pupils from working-class backgrounds (illustrated well in work by for example Hymes 1974 and Labov 1970).
3. The availability of relatively inexpensive technology whereby recordings of talk were made possible (Labov 1966) and which, whilst taken for granted today, enabled researchers to move from a focus on language as represented in written texts to actual recordings of speech and thus enabled spoken language to become 'studyable'.[2]

The importance of studying spoken language in a field dedicated to exploring the relationship between language and society is clearly self-evident. However, it is equally important to explore other communicative practices and the goal of this book is to focus on one (as we shall see, multimodal) practice: writing. In order to justify this focus, it's worth considering the key principles underpinning sociolinguistics and in this way question any assumption that such principles necessarily demand a focus on spoken language, to the exclusion of writing.

KEY PRINCIPLES IN SOCIOLINGUISTICS

The importance of the social

As the *socio* attached to linguistics indicates, the social is central to the study of language in sociolinguistics. Sociolinguistics works with the social in a wide range of ways, most obviously at a micro level (the language of immediate situations, people and contexts) and/or macro level (theorising the relationship between language, social systems and ideologies). In emphasising and engaging with the thorny question of 'the social', sociolinguistics defines itself in contradistinction to the field of linguistics: whereas linguistics looks at language through the lenses of system, structure or grammar, sociolinguistics sets out to pay attention to context, users, functions (see discussions in Paulston and Tucker (eds) 2003, particularly chapters by Calvert and Shuy). The distinction between the two fields (or branches of study) is reflected in the oft-quoted difference in the positions of Chomsky and Hymes, the latter conventionally referred to as a 'founding father' of sociolinguistics. Chomsky's theoretical interest in a universal grammar of language is built explicitly on an idealisation of language use and its users, famously encapsulated in a widely quoted comment: 'Linguistic theory is concerned primarily with an ideal speaker-listener, in a completely homogeneous speech-community, who knows its language perfectly' (Chomsky 1965: 3). Chomsky argued that linguistic *competence* ('native' speakers' implicit knowledge of the grammatical rules governing their language) rather than *performance* (actual language usage, that is what people actually say and hear with all the errors, false starts, unfinished sentences) was the proper object of linguistic inquiry. Hymes was highly critical of a theory that explicitly set out to ignore the impact of social context on the language actually used (Hymes 1968, 1971, 1974). He categorically challenged the view that performance was of lesser or secondary importance or academic interest, by, not least, juxtaposing the word 'communicative' with 'competence' to emphasise that the ability to use a language well involves knowing (either explicitly or implicitly) how to use language appropriately in any given context and is not based – as Chomsky implied – solely on grammatical knowledge. Hymes argued that 'performance data', the messy, apparently chaotic language that we use in everyday encounters, should indeed be a legitimate focus of study.[3] Whilst spoken language is not the only performance data referred to by Hymes, spoken language is the pre-eminent empirical focus in Hymes's work. This empirical work has been widely taken up in subsequent studies of spoken language, but more recently his theorising and work in general is being seen as equally foundational for the study of writing (see for example Blommaert 2008).

The study of everyday language in social context therefore is a defining principle of sociolinguistics but, whilst the 'language' studied has primarily been spoken language, there is clearly no reason to justify the exclusion of other communicative modes, including writing, the topic of this book. Exactly how the 'social' or 'social context' is defined, as already indicated, is a hotly contested debate both empirically (what we can actually observe) and theoretically (how we make sense of what we observe), a key tension being between the amount of scholarly attention that should be directed to language use or to society (or aspects of society). There have been some attempts at establishing clear demarcations in this respect, notably Fasold's distinctions (1984, 1990) between orientations that foreground language and linguistic categorisations (what language can tell us about society) and orientations that foreground society and sociological categorisations (what society can tell us about language). But in general scholars have not been convinced by such demarcations and there continues to be lively debate around the 'social' in sociolinguistics, including specific questions about the following: the nature of communicative practice as both individual and socially structured activity; the nature of communities and how these can be conceptualised; power and agency and how these are played out in interaction; tensions between societal norms and individual or collective creativity;

issues of access and participation in linguistic and semiotic processes, locally and globally. These are just some of the debates that continue to figure in sociolinguistics and are picked up across this book with specific reference to writing.

The empirical study of naturally occurring language

A second distinguishing feature of sociolinguistics as a field, layered on, and related to the importance of getting at the social dimension of language use, is a commitment to the empirical study of 'naturally occurring' language. In contrast to claims made on the basis of either abstractions of language or 'armchair' hypothesising about what language is or does ('armchair linguistics' is a term sometimes used to refer to a 'native' speaker reaching conclusions about language based on reflection on his/her usage), a key goal is to attempt to explore language as it is actually used and to develop methodologies that facilitate the collection and analysis of such language. Whilst the mainstay for some time in sociolinguistics was a quantitative approach, a range of methodologies is now in use, from large scale survey data to in-depth ethnographic studies (for overviews, see Johnstone 2000; Mesthrie 2001b; Milroy and Gordon 2003). Whatever the methodologies used, this emphasis on understanding language through empirical study is a key principle in sociolinguistics, connecting in a fundamental way with another key principle, that of the stated *descriptive* rather than prescriptive goal of sociolinguistics. This distinction between description and prescription has long since been acknowledged as more complex than might initially appear, but it takes on a particular hue when it comes to discussions of writing. This is an issue I return to below and at different points in the book.

Everyday language as worthy of study

The idea that the language that we use in going about our everyday business is a worthy object of study is central to sociolinguistics, and whilst an apparently innocuous enough position is in fact a historically radical one. It is a position that had to be forged, not least, against an assumption that only certain kinds of 'high status' language(s) used by certain kinds of people merited academic study. Such 'high status' language examples were drawn primarily from written texts. Samuel Johnson in compiling his dictionary of the English language (1755) states that he aimed to collect examples of language from 'the writers before the Restoration' explicitly dismissing the everyday speech of working and merchant classes as 'casual and mutable diction . . . fugitive cant, which is always in a state of increase or decay . . . and therefore must be suffered to perish with other things unworthy of preservation' (Johnson 1755; quoted and discussed in Stubbs 1980: Chapter 2). Mugglestone (2001) gives an overview of the rise of national academies of language that devoted themselves to the maintenance and regulation of individual languages. Whilst a key goal in the establishment of such academies in Europe was to claim a legitimacy for vernacular languages, in contrast to Latin, a further key goal was to set up a distinction between good and bad uses of the vernacular. The Italian Accademia della Crusca in 1584 was the first academy to be established (followed by the Académie Française in 1635) and its dictionary of the Italian academy, *Vocabulario degli accademici della Crusca* (1612), records words which 'are supported by the written authority of great works rather than by current usage' (Mugglestone 2001: 615). Likewise, the Preface to the seventh edition of the dictionary of the Académie Française (1877) states: 'A word is not dead because we no longer employ it, if it lives on in the work of Molière, La Fontaine, Pascal . . .' [*Un mot n'est pas mort parce que nous ne l'employons plus, s'il vit dans les oeuvres d'un Molière, d'un la Fontaine, d'un Pascal . . .*].[4] Thus as Mugglestone summarises, the academy dictionaries were not attempts to describe language as it was used, but rather to capture 'the words felt to merit existence in that language' (Muggletone 2001: 615). Such merit or worth was (is) often based on 'high status' written texts, such as literary or religious writing and is most obvious in dictionary compilation (although more recent approaches to dictionary compilation based on corpora of language usage challenge this approach – see for example a discussion of the Cobuild project, Moon 2007).

In many ways, sociolinguistics turns the worthiness argument on its head by explicitly setting out to describe, document and theorise 'unworthy' language, that is everyday language, the most emblematic of which is spoken language, with its apparent messiness and 'errors'. However, one of the effects of this position is that much writing has escaped the (mainstream) gaze of sociolinguistics because writing has been considered either too worthy (high status written texts) or not unworthy enough (not spoken language). I argue that much writing can be considered as everyday a communicative practice as speaking and therefore merits a central place in sociolinguistics.

Variety as a core dimension to language

In contrast to an idealised or abstract notion of language, a focus on the everyday uses of language necessarily leads to an interest in varieties of language(s) and language usage(s). Variety is a key notion in sociolinguistics, articulated at a number of levels: at the level of use, for example in its emphasis on functions, genres, practices; at the level of user, for example, in signalling the importance of age, social class, gender, ethnicity; and at the level of linguistic phenomena, in the use of categories such as monolingualism, multilingualism, dialect, accent. *Variation* is a related notion that reflects a specific tradition in sociolinguistics and a concern to explore and measure patterns of linguistic variety, mainly through the use of quantitative approaches mapping the use of specific linguistic variables across speakers, groups and domains of use. Foundational work in this tradition (notably Labov 1972) showed that far from the huge amount of variety in everyday language use being idiosyncratic or chaotic, there is considerable order, and such variety can more accurately be described as 'structured heterogeneity' (discussed in Mesthrie 2001a: 378) or 'orderly heterogeneity' (Weinrich et al. 1968; for recent overview of variationist approaches, see Kiesling 2011).

Of course, different approaches to mapping, tracking and conceptualising variety and variation have developed over time: most obviously whilst variationist approaches have tended to work with mapping specific clusters of linguistic variables against quite rigid social categories – notably social class, gender, ethnicity – more recent approaches, drawing on postmodernist understandings of language and identity, emphasise fluidity and change. What we might term the *performative* aspect of variety is emphasised in current work, that is the performing or enacting of identity through language rather than language use simply mirroring existing identities (see for examples of discussions Rampton 1995, Cameron 2010). At this juncture the notion of *variety* fades somewhat in sociolinguistic discussions and *diversity* (and more recently *super-diversity*) comes more sharply into view, albeit with different emphases: for example *language diversity* is often used in the context of language policy and planning to refer to the 'co-existence of sociolinguistically varied linguistic codes (dialects and languages) within a speech community' (Swann et al. 2004: 169). But diversity is also used to signal a hierarchical relation between different types and usages of language, including concerns about differential access to and use of resources (for example Blommaert 2005). It is this latter angle on diversity with regard to writing that I will emphasise in some chapters in this book.

The above four principles are what we might consider to be foundational in establishing and sustaining sociolinguistics as a field and whilst they have been used to justify the central focus on spoken language, this book argues that all four defining principles can be applied to the study of writing. But first it's important to consider the position currently occupied by writing which in many ways is at odds with these very principles and continues therefore to justify (implicitly and explicitly) the exclusion of writing from mainstream sociolinguistics.

THE POSITION(ING) OF WRITING IN SOCIOLINGUISTICS

Despite the central focus on spoken language in sociolinguistics, writing has always been present in sociolinguistic study albeit positioned in specific ways, as I outline here.

Standardisation and codification

Canonical and introductory sociolinguistic texts foreground the role played by writing in standardisation and codification practices. There is a strong tradition of exploring histories of writing systems and the use of such systems in language and literacy planning, often in the context of debates surrounding nation states. What is meant by 'writing systems' is explored in Chapter 2 in the context of a broader discussion of the multimodal nature of writing. The point to note here is the way in which a link is often made between literacy and standardisation, as illustrated in the following statement: 'Standardization and literacy go hand in hand since the acquisition of literacy presupposes the existence of a codified written standard, and standardization depends on the existence of a written form of language' (Romaine 2000: 90). The link between standardisation and literacy is often nested in the primacy argument discussed earlier – speech comes before writing and is therefore more 'natural'– and linked to specific, if often vaguely articulated claims about functions (usually 'formal'), as illustrated in the following definition:

> A standard variety is generally one which is written, and which has undergone some degree of regularisation or codification . . . Only a minority of the world's languages are written, and an even smaller minority are standardised in the sense of codified and accepted by the community as suitable for formal functions.
>
> (Holmes 2001: 76)

What is not in dispute here is the central role written texts/writing play historically in processes of codification, standardisation and the inevitably strongly prescriptive dimension inherent in such processes; after all, decisions are made (for political and economic reasons) about what variety should constitute the 'standard', should be codified and should become the medium of formal schooling. What is up for debate, however, is whether literacy – and more specifically writing – should *only* or *primarily* be positioned in this way in a disciplinary field that aims to explore the relationship between language and society. The focus on writing in processes of standardisation and codification hides other ways of noticing and understanding what writing is and does in social context, thus potentially limiting our understanding of 'everyday' writing. This is not a new argument (see Hymes [1973] 1996) but it is an argument that still needs to be made and to which this book contributes.

Speech and writing in binary opposition

Exactly what writing is and does, and its relationship to spoken language (in different contexts, involving different participants) is a topic that still requires much attention, as is illustrated across this book. Yet within sociolinguistics we often continue to find quite categorical statements about writing; an early categorical view from linguistics is that writing is simply speech recorded or written down, as illustrated in the oft quoted comment by Bloomfield: 'Writing is not language but merely a way of recording language by means of visible marks' (Bloomfield 1933: 21). Here the specific nature of writing and what it does in and for communication in social context is ignored entirely. A much more widespread categorical position in sociolinguistics is to use 'writing' as a stark counterpoint from which to explore and describe spoken language, layered onto the primacy/secondary dichotomy discussed above. The decontextualised or, as Street (1984, 2001) describes it 'autonomous', position on writing put forward by Goody (1977) and Ong (1982) is echoed explicitly in some sociolinguistic discussions:

> A piece of writing typically has to stand on its own entirely, without any help from the situation, and therefore has to supply all the necessary contextual information explicitly [. . .] normal language is usually heavily context dependent, whereas written language has to be context-free as far as possible.
>
> (Stubbs 1980: 109)

Here writing is contrasted with 'normal' language, a point I return to below. We find in many sociolinguistic texts that specific features and functions are attributed to spoken and written language from a binary perspective, usually regardless of other key dimensions, such as modes, registers, contexts. A list of the typical binary set of attributes is in Figure 1.1.[5]

Figure 1.1 The binary framing of spoken language and writing

Spoken language as . . .	Writing as . . .
Transient	Permanent
Multimodal	Monomodal
Informal	Formal
Grammatically complex	Lexically dense
Local	Distant
Context dependent	Context independent
Dialogic	Monologic
Involved	Detached
Personal	Impersonal

A key problem here is not only that this binary framing is powerful, but that the descriptors constituting such binaries are treated as self-evidently meaningful; an obvious example is *formality* where the binary between what constitutes formal/informal seems to be in widespread use in sociolinguistic texts yet is rarely precisely defined (for useful discussion, see Barton 2007: Chapter 6). What we tend to find are circular arguments, where features of writing or spoken language are defined as X and then the identification of X is used to define a specific instance of written or spoken language. This is illustrated in the following sociolinguistics encyclopaedic entry, where, furthermore, we see how evaluative notions also creep in – in this case 'genuine':

> Not every text that is spoken counts as genuine spoken language. The most interesting examples, because furthest from written language, are informal spontaneous conversation and a dialog produced during the performance of a task.
>
> (Miller 2001: 271)

The definition of what counts as 'genuine' spoken language as being determined by an analyst's dichotomous stance on speech vs writing is evident in many comments, including attempts to provide more nuanced categorisations. So, for example, we find statements that written language that is characterised by 'involvement' is described as 'oral-like', whereas oral language characterised by detachment is 'written like' (Chafe 1982). What such circular categorisations illustrate is not so much an unwillingness to provide accurate characterisations of what written language is and does, but the powerful nature of the binary lens framing our thinking.

One way of engaging with and testing the validity of this binary framing is to work with it and one empirical goal could be to map the differences between written and spoken language. Such a task was carried out by Biber (1988), from a linguistic perspective, who asked the question: 'Is there a linguistic dimension of co-occurring features that distinguishes between spoken and written texts?' Usefully, but perhaps unsurprisingly, his study showed that 'the variation among texts within speech and writing is often as great as the variation across the two modes' (Biber 1988: 24).

Yet the binary framing around spoken language and writing is strongly evident in contemporary sociolinguistic work, signalling a key dimension to this particular paradigmatic imaginary: by imaginary I mean the particular ways in which 'sociolinguistics' has come to be conceptualised (or imagined) as a field, including what its objects of study are, and importantly, can or should be. Thus writing has been imagined in particular ways: where writing has figured as an object of inquiry, for example as writing systems, it is often treated as a neutral system of representation, thus curiously decontextualised, that is separated from the social dimension which is of such central concern in sociolinguistics. Exceptions to this decontextualised approach to writing are found in some more recent work, but usually where writing gets marked as 'vernacular', often used to mean more 'spoken like', as in for example studies of graffiti, or the use of new technologies as in text messaging (see Chapters 2 and 4). What we generally find is that what is often referred to as the 'Great Divide' – which refers not only to the spoken/written language binary but the grand claims that are made about so-called oral and literate traditions – remains powerful, as I discuss below.[6]

The acceptable site for 'closet prescriptivism'?

A key claim in sociolinguistics, as mentioned above, is that the goal of language study is description – that is to describe language as it is used – not prescription – that is to state how language should be used. Whilst an appealingly simple position, matters are, of course, far more complex. Indeed whether such a position is possible, or even desirable, has been challenged, most notably by Cameron (2012), who has argued that evaluation – making value judgements about language – is central to traditions in both 'folk' and 'expert' (i.e. linguists') commentary on language. Consider the regular outbursts in the media about common features of texting, illustrated in the headline 'I h8 txt msgs: How texting is wrecking our language'.[7] Language and particular uses of language have long since been evaluated in terms indicating concerns that go well beyond any notion of language per se. Consider the following statement on the power of a very specific kind of writing, 'English literature':

> England is sick, and [. . .] English literature must save it. The Churches (as I understand) having failed, and social remedies being slow, English literature has now a triple function: still, I suppose, to delight and instruct us, but also, and above all, to save our souls and heal the State.
>
> (George Gordon, early Professor of English literature at Oxford, quoted in Eagleton 1983: 23)

And this link between language use and social and moral behaviour continues to surface, as documented by Cameron and illustrated in the comment by a member of UK royalty:

> All the letters sent from my office I have to correct myself, and that is because English is taught so bloody badly [. . .] We must educate for character. That's the trouble with schools. They don't educate for character.
>
> (Prince Charles 1989, quoted in Cameron 2012: 94)

But rather than dismissing such comments or stating that evaluation should hold no place in the study of language, Cameron argues that we should accept that both the use and the study of language necessarily involve evaluation – or to use her phrase 'verbal hygiene' – and that such evaluation should form part of any discussions about language:

> If we accept that evaluation and verbal hygiene are integral parts of language-using, sociolinguistics must engage in critical debates about the grounds for particular evaluations rather than denying the legitimacy of evaluation itself.
>
> (Cameron 2001: 690)

Thus whilst sociolinguists may strive to describe everyday language use, and to move away from the strongly normative (evaluative) positions on language found in public discourse (for example the media), they/we should also recognise that evaluation will always be part of the work that we do. This position presents two significant challenges. The first challenge is to make our own evaluative practices – as sociolinguists, as researchers and students of language – visible, and thus to confront: 'the tendency of linguists to deny that their terms have any evaluative content or normative intent, when in reality they have both' (Cameron 2012: 234).

The second challenge is: 'to persuade people that there are other values and other standards that might underpin the use and the teaching of language' (Cameron 2012: 82). Examples given by Cameron of the range of values that might be called on, in addition to or instead of the conventional value of 'correctness', are those of utility, aesthetics and morality (Cameron 2001). I return to the question of values at different points in the book, particularly in Chapter 7 and the concluding chapter.

Cameron's questions about evaluation are clearly relevant to the study of any aspect or mode of language use, but they seem particularly pertinent with regard to the way writing still tends to be positioned within both public discourse and the sociolinguistic imaginary. Indeed, I think Cameron's comment that: 'we are all closet prescriptivists – or as I prefer to put it, verbal hygienists' (Cameron 2012: 9) could be used to apply specifically to the way in which writing is positioned in sociolinguistics with, in particular, two specific consequences:

- Firstly, positioned within the sociolinguistic imaginary as fundamentally distinct from spoken language, the potential of writing in communication and meaning making is backgrounded and denied the clusters of explicitly positive evaluative comments reserved for speech (in sociolinguistics). For the 'attributes' of speech and writing listed in Figure 1.1. not only carry clear evaluative overtones, they also tend to get aligned differentially with other more explicitly 'positive' evaluative notions: consider the wordings from quotes included so far in this chapter where spoken language is construed as being 'genuine', 'authentic', 'natural' and 'normal' (and by implication, writing is presumably none of these).

- Secondly, precisely because writing is marginalised as an object of study, there is a danger that it tends to get treated in sociolinguistics in much the same way as it does in the public media or common sense discourse; that is, as already discussed, in terms of standardisation and codification, and, therefore, through a particular emphasis on correctness.

To sum up. The binary framing around spoken and written language use may have served a particular purpose historically in sociolinguistics, to make everyday spoken language a worthy object of study. But writing also seems to have served sociolinguistics as a particular and convenient location for 'closet prescriptivism', that is, as a place to dump evaluative, prescriptive tendencies (so as, perhaps, to free up a more open and descriptive stance towards speech?). And this has consequences for the field and what the field can offer to public debates about writing. For whilst there is evidence that sociolinguists strive to adopt a descriptive approach towards varieties of spoken language – albeit often nested within this is a strong tendency towards a particular evaluative stance which can be summarised as 'the more vernacular the better' – they (we) seem less at ease with this position when it comes to writing. There is a need to adopt a more inclusive and open stance towards writing, particularly at a historical moment where there is a considerable amount of writing taking place within and across different contexts of production and systems of evaluation globally.[8]

LEGITIMISING WRITING AS AN OBJECT OF SOCIOLINGUISTIC INQUIRY

The picture presented so far of the current place of writing within sociolinguistics is drawn from overview textbooks and mainstream journals which inevitably reflect the more canonical works and positions within the field. If we consider the stuff around the edges – most obviously studies presented at sociolinguistic conferences and seminars – it is true to say that writing occupies a much larger and contested space and in part it is some of the 'stuff around the edges' of sociolinguistics that this book seeks to represent. That the stuff of particular focus here, writing, should constitute a legitimate object of inquiry should not be surprising if we start from the premise that the focus on spoken language in sociolinguistics was not (or does not need to be) a category move towards a specific mode, but rather a move towards the legitimisation of the study of 'everyday language' in social context. Indeed, within this frame, writing – along with other modes – has long since been considered an important aspect of everyday language in one tradition of sociolinguistics, that is the tradition of 'ethnography of communication' (see Gumperz and Hymes 1972). This can be thought of not only as a specific tradition in its own right but as, more broadly, reflecting what can be described as the ethnographic 'pull' in sociolinguistics and developed in more recent times with specific reference to writing in 'New Literacy Studies' (NLS), as I outline below.

The ethnographic pull in sociolinguistics

In broad terms, ethnography 'is an attempt to study systematically the beliefs and practices of a community or social group' (Swann et al. 2004: 101) and there is general agreement that doing ethnography or adopting an ethnographic approach involves a commitment to observing real-life events as they unfold, using a range of methods. Given the commitment to exploring everyday language, it is not surprising that ethnography should be of such interest to sociolinguists. As Hymes pointed out, this concern with language in context demands the need to go beyond any narrow definition of language as a focus of analysis and understanding:

> One cannot take linguistic form, a given code, or even speech itself, as a limiting frame of reference. One must take as context a community, or network of persons, investigating its communicative activities as a whole, so that any use of channel and code takes its place as part of the resources upon which the members draw.
>
> (Hymes 1974: 4)

The need to develop analytical tools that focus on language whilst locating language within social context is of course one of the major challenges for sociolinguists, giving rise to a wide range of analytical tools and theoretical frameworks (see for example Hymes's 1972 essay for his 'SPEAKING' analytical device). Ethnography has long since provided both methodological and theoretical frameworks for exploring context and is continuing to drive scholarly debate with specific regard to everyday language in terms of specific ethnographic concepts, for example the importance of the 'emic' in sociolinguistics:

> Sociolinguistic analysis needs to be 'emic' (explaining meaningful differences) rather than simply 'etic' (describing formal differences and distributions) and an analyst's 'etic' categories may not match speakers' 'emic' understandings.
>
> (Coupland and Jaworksi 2009: 7)

And this critical interest in specific tools and notions from ethnography is part of a larger tradition that is explicitly connected with anthropology and anthropological debate, as illustrated in the increasingly prominent work in linguistic ethnography in the UK (see Rampton et al. 2004; Rampton 2007).

There are three specific points I want to make here about the significance of this ethnographic pull with regard to writing:

1. The ethnographic pull necessarily leads to an opening up of what we are looking at, including – of specific relevance to the discussion here – a

problematisation of the focus on language through one specific mode. As Roberts and Street (1997) point out, once *context* becomes as significant as *language* in exploring language use, this: 'shifts the focus away from a traditional concern with differences between the channels and onto the ways in which meanings are constructed locally within particular contexts' (Roberts and Street 1997: 169). This echoes a point made by Basso, a lone voice, some twenty years earlier (1974) in a paper arguing for a more sustained and ethnographic approach to writing as part of the study of communication more generally. An ethnographic interest not only leads to an attention to the contextual dimension of one pre-determined object (i.e. mode) of study – for example spoken language – but necessarily serves to open up what counts as the object of study: thus, for example, in looking at how people use language we find that writing is a key dimension of everyday language use and practice.

2. Moving beyond a (mono)modal framing enables the interconnections between modes to come to the fore. A good example of this is work by Cook-Gumperz focusing on the relationship between spoken language and literacy in schooling (2006). Hers – and colleagues' – strongly educationally driven work challenged the deficit views on literacy and schooling which were often premised on assumptions/prejudices towards spoken language; for example if a child speaks in non-standard language she must be incapable of thinking in full sentences or becoming 'fully literate', or the related notion that people need to speak the standard language in order to write standard language. What was needed, they argued, was not an understanding of oral and written practice 'as opposites' but rather 'a theory of communication that has literacy at its core' (Cook-Gumperz 2006: 15). The more recent and growing work on multimodality has likewise challenged the emphasis on monomodal framings – in particular over-emphasis on the verbal as the key or primary mode – pointing to the considerable communicative work that a range of modal dimensions bring to bear on communication (Kress and van Leuwen 2001; Jewitt (ed.) 2009; Kress 2010). Definitions of 'mode' and how these relate to the study of writing are discussed in Chapter 2.

3. With regard to writing, and more broadly everyday literacy, ethnography has helped to provide methodological tools for analysing writing in context, some of which have derived from those developed by Hymes for analysing spoken language, such as *literacy event* (see Heath 1983); a point to note here is that this notion has largely been taken up in terms of action (analysis of what literacy is doing) rather than the 'stuff' of literacy (detailed analysis of the linguistic and semiotic resources used), as I discuss across several chapters in this book. At a theoretical level, ethnography, with its fundamental attention to context, has served to open up what we mean by writing and literacy, and challenges in particular what Street, already mentioned above, termed the 'autonomous' approach to literacy. In contrast to an autonomous view of literacy where literacy is viewed as having consequences (cognitive, social etc.) irrespective of, or *autonomous* of context, Street argues for the need to adopt

an *ideological* model of literacy which is built on ethnographic accounts and foregrounds literacy as social practice:

> Literacy is a social practice, not simply a technical and neutral skill [. . .] it is always embedded in socially constructed epistemological principles. It is about knowledge: the ways in which people address reading and writing are themselves rooted in conceptions of knowledge, identity, being. Literacy, in this sense, is always contested, both its meanings and its practices, hence particular versions of it are always 'ideological', they are always rooted in a particular world view.
>
> (Street 2001: 8)

There has been considerable work carried out in the ethnographic study of literacy in the past twenty years, often referred to as New Literacy Studies, which has worked with this 'ideological' notion of literacy (see Chapter 4). Such work, drawing on and engaging with key principles in sociolinguistics, whilst at the same time challenging assumptions about writing, has gone some way to responding to the concern by Basso (1974), that: 'The most conspicuous shortcomings of traditional studies of writing is that they reveal very little about the social patterning of this activity or the contributions it makes to the maintenance of social systems' (Basso 1974: 431). The way in which writing as resource and action is linked to 'social patterning' is illustrated across the book, including specific attention to institutional practices (Chapters 4 and 5) and to issues of identity, regulation and agency (Chapter 6).

BACKGROUND AND AIMS OF THIS BOOK

The aim of this book is to provide an introductory overview of approaches to writing which engage directly with the project of sociolinguistics, as reflected in the key principles outlined above: the importance of the 'social'; the empirical study of naturally occurring language; the 'everyday' as worthy of study; variety as a core dimension to language use. Writing an introductory book about a (sub)field that is emergent and highly contested has proved challenging and this book must be viewed as a contribution to current debate rather than an attempt at laying out any canonical boundaries. In conceptualising what writing is and does, the book draws on work in New Literacy Studies, multimodality and semiotics and on academic fields that have paid particular attention to writing and written texts, such as discourse and genre studies, stylistics, new rhetoric and contrastive rhetoric(s) and academic literacies. Examples are drawn from across these fields, from both more recent as well as more established work, in an attempt to give a strong sense of the range of relevant and interesting research studies, data, theories and analytical tools from which those of us interested in writing can draw.

The book is overlain with my specific interests in a number of ways. My empirical research interests will be evident in some of the areas I cover – for example student writing, scholarly writing for publication and work based writing, drawn from my research (for example, Lillis 2001, 2011; Lillis and Curry 2010; Lillis and Rai 2011);

and extracts from some of these are used as illustrations in some chapters of the book. My background and interest in education and pedagogy influence the way I frame some discussions about the importance of focusing on writing. And my particular 'take' on writing, which is that of writing as a 'social practice' (Street 1984; see Chapter 4), forms the basis of many of my arguments. This take involves two positions, which are easily recognisable as 'mainstream' or canonical sociolinguistic positions (and evident if you swap the words 'spoken language' for 'writing' below):

1. A *theoretical position* on writing which states that writing cannot and should not be viewed as separate from contexts of use and users.
2. An *empirical position* which states that texts, uses and users need to be the subjects of empirical research rather than being driven by *a priori* assumptions and value positions.

These theoretical and empirical positions on writing are in tune with sociolinguistic epistemology – that language cannot be separate from context and that its meanings and purposes are always bound up with specific contexts of use. Of course, debates around context are ongoing: What counts as 'context'? To what extent is 'it' observable? To what extent does context need to be theorised? What is the relationship between language and context? Which bits of 'context' are significant in any use and analysis of language and which aren't? Such questions are at the heart of sociolinguistics (see for example Coupland et al. 2001) and apply equally to studies of writing, even though much has been claimed about the decontextualised nature of writing, as I discuss across the chapters in this book.

A third more contested position I adopt as part of a social practice approach is as follows:

3. An *ideological position on writing* which posits that issues of power, identity, participation and access are central to writing practices and as such need to be taken account of in exploring what writing is and does.

This ideological position raises further difficult questions about the language–context relationship, in particular how to connect micro contextual details and understandings with macro analytical frameworks. This position is in tune with the more recent and explicit concern in sociolinguistics with ideology and theory and debates around the ways in which language keys into local and globalising communicative practices (Blommaert 2010). This ideological interest in issues of access and participation is strongly evident in some strands of sociolinguistic inquiry and is also a driving imperative in my own interests around writing.

Finally, and in tune with my ongoing interest in ethnography, the book reflects particular concerns I have about key analytic categories or tropes in sociolinguistics which I think socially situated approaches to writing bring into strong relief and which need some critical attention, a key one being that of 'function'. A normative approach to function is strongly evident in approaches to writing, and most obviously captured in snatches of evolutionary discourse which frame some linguistic approaches to writing and language more generally.[9] Such a view necessarily downplays tensions around functions, such as who has the power to decide which functions are being served, on what terms, in what contexts. This book argues that questions about functions must always be to the fore: What are the 'functions' of any instance of language use, and, given the focus of this book, specifically, writing? How are functions (mis)recognised in specific contexts and with what consequences? How can we (as analysts) know what these functions are, particularly given that deciding on function is not separate from our practices of evaluation?

This book has four key aims: to claim a more central place for the study of writing in sociolinguistics on the grounds that many of the basic premises of sociolinguistics justify its legitimisation as an object of inquiry; to bring together ideas and research on writing from a number of disciplinary fields to explore what they may offer to those of us interested in understanding and researching writing within and across diverse domains of practice; to illustrate some of the methodologies and analytical tools available for researching and analysing writing; and to consider how a focus on writing can inform and contribute to key debates within sociolinguistics more generally. In the discussions in this book, I find it useful to work with the ambiguity in English of the word 'writing', that is as referring to both writing as written texts and the activity of writing, including who does it and why. Where I use 'writing' with a particular meaning, for example a written text, I state this.

OVERVIEW OF THE BOOK

Chapter 2 begins to explore the question that concerns the book as a whole – what do we mean by 'writing'? – focusing in particular on the question of 'mode'. The chapter outlines the range of key modal dimensions to writing, drawing on work in multimodality and emphasising the analytical value of adopting a semiotic rather than a linguistic take on writing. This chapter seeks to challenge the positioning of writing as 'one mode' – historically and currently – and to consider what a focus on multiple modal dimensions brings to our understandings of writing. It argues for the need to draw on semiotic and multimodal understandings when exploring writing as everyday practice and at the same time to socially situate any multimodal analysis.

Chapter 3 focuses on the modal dimension that is most commonly foregrounded with regard to writing, that is the verbal dimension, exploring in particular the way in which verbal 'form' is anchored to social context through an articulation with 'function'. The chapter discusses three ways in which this relationship is often articulated: function layered on to form, form and function collapsed or elided, form elevated over function. It offers brief overviews of some of the different disciplinary-based ways in which the verbal dimension has been explored, including critical discourse analysis, rhetoric and stylistics. The chapter concludes by pointing to the importance attached to *typification* in studies of writing, most notably through the use of *genre*, and considers tensions surrounding the use of this notion, including the way in which it is conceptualised along a continuum from text to activity to practice.

Chapter 4 shifts the emphasis away from a primary focus on the internal workings of written texts towards the ways in which writing is used in everyday practice. Drawing on research from New Literacy Studies as well as studies indicating the considerable growth in writing across all media, the chapter seeks to position writing as being of considerable importance to all interested in communication in contemporary society. It illustrates some of the ways in which writing is an everyday activity and offers examples of how writing mediates different domains of our life worlds – home, schooling, work, political activity, personal relationships – using a range of materialities and both traditional and digital technologies. The chapter outlines what it means to construe writing as a 'social practice' and illustrates some of the key analytical tools currently available.

Chapter 5 focuses on the *dynamic* rather than the (often) assumed fixed nature of writing in three main ways: in terms of its specific texture, in that any text is built on and out of a range of existing resources; in terms of the processes surrounding production, in that writing often involves many people across space and time; in terms of its mobile potential, for the material nature of writing means that it is portable or mobile – travelling along with the people who produced it or alone – although as it moves the meanings attached to it and the ways in which it is evaluated may shift and vary in complex ways. This chapter explores the resources needed for writing and some of the ways in which these are tied into specific communities, practices and values in processes surrounding the making of texts, that is as *entextualisation* and *recontextualisation*. It argues for the importance of understanding writing through the lens of 'text trajectories' and in so doing also revisits the question of 'genre' discussed in Chapter 3.

Chapter 6 returns to the notion of writing as inscription discussed in Chapter 2 but turns from the material act of inscription to consider writing as the making, or inscription, of the self. The chapter considers why identity has become a key focus in studies of writing and discusses how identity is theorised and explored, using as a central analytical tool the notion of writing as 'identity work'. The chapter considers some of the different ways in which writing involves the doing of 'identity work', exploring the ways in which existing semiotic resources for writing are inscribed with particular (resources for) identities. Using examples from old and new technologies of writing, the chapter considers the ways and extent to which writing practices are regulated more strongly or more weakly in different social semiotic spaces and the importance of ownership of the material resources of writing – as well as control over evaluation and regulation practices – for the possibility of agency.

Chapter 7 draws together work from different academic domains touched on in previous chapters to outline the key ways in which writing and relations around writing – as writer/reader/text, or, producer/materials/uptake – are conceptualised and theorised. It summarises eight key approaches to writing, including those most evident across the book – writing as a social semiotic and social practice – as well as approaches that are highly influential in both academic and public discourses – writing as poetic-aesthetic, writing as transactional-rationalist – and an approach less discussed to date in relation to writing, that of 'participatory culture' (i.e. Jenkins 2006). The chapter argues that there is a tendency in writing research to conflate the domain of writing activity being observed with the domain (or analytical frame) through which such observation is being made. The chapter argues for the importance of bringing to bear a range of different analytical frameworks in order to make visible and critically explore what's involved in any act(s) of writing.

Chapter 8 draws the book to a conclusion by summarising the key points made about writing across the chapters, revisiting in particular debates about the identification of *function* and the ways in which such identification is nested within academic, institutional and common sense practices of *evaluation*. The book closes by indicating opportunities and challenges for future research on writing.

NOTES

1. This claim is based on a review of key sociolinguistic texts and journals including the following: Coupland and Jaworski 2009; Holmes 2001; Hudson 1996; Mesthrie 2001b; Mesthrie et al. 2009; Meyerhoff 2006; Meyerhoff and Schleef 2010; Paulston and Tucker 2003; Romaine 2000; Trudgill 1974, 1983, 1995, 2000; Trudgill and Cheshire 1998a, b; the *Journal of Sociolinguistics*.
2. Of course the issue of how such recorded speech then gets transformed into objects for analysis and the implications of specific representations is an ongoing discussion in sociolinguistics and one that continues to merit attention. This is an important area but one that I am not able to deal with within the scope of this book. For interesting discussions, see Ochs 1979; Roberts 1997.
3. Hymes acknowledged the value of the more abstract and idealised approach that Chomsky advocated, not least that such a universalistic approach challenged any theories of language or language difference based on genetic differences or notions of a racial hierarchy (Hymes 1971: 4).
4. Preface to 1877 edition available online, at http://homes.chass.utoronto.ca/~wulfric/academie/pref7.htm (accessed 1 Jan. 2012).
5. For a longer list framed within a critical discussion of this binary, see Baron 2000 and Holmes 2004.
6. The introductory text on sociolinguistics by Coulmas 1997 stands out in including a chapter, by Roberts and Street, which challenges this great divide.
7. This is taken from an online newspaper article by a well-known UK broadcaster, http://www.dailymail.co.uk/news/article-483511/I-h8-txt-msgs-How-texting-wrecking-language.html (accessed 1 May 2012). Statements such as these regularly appear in the UK press.
8. In mapping traditions of the more prescriptive or 'how to' approaches to writing – of which indeed sociolinguists would be critical – I recognise that there is considerable variety, historically and geographically. It's interesting to note, for example, that the prescriptively entitled 1939 book by the scholar, C. E. M. Joad, *How to Write, Think and Speak Correctly*, includes sections on how ideology and interests shape how we think and write, parts of which would be in tune with more recent discussions on writing, habitus and identity, discussed in this book in Chapter 6. Individual scholarly positions are therefore often more internally hybrid and self-contesting than canonical accounts of disciplinary subfields may encourage us to believe.
9. I am thinking here of those approaches to writing, literacy and linguistics more generally which attribute specific cognitive/intellectual capacities of whole societies/civilisations to the development and use of writing systems. For example with regard to writing and

literacy see Ong 1982 and for useful critical overview of the significance of evolutionary metaphor and discourse, see Barton 2007 Chapter 8; for example of linguistic approach to language more generally which uses an evolutionary metaphor, see Halliday 1993, 1994; and for useful critique, see Street 1995: Chapter 1. For discussion of the treatment of the origins of writing, see Harris 1986.

Chapter 2

The question of mode

INTRODUCTION

The aim of this chapter is to begin to explore what we mean by 'writing', by focusing in particular on the question of mode. As discussed in Chapter 1, writing is often positioned as being distinct from spoken language on the grounds of 'mode' (sometimes also referred to as modality), with spoken language being construed as one mode and writing another. Yet this modal distinction between speech and writing may not be helpful given that there are many more modal dimensions to language than just 'speech' or 'writing', any or all of which may be significant in any specific instance of language use.

Much has been claimed about what writing is and does, on the basis of assumptions about particular modal-material dimensions, notably, its verbal nature and its object-like (or material-permanence) existence. However, as this chapter discusses, whilst it is important to discuss writing as a verbal-object, there are other important modal dimensions to consider, as well as a need to explore the meanings attached to these different dimensions by users, writers (producers) and readers (lookers, readers, consumers).

The aims of this chapter are:

- to tease out the significance attached to mode when conceptualising writing
- to consider what a focus on specific modal dimensions brings to our understandings of writing
- to illustrate the importance of avoiding what can be described as a 'modalist' approach to writing whilst at the same time taking account of the potential significance of different modal dimensions when seeking to understand writing as everyday practice.

WHAT'S IN A MODE?

Writing in sociolinguistics is commonly distinguished from speech or spoken language on the basis of mode or medium. *Mode* or *medium* are often used interchangeably to emphasise the differences in certain aspects of the material nature of speech and writing; most obviously the fact of speech being produced through vibrations in the air ('channel' is also used when referring to the physical material and properties involved in speech, for example sound waves) in contrast to writing which involves making marks on material of some kind, such as stone, paper and screen. That there are such material differences between speech and writing is obvious but what are questionable are the nature and strength of claims that are made on the basis of such differences. What we tend to find are a series of nested claims about writing made on the grounds of (a certain dimension of) *mode*, some perhaps more obviously warrant-able than others but which very quickly spill over into larger, vaguer and unfounded claims about what writing is and does (or can/can't do). For example, because writing involves marks on paper (or screen) as compared with sound waves in the air, it may seem reasonable enough to conclude that writing is more permanent and object-like in nature than speech which is assumed to be transitory and disappears once con-cluded. Yet it is a significant step from the description of the existence of writing as an object or product (a letter, a book, a word file) to claim that writing is necessarily more permanent than speech (letters can be destroyed, speeches can be recorded). It is a further leap to claim that on the basis of its (potential) material permanence in the world that writing is necessarily more *context free* than speech. And on the basis of this context free notion of writing, along with descriptions of specific features of particular kinds of writing, it is an even greater leap to make broad claims about the cognitive and cultural impact of writing on large groups of people and whole societies (Goody 1977; Goody and Watt 1963; Ong 1982; Olson 1994). As Hymes stated some time ago: 'many generalisations about the consequences of writing and the properties of speaking make necessities out of possibilities' (Hymes 1996: 40).

Yet these kinds of slippages about what writing is and does are quite common in many discussions about writing. A key goal in this chapter is to explore the range of different modal dimensions to writing, highlighting which aspects tend to be foregrounded and backgrounded in mainstream sociolinguistics, and in discussions about writing more generally. To begin with, a cautionary note is needed with regard to definitions and uses of the word 'mode'. Definitions of mode vary, as does the specific level or layer of mode invoked. As already stated, mode has often been used to refer to and distinguish between speech and writing. In more recent times, specific dimensions of mode in communication have been emphasised according to the study being carried out. For example, Kress et al. (1998) foregrounded the importance of the visual mode in their study of science textbooks and challenged the sole (or primary) emphasis on written verbal language. Cook identified three main modes in his study of advertising – music, pictures and language – with each of these having 'sub modes', for example, pictures can be still or moving (Cook 2001). There is clearly a range of modal dimensions to writing, as I outline below, but it's impor-tant from the outset to be aware that definitions of mode (and sub-modal elements) and questions about these vary; for example, should we consider the layout of a written text an aspect of the visual mode or a modal element in its own terms? The answer to this question lies to a great extent in the specific interests of the researcher or the phenomena being studied (see Kress 2010: 88ff.).

In this chapter I am using mode in a broad way to open up discussion about the many potential semiotic dimensions to writing, some of which tend to be ignored more than others. 'Semiotic' is a useful term to bring in here for two reasons: it is a broader category than aspects we typically think of as 'language', that is, it includes but does not start from a primary focus on verbal language and also includes the material substance, colour, shape and size of writing (it is also used, of course, to refer to signs beyond language such as music, dress, food); semiotic refers to form *and* meaning, thus usefully emphasising that modes or modal dimensions are always bound up with meaning, rather than being neutral or autonomous. By increasing the range of modal descriptions and dimensions we apply to the study of writing, we can enrich our understandings about 'everyday' or 'ordinary' writing, as well as those kinds of writing that are awarded privileged status in society. Paying attention to modal dimensions can thus enable us to explore in more nuanced ways the work that writing does in any given context, for whom, with what purposes in mind and with what consequences.

I begin with the two modal dimensions that are most commonly (if sometimes implicitly) emphasised in sociolinguistics; these are writing as material *inscription* and writing as *verbal*, and the representational significance attached to both of these. I then outline other less widely acknowledged modal dimensions that need to be considered as potentially relevant to any study or account of writing.

WRITING AS INSCRIPTION

One important way of categorising writing (and of distinguishing it, for example, sharply from speech) is as mark-making or inscription. Early evidence is found in many parts of the world with markings or inscriptions discovered on materials of different kinds – stone, clay, bone, wood, shell – using tools such as sharpened stone, bamboo, reed. The etymology of the word *writing* in English indexes this notion of marking (see Box 2.1). Debates exist about where the earliest examples are to be found, with mention made of Egypt, China and Pakistan. More recently, inscriptions have been found on ostrich shells in South Africa, dating back some 60,000 years (Texier et al. 2010). The oldest known piece of writing in English may be a carving on a roe-deer's ankle bone, found in Norfolk from AD 400 (Graddol 2007:161).

The meaning of early markings is often difficult to decipher, but that meanings were attached to such markings is signalled by their very existence – reflecting a human symbolic intent – and the repetitive patterning of particular shapes (for examples, see http://www.britishmuseum.org/explore/themes/writing/historic_writing.aspx (accessed February 6 2010)).

An interest in writing as inscription is evident in sociolinguistics, through the focus on the development of writing as 'scripts', 'systems', 'spelling' and 'orthography', discussions of all of which appear in most overview text books and encyclopaedias. Definitions of these are in Box 2.2. These particular interests reflect a concern with inscription as *representation* of language, rather than a concern with the material dimension of inscription, which is signalled in the etymology of the

Box 2.1

O.E. *writan* 'to score, outline, draw the figure of', later 'to set down in writing'
(class I strong verb; past tense *wrat*, pp. *writen*), from P.Gmc. **writanan*
'tear, scratch' (cf. O.Fris. *writa* 'to write', O.S. *writan* 'to tear, scratch, write',
O.N. *rita* 'write, scratch, outline', O.H.G. *rizan* 'to write, scratch, tear', Ger.
reißen 'to tear, pull, tug, sketch, draw, design'). Words for 'write' in most I.E.
languages originally mean 'carve, scratch, cut' (cf. L. *scribere*, Gk *grapho*, Skt.
rikh-); a few originally meant 'paint' (cf. Goth. *meljan*, O.C.S. *pisati*, and
most of the modern Slavic cognates). Source: Write/Writing (for full details,
see www.etymonline.com/ (accessed 15 August 2010))

Box 2.2 Writing system, script, orthography, spelling

Writing system: A means of representing graphically a language or group of
languages. Logographic (based on words and morphemes), syllabic (based on
syllables), alphabetic (based on vowels and consonants as individual units) (see
Mesthrie et al. 2009: 375)

Script: Usually taken to be a synonym for writing system

Orthography:
1. A writing system specifically intended for a particular language
2. A particular way of performing/producing a writing system of a particular
   language (for example, types of handwriting, fonts, spelling conventions
   used to represent verbal language)

Spelling: Conventions governing the representation of specific features of a
specific language

Sebba usefully illustrates distinctions between terms as follows: 'I am spelling
the words of this sentence according to the orthography of English using the
Roman writing system or script' (Sebba 2007: 11). He also points out that
'orthography' – including 'spelling' – often signals a clearly evaluative stance,
that is an emphasis on 'correct' orthography. *Orthographia* (Greek = 'correct
writing' Sebba 2007: 10)

word 'writing'. The representational dimension to inscription is evident in work
that focuses on the ways in which oral language is/should be represented in written
form and in the debates surrounding questions such as which writing system to
adopt – logographic, syllabic, alphabetic? Should an existing or a new system be
adopted? Some studies in sociolinguistics also pay attention to the social and political reasons surrounding representation (for example, see Mesthrie et al. 2009: 388

ff. for accounts of the script reforms in twentieth-century China), including discussion of the fact that there is not necessarily a 1–1 correspondence between languages and writing systems and scripts. Some languages are represented contemporaneously in several scripts (see Juffermans 2010 for Mandinka in the Gambia, written both in Latin and Arabic scripts). However, it is the symbolic or representational dimension to inscription that has tended to receive most attention in the study of writing, with a normative position strongly evident. Thus for example, significant attention has been paid to *graphisation* – the processes whereby specific writing systems are developed as ways of representing oral language or existing written language – with graphisation often discussed as part of language codification, language planning and standardisation practices (Mesthrie et al. 2009: 375 ff.; Sebba 2007).

The focus on writing systems and orthography justifiably holds an important place in sociolinguistics. However we need to be aware of some of the limitations in this particular *representational* take on writing-as-inscription:

1. The emphasis tends to be on exploring inscription-representation in practices which are strongly normative, that is in describing which kinds of systems of representation are used to fix language towards 'standards', with the effect of backgrounding debates around what might be considered non-normative or 'centrifugal' inscription practices. (See Chapter 6 for further discussion of 'centripetal' and 'centrifugal'.)

2. There is a danger that in focusing only on standardisation processes the notion of inscription itself gets treated normatively/neutrally, as if inscription were only ever about standardisation processes. This means that even when 'non-normative' or 'vernacular' inscription practices have been explored within sociolinguistics, notably 'graffiti', these still tend to be explored from a normative standpoint, that is in terms of a set of assumptions about what writing should (or shouldn't) be (see Sebba 2007).

3. Within this representational emphasis, two important aspects of inscription can get lost: these are the materiality of inscription – at the most obvious level the significance of the material stuff and tools used for writing, an issue that has come to the fore in some recent work in multimodality and New Literacy Studies and to which I return below; and the significance of inscription as 'identity work', that is of writing as inscribing (writing) the self, as I discuss in Chapter 6.

As a field of inquiry, therefore, a focus on writing as inscription needs to include studies that extend beyond both the representational and normative to include other modal dimensions – including materiality – in order to understand the potential significance of writing in everyday practices.

WRITING AS VERBAL

The verbal dimension to written language has obviously been central in studies of writing, including linguistic and sociolinguistic approaches, where language (and communication more generally) has been defined in terms of its verbal nature. Not surprisingly, therefore, the verbal dimension of writing has been a primary analytical focus and a wide range of tools and traditions has been developed in order to analyse this dimension: these include sentence level grammars, text grammars, argument, rhetoric, different genre theories, literary studies, stylistics. Attempts to get at the verbal nature of writing are clearly important for understanding the potential for meaning making that writing – and indeed speech – offers. Focusing on the verbal nature of writing is crucial for making the work that verbal language does visible and it is also central to challenging the common sense idea that language is a transparent tool for conveying, rather than constructing meanings (see Chapter 7 for discussion of transparency models). I focus in some detail on the verbal dimension in Chapter 3.

However, there are several points to bear in mind when foregrounding the verbal dimension to writing which raise important questions for sociolinguistics as a field as well as for individual researchers. Firstly, an emphasis on the verbal dimension of writing can lead to a 'textualist' approach to writing (Collins 1996; Horner 1999) whereby the primary focus becomes the text – or the text as instantiation of a grammatical system – rather than a seeking to understand the significance of a text in its specific social context. A good example of this in an educational context is the common way in which student writing is approached. Often, conclusions about the writing are based on a reading or analysis of the text alone, rather than an exploration of why a student has written as she has, including her reasons and perspectives on specific features of the text, or considering the writing from a broader contextual perspective by, for example, focusing on the rhetorical conventions privileged by the institution. There are good pedagogical reasons for not adopting this textualist approach and for drawing on writers' perspectives in understanding the written text (see discussions in Lillis 2001, 2003, 2009). But the methodological and epistemological point I am emphasising here is that we need to be aware both of what text based approaches make visible and also obscure. At a more fundamental level, a textualist approach necessarily leads to a decontextualised orientation to writing which stands in contrast to the sociolinguistic interest in exploring language use in/as context (see Chapter 4 for further discussion of context).

Secondly, and of relevance to how sociolinguistics (or any field dealing with writing) construes writing as a phenomenon, it is not just that the verbal dimension to writing has tended to be foregrounded over others but that specific kinds of verbal dimensions have been attributed to writing. After all, speech is also (in part) verbal but it is the differences between the verbal nature of speech and writing, and the way these are categorised, that have been emphasised: a good example here is that written texts are often construed in terms of 'sentences' and 'grammaticality', as compared with the focus on 'utterances' and 'acceptability' in speech (Barton 2007: 88).[1] These quite different categories feed into the binary assumptions about what speech and writing are or should be, discussed in Chapter 1, with claims about writing, often based on *a priori* assumptions about very particular kinds of texts, such as literary texts. Once writing is analysed from the perspective not just of the texts but of the contexts in and for which these are produced, the binaries break down. A good example here is the work by Besnier (1988, 1995) exploring the language and literary practices of people in the Pacific atoll of Nukulaelae. Arguing for the importance of focusing on what people do with language (rather than assuming any clear dichotomy between speech and writing), he identified the practice of personal letter writing in Nukulaelae Tuvaluan and analysed the specific textual features. Challenging the common binary characterisation of speech as 'involved' and 'personal', in contrast to writing as 'detached' and 'impersonal', he found (perhaps not surprisingly) that personal letters displayed considerably more involvement than everyday spoken language. 'Involvement' here is defined in terms of the use of features such as first and second person pronoun and as illustrated in the letter extracts in Figure 2.1 (the bolding of features in Nukulaelae Tuvaluan follows the original publication; for full details of the features analysed, see Besnier 1988).[2]

Figure 2.1   Personal letters (Besnier 1988: 728)

Talu mai te aso ne maavvae ei taatou, i te afiafi teenaa, a maatou **mo** S, 0, T, S, **mo** tamaliki katoa, koo ttagi i te masausau atu kiaa **koe. I** te paleleega o temotou lotu, **a** ko 0 koo fakamasau aka nee ia a **tau** maasani i taimi o ttou lotu afiafi, a **koe** e see mafai loa o fano ki se koga fakaaatea [. . .] A S i te taimi teenaa koo tagi, **a** ko **au** foki koo tagi, a maatou koo ttagi katoa loa i te maafau-fau **atu** ki **ou** uiga ggali **mo ou** faifaiga llei ne fai i loto i te kaaiga, peelaa foki ki tefenua.

On the day when we parted, that evening, all of us including S, O, T, S, and all the children, we cried from reminiscing about you. Our evening prayer was over, and O started reminiscing about your habit of not going off anywhere else during prayer [. . .] S then started crying at that time, and I cried too, and all of us cried thinking [thither] about your nice attitude and the nice things that you did at the heart of the kin group, and also in the island community.

Besnier makes the important sociolinguistic point:

in order to provide cross-linguistically valid explanations for the structural characteristics of spoken and written language, we must take into account how, why, where, and by whom the discourse is produced, and we must pay particular attention to the norms of communication at play in each context of production.
(Besnier 1988: 709)

Thus, if the goal is to develop context sensitive approaches to writing, analyses of the verbal dimension to writing needs to be accompanied by attention to the social context and purposes in which specific writing occurs.

Thirdly, considerable attention has been paid to the way in which the verbal dimension of writing links with cognition, at an individual level, and the development of knowledge and science, at societal levels. A key claim is made for the power of writing to advance thinking, whereby writing is viewed as a 'way of bringing speech into consciousness' (Olson 2003: 70). Powerful arguments have been made about the link between writing (and literacy), the development of scientific thinking and the development of societies (see for key examples Goody 1977; Ong 1982; Havelock 1976; see *Language and Communication* special issue 1989). I return to this focus on writing and science in Chapter 5.

That the verbal is a key dimension to language is clear. Spoken and written language are verbal, involving words and phrases and ways of putting these together. At the same time, they differ in the involvement of other modal dimensions: most obviously, spoken language generally includes sound,[3] whereas written language involves visual dimensions, such as colour, layout, handwriting style or font. Exactly how the different modal dimensions cluster together to enable meaning making or to constitute a specific instance of communication is a question that needs to be explored. A key position in developing a sociolinguistic approach to writing, therefore, is to acknowledge that the verbal mode is an important resource or affordance (see Box 2.3) for meaning making and communication, but that it needs to be considered alongside other modal dimensions. In tune with the key principles of sociolinguistics, any claims made about what writing is and can do needs to be based on a careful study of specific instances of writing use and the specific practices in which writing is embedded (See Box 2.3).

Box 2.3 Writing as *resource*, *affordance* and *practice*

Resource: A focus on the material, tool, technology available to people that can be used for meaning making and communication

Affordance: A focus on what a particular resource or cluster of resources can potentially enable people to do

Practice: A focus on what people do with writing and how specific practices reflect and instantiate conventions and relations

Resources, affordances and practice help us to make several conceptual shifts when thinking about writing:

1. From an emphasis on writing as one single mode to multimodal.
2. From writing as a transparent medium that emerges from the individual mind towards writing as a socially available resource or affordance.
3. From an emphasis on system or text towards a focus on use – *practice* – and towards what people do.

WRITING AS MATERIAL

The materiality of writing is powerfully evident when we look at examples of early writing, where our attention is directed to the materials used to make marks and the materials on which such marks are made. This material dimension to writing, however, remains invisible for some time in the development of sociolinguistics as a discipline where, as I have discussed, a concern with inscription as representation is dominant, along with an emphasis on specific verbal dimensions to writing. Where the material dimension to writing has consistently been taken up has been in relation to its object-like permanency, which has been attributed specific importance with regard to individual cognition and societal development (as briefly discussed above). However, in this frame it is an *abstracted* notion of materiality that gets foregrounded, that is the fact of the material existence of writing (as compared with the transitory existence of speech) rather than attention being paid to the specifics of its material, situated nature and the meanings attributed by users. An example of this kind of abstracted claim is when Olson (2003: 75) for example states: 'The legacy of Western literacy is the ability, on occasion, to take utterances literally according to the narrow meaning of the words employed.'

A focus on the material nature and the 'stuff' of writing (Kress 2010: Chapter 5) has resurfaced more recently, however, in part because of the growth in contextualised empirical studies (see Chapter 4) and theorisations of the multimodal nature of communication (for overviews, see Jewitt 2009) and in part because of the growth in the use of 'new' or digital technologies which are forcing us to reconsider how we think about language and communication. In seeking to describe and account for the ways these new technologies are used in communication, such work challenges assumptions and expectations built from the continued emphasis on the speech/writing dichotomy or the so-called 'Great divide' between orality and literacy emphasised in much (socio)linguistic work (an issue already discussed in Chapter 1; examples of digitally mediated writing are discussed across the book and in Chapter 6).

Aspects of this situated materiality of writing are increasingly being brought to bear under the umbrellas of multimodality and New Literacy Studies. These include accounts of contemporary practices in schools, as in work by Stein (2008) in South Africa and by Ormerod and Ivanič (2002) in the UK (see also discussion in Chapter 4 on findings from the latter research);[4] work by Wilson (2000, 2003, 2010) on prison literacies, including the ways in which some literacy objects are used to transform institutional spaces (see Figure 2.2), and an issue I return to in Chapter 6; and work by Pahl and Rowsell (2010) who explore the meanings attached to literacy (and other) artefacts, in particular the ways in which these bridge geocultural, linguistic and institutional boundaries. This attention paid to the material dimensions in contemporary practices is mirrored by the historical work being carried out in reviewing pre-European writing practices, such as work on Mesoamerica (see Baca 2008, Baca and Villanueva 2010).

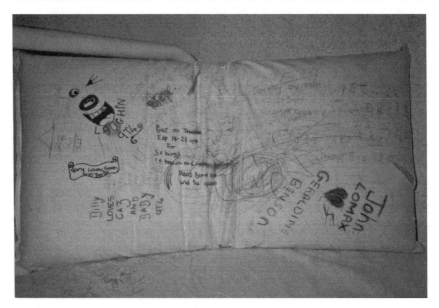

Figure 2.2   Pillow as site of graffiti (Wilson 2003: 298: see discussion in
            Chapter 6)

WRITING AS TECHNOLOGIES

The material nature of writing clearly overlaps with the notion of writing as a technology or more precisely as involving a range of technologies. Technologies – tools, materials and ways of using these – are material, after all (see Box 2.4 for some distinctions made). But it can be useful to foreground the specific notion of *technology* for the purposes of making visible what's involved in writing and the affordances that different kinds of specific technologies facilitate. Ivanič et al. (2009) distinguish between mode and technologies in their research setting out to explore the kinds of resources and practices in which people engage inside and outside formal contexts of learning. Their frame of reference seeks to be inclusive, asking, 'which semiotic modes (spoken language, written language, visual, material and/or animation) are employed, in what ways, using what technologies and associated media, tools, materials and physical resources such as computers, notebooks, glitter pens, textbooks' (Ivanič et al. 2009: 51).

An obvious illustration of the nature and affordances of different technologies for writing is to compare 'writing on walls' in two contexts: the use of a spray can on the wall of a government building and the posting of a message on a Facebook virtual wall. Both involve writing on pre-existing spaces but they both use particular kinds of technologies for writing, for example, a spray can in the first case and text/ image/sound produced for and accessed via the screen in the second. In the first case the inscription has to be large enough in order to be seen by passers-by, whereas in

Figure 2.3   Extracts from the status updates on a Facebook wall
(see discussion in Chapter 5)

the second, size or amount of semiotic signs is not an issue because both writers and readers can scroll up and down, use hyperlinks etc. In both cases, there may be more than one writer-producer inscribing on the same wall – and in Facebook of course, the use of walls as an interactive site is a key affordance of this particular techno-logical design. Figure 2.3 shows the status updates on one person's wall, as well as comments posted by others (see also Chapter 5).

Exactly what meanings are afforded by such technologies is of course a ques-tion for exploration but it seems clear that whereas graffiti continues to work as marginal or oppositional, Facebook walls are both 'personal' sites for social interaction and also increasingly sites for commercial enterprise (see for example of study on how businesses can use Facebookwalls http://www.buddymedia.com/newsroom/2011/09/introducing-our-latest-research-a-statistical-review-for-the-retail-industry-strategies-for-effective-facebook-wall-posts/ (accessed 7 November 2011)).

Specific attention is being paid more recently to the way in which 'new' or online technologies – in which writing plays a key role – are mediating people's everyday lives. Such work emphasises both the constraining and the creative potential of new technologies for individuals and their meaning making. Clear examples of the more regulatory/ed kind are centralised information systems designed for the recording of information, evident in many work based contexts and which call on users to use rigid templates, such as for example the storing of medical information in databases (Pontille 2010: Chapter 6). In contrast, examples of the more open ended spaces

---

Box 2.4 Mode and Technologies

Kress (2009) on modes: '*Mode* is a socially shaped and culturally given resource for making meaning. *Image, writing, layout, music, gesture, speech, moving image, soundtrack* are examples of modes used in representation and communication' (p. 54).

Ivanič et al. (2009) distinguish between mode and technologies:

'**Modes:** refers to the range of semiotic resources which can be employed to make meaning, e.g. spoken language, written language, visual, material and/ or animation.

Technologies: includes not only electronic media but also the material media and resources of "old technologies" such as books, newspapers, magazines, pens, chalk and different types of paper' (p. 61).

O'Halloran (2009) distinguishes between 'semiotic resources and the modalities of their materialisation' (p. 99). Example: Language is a semiotic resource which can be realised through different modes – speech, writing.

---

that online technologies provide are web spaces into which users insert or upload their own content, material, ideas and genres – such as in social networking sites – and over which users have considerably more freedom and control. An example of the latter is described by Barton (2010) in his study of Flickr, a photo sharing site www.flickr.com. Of course, the fact that these are all pre-designed spaces means that they are never entirely 'open', that is entirely free for the users to do what they want (for further discussion see Chapter 6). Debates about the specific ways in which technologies impact on meaning making and communication are taking place both in studies of language use (see, for interesting earlier example, special issue of *Language and Communication* 1989) and, in relation to human action more widely, as reflected in discussions about the 'posthuman' condition (Haraway 1991 and Hayles 1999).

WRITING AS VISUAL

As part of the increasing awareness of the multimodal nature of all communication, the visual aspect of writing has more recently come to be emphasised. The visual, like other modal aspects, has tended to be backgrounded historically or glossed over in analysis of written language, with considerable emphasis on the verbal dimension. Attention to the visual has mostly been reserved for particular aspects of the visual or look of writing, that is spelling and orthography, and these through a normative lens (that is analysed or explored in terms of what is correct or appropriate). Sebba (2007) has challenged this default normative approach to spelling and orthography, which he says dominates in sociolinguistics and he argues instead for a social practice account of orthography, to include questions about what people do with signs, and why, and the social meanings attached to these. He offers empirical case studies of particular spelling practices, including for example what he refers to as the 'subcultural use of use of <k>' in areas of the Iberian peninsula to mark political resistance to central or mainstream Castilian Spanish culture (Sebba 2007: 49–50; see also Chapter 6). Other researchers point to the ways in which orthography (as form and spelling, see Box 2.2) is played with in what we can think of as 'verbal light' modes of production such as digital storytelling: for example, Hull and Nelson (2005) give an example of the juxtaposition of the (highly conventional) use of Times New Roman font with 'radically unconventional spelling' LYFE-N-RHYME.

Sebba's concerns about the normative approach to orthography echo those of Blommaert (2005) who uses the term 'hetero-graphy' (see Box 2.5) to emphasise the need to engage with (rather than dismiss) the visual nature of writing, as well as the importance of taking account of what happens when people 'look at' writing – rather than or in addition to – 'reading' writing (for example of the consequences of different ways of reading/looking, see discussion in Chapter 5).

Box 2.5 Hetero-graphy and looking at written texts

Hetero-graphy: Used by Blommaert 2010 to refer to 'the deployment of literacy techniques and instruments in ways that do not respond to institutional orthographic norms, but that nevertheless are not completely chaotic, even if such chaos appears to be the most conspicuous feature' (p. 87)

Reading: Foregrounds the verbal or propositional dimension to engagement with written texts

Looking: Foregrounds the importance attached to attention paid to the visual aspects of a written text

---

Drawing on a semiotic perspective, Goodman (2007) powerfully illustrates the many visual aspects to written language which include colour, size, layout and font – or what she refers to as 'the semiotics of typography', that is the meanings that different fonts, signs and typefaces index, an area of growing interest with regard to public signs (see Shohamy and Gorter 2009). Consider for example, Figures 2.4 and 2.5. Figure 2.4 involves a cluster of signs on a London pub; Figure 2.5 is a sign outside Dublin City Hall. The verbal features in Figure 2.4 are in English and in Figure 2.5 in Irish and English. What is noticeable in the English medium sign are the instances of Celtic script features of Irish medium texts (see Lynam 1969) such as those in the City Hall sign. Whilst not identical, some features are clearly discernible: the use of 'upper case' R, the stylised marking at the top of the <n>, the rising of <ll> above all other characters, the use of accents – on the <i>, the curved <t>. It's also interesting to note both the brand (markedly 'non Celtic') typeface in the

Figure 2.4   Example of public sign using English with features of Celtic typeface

drinks/companies advertised on the window and the use of a more standard English typeface in the sign advertising breakfast – although these are also mixed in that there is a clearly marked Celtic feature in the low <g>.

The Celtic features in the Irish medium sign are strongly linked to the verbal meaning. In contrast, whilst the sign in Figure 2.4 has verbal meaning – the name of the pub and details of what's on offer – the Celtic script features (along with reference to key brands and Celtic patterning framing the windows) have indexical meaning, here indexing Irishness in a way which the English medium text in other script features would not do. Irishness here includes drink – notably Irish brands such as Guinness – music, fun (or the 'craic'), all of which have been heavily commercialised as an 'Irish package' in the past twenty years (see Negra 2006).

In some instances signs seem to be emptied of their (potential) verbal meaning altogether with meaning attached purely to the visual-indexical. Blommaert (2010: 29) exemplifies this with a sign over an expensive chocolate shop in Tokyo, 'Nina's *derrière*', with *derrière* in a handwritten type font. He argues that the sign is not for verbal linguistic purposes (his assumption is that an expensive chocolate shop would not be called 'Nina's backside') but rather for symbolic purposes, to index a cluster of cultural meanings –French/France/European/chic/ expensive. Whether signs are iconic, symbolic or indexical (see Box 2.6) is not just a formal issue (to be identified through analysis of the signs) but also an empirical or ethnographic question, as I discuss below.

Figure 2.5   Example of public sign using Irish with Celtic typeface

---

Box 2.6 Types of Signs (from Scollon and Scollon 2003)

Icon: Sign which denotes, represents some aspect of the object itself/a picture of the thing in the world, for example :) = smiley face (Scollon and Scollon 2003: vi)

Symbol: Sign which is an arbitrary representation of the thing in the world for example green traffic lights mean keep moving

Index: Sign which means something because of where it is located in the world, for example an arrow pointing one direction down a street shows the direction in which traffic should go.

'To put it briefly, a sign can resemble the object (icon), it can point to or be attached to the object (index), or it can be only arbitrarily or conventionally associated with the object (symbol)' (Scollon and Scollon 2003: 25)

Notes

1. Indexicality is a property of all signs. All signs must be located in the material world to exist.
2. At an analytical level some writers, like Scollon and Scollon (2003), make a sharp distinction between indexicality and symbolisation in analysis of signs. Within their framework, indexicality takes on a more literal meaning, for example a sign above a shop in English indexes an English speaking community and/or services. This contrasts with a symbolic meaning of the same sign where, for example, a typeface/font is used to symbolise foreignness.

Particular emphasis has been placed in the past fifteen years on explorations of the relationship between aspects of the visual and the verbal occurring in the same textual space, and a range of analytical tools has been developed to do this. They include 'vectors' or lines that guide the eye – to track transitivity (who does what to whom, and in what circumstances) – in a wide range of publicly available images; and attention to colour and shades of colour to explore modality, used here to signal a perspective on reality and truth value, including 'real' versus 'ideal' as is often evident in advertisements (see Kress and van Leuwen 1996, 2001). Of course whilst this interest from Western applied linguistics/semiotics is recent, semiotic communicative practices that foreground the visual have long since been practised: consider for example systems as documented and reflected in the work of sixteenth-century chroniclers in American Andean regions, such as Guaman Poma de Ayala (see Quispe-Agnoli 2010) and accounts of more recent practices by Menezes de Souza (2003) on the text making of the Kashinawá people in Brazil and Peru. With regard to the last, de Souza identified six possible multimodal combinations of Kashinawá writing on paper, including a geometric pattern standing alone; a geometric pattern plus an alphabetic text; a figurative image standing alone; a figurative image with alphabetic text (for digitally available examples of the hybridity in the work of Guaman Poma, see http://www.kb.dk/permalink/2006/poma/22/en/text/?open=id2972347 (accessed 7 November 2011)).

WRITING AS SPATIAL

Closely linked to the visual dimension to writing – and often considered an aspect of the visual – is the spatial dimension, that is the way in which writing occupies space including the organisation of writing, whether from left to right, right to left, vertical or horizontal. This spatial configuration seems to distinguish writing clearly from speech, a key dimension to the latter being sequentiality; speech occurs sequentially in time, whereas writing is organised in units across space. However, sequentiality may also be evident in some writing that draws on the temporal dimension evident in spoken language in its spatial configuration. Kress argues that this is particularly the case with alphabetic writing, which can be considered a 'border' category:

> Alphabetic writing is a border category in this respect: it is spatially displayed, yet it 'leans on' speech in its logic of sequence in time, which is 'mimicked' in writing by the spatial sequence of elements on the 'line' on which writing is displayed.
>
> (Kress 2009: 56)

This 'leaning on' speech connects writing in some powerful ways with speech and can – in specific instances – signal the greater proximity of writing to spoken language than to other modes, for example, image. However, as discussed above, whilst the verbal–spatial dimension may intend to encourage a sequential *reading*, visual dimensions which involve looking (see Box 2.5) may not involve sequential engagement at all.

WRITING AND OTHER MODAL DIMENSIONS

Once the representational and verbal dimensions are understood as just some – albeit important – modal dimensions to writing, and other dimensions are considered as potentially relevant to definitions and characterisations of writing, other perhaps even less obvious dimensions also come to the fore. For example, the olfactory dimension has been mentioned in some work, as by Wilson (2003) in her work on literacy practices in prisons and the way in which the smell (and taste) of paper and envelopes powerfully evokes other people, places and experiences. These are referred to by Wilson as 'intra-literacy' features, which she uses to 'describe qualities within texts and attached to texts and the activities and practices associated with them that form part of prisoners' meaning making' (Wilson 2003: 301).

Audio/aural modes may also be important, not least because the writing we produce and read/look at involves hearing the words associated with others – not disembodied voices but often attached to real and imagined people and moments (the issue of identity and imagining is picked up in Chapter 6). These lesser researched modal dimensions can be considered perceptual dimensions that are under the surface or 'outside of our awareness' (Hall 1959; discussed by Scollon and Scollon 2003: 48); that is, they are dimensions which are (or may be) significant but are often ignored in the study of communication.

MODES IN PRACTICE: AN EXAMPLE FROM GEOSEMIOTICS

Given the discussion above, it is clear that writing as a phenomenon must always be considered multimodal. In exploring specific instances of writing, it is important to take account of the potential significance of different modal dimensions whilst at the same time avoiding adopting what we might describe as a 'modalist' analytical bias in our approach to writing, akin to the common 'textualist' (Collins 1996; Horner 1999) bias evident in many approaches to writing; that is, we need to avoid assuming that because a particular visual dimension seems salient to an analyst, that it is necessarily salient or significant (or significant in the same way) to producers and viewers. (The question of analytical frames is an issue I return to in Chapter 7.) The significance attached to any specific modal dimension in any specific instance of communication and conclusions about the affordances of mode need to be built on a study of where and how the modes of writing figure in everyday practice.

Perhaps one of the most obvious ways in which the multimodal nature of writing is evident in our everyday lives is in the signs that surround us, captured in the phrases 'geosemiotics' of space (Scollon and Scollon 2003), 'linguistic landscapes' (Shohamy and Gorter 2009) and 'displayed writing' (Beroujon 2010). The labels themselves signal different emphases, most obviously, the 'linguistic' seems to emphasise the verbal nature of signs whereas 'geosemiotics' clearly signals a broader spatially located semiotic perspective.[5] However, together this work (focusing on the signs that surround us – shop signs, road signs, advertisements, travel information) reflects a recognition that writing – understood as a multimodal phenomenon – is ubiquitous. (For example of ongoing research project on signs in public spaces in France, see www.iiac.cnrs.fr/ecriture/)

The importance of the term 'geosemiotics' by Scollon and Scollon to our discussion in this chapter is that they use it to point to the need not only to describe and analyse the nature of these public writings but to explore the ways in which such signs are 'read' or attributed meaning.[6] In this way they explicitly link their analysis of signs within a broader interest in what Goffman called the 'interaction order' (Goffman 1971), that is how we use and 'take up' the meaning of signs in specific contexts.

To illustrate the relationship between signs and readers/lookers, it is useful to consider their research into the ways in which people responded to 'traditional' and 'simplified' characters in Chinese signs in Hong Kong and China. Examples of a company name as it appeared in a street in Hong Kong (TE OU DIAN XUN), and the simplified characters it uses, are provided in Figure 2.6. Figure 2.6a shows the simplified characters used in the sign alongside traditional characters. Scollon and Scollon conducted focus group discussions and interviews with four groups of

Figure 2.6   Shop sign using simplified Chinese characters (Scollon and Scollon 2003: 131–2)

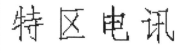 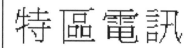

Figure 2.6a   Simplified and traditional Chinese characters (Scollon and Scollon 2003: 131–2)

people from different age groups in China and Hong Kong in which they discussed a variety of photographs of signs from both contexts. Their findings can be summarised as follows:

- The oldest group[7] in China felt that the choice of traditional over simplified characters was motivated by aesthetics, describing the former as more beautiful
- The 'middle group', people who were more clearly associated with the 'Cultural Revolution', offered a political explanation, suggesting that the use of traditional characters 'symbolised the winds of political change from a conservative revolutionary discourse to a more progressive reform discourse' (Scollon and Scollon 2003: 134)
- The young people in China felt that decisions about characters were based purely on pragmatic concerns of businesses – which characters would attract the most attention?
- The young people in Hong Kong emphasised that it wasn't the characters/font that were important but the overall quality of the design and materials: 'if it

was high quality it indexed Hong Kong and if it was of low quality it indexed mainland China' (Scollon and Scollon 2003: 134).

Scollon and Scollon conclude as follows:

> We have concluded that virtually any sign in virtually any font will have all three kinds of meaning potentially available – the meaning that comes from where the sign or font is located in the actual world, the meaning that comes from what the font, design and materials symbolize, and the meaning that comes from the interpretive frames of the users – viewers – readers of these signs. We believe that it would be futile to think that we could isolate these meanings from each other.
>
> (Scollon and Scollon 2003: 135)

CONCLUSION

Writing is a multimodal phenomenon. In addition to those modal dimensions to writing most commonly foregrounded in (socio)linguistic discussions – that is writing as inscription (marking of forms and symbols) and as verbal (grammar, syntax, discourse) – this chapter has argued that there is a need to be aware of, and take account of, a range of modal dimensions including the visual, material and technological. Acknowledging this multimodality has important implications for sociolinguistics as a field – and indeed any disciplinary field dealing with writing – as well as for individual researchers. Disciplinary fields dealing with writing need to open up debate about what writing is and does, including questioning which modal dimensions to writing are significant – and how – in specific instances of use. A focus on the different modal dimensions to writing opens up a theoretical discussion about the affordances or potential 'reach' of modes (Kress 2010: Chapter 1) as well as empirical and theoretical debate about why some modal dimensions to writing are conventionally used and/or privileged in certain contexts rather than others. This in turn raises more general questions about which kinds of semiotic resources are used and valued and why.

For individual researchers, the multimodal – and therefore far more complex – nature of writing presents challenges of both a practical and theoretical nature. As individuals, or even groups of researchers, it is impossible to research all aspects of a phenomenon so choices have to be made. We may choose for particular reasons to focus on one dimension, for example the verbal (as discussed in detail in Chapter 3), but in so doing we need to acknowledge the inevitable limitations of the frame we are imposing. A larger challenge is to seek to approach writing without determining *a priori* which modal dimensions may be the most significant. This means, most obviously, that as researchers and analysts we should not assume that the verbal dimension is always central to writing; but equally, we should not assume that in any specific instance it is not central. So, for example, to the question: Is there a case for 'reading' off the verbal dimension, separate from its materiality? Yes of course; just as a pillow can be turned into a site for graffiti and thus become a semi-public display of comment, emotion and decoration (see Figure 2.2.), a scrappy bit of toilet paper can be used to record ideas and experiences and be removed from its initial material context of production to another, to be rematerialised as a book (see Chapter 6). So whilst materiality constitutes a written text, a text is not necessarily bound/restricted/ by this materiality but rather connects to context in more than one way; a text may index as well as override the specific context of its own materiality.

At any one point or instance in communication, a particular modal dimension to writing – or to writing as compared with other juxtaposed modal elements, such as moving image (e.g. in online spaces, see Chapters 4 and 6) – may be more or less significant to those involved (e.g. as writers, readers, producers, lookers). Being aware of the possible range of modal dimensions to writing as well as other modes alongside writing helps us to avoid any simple categorisations or claims about writing and encourages us – as individual researchers and as researchers contributing to building a field of inquiry – to ask questions rather than make assumptions about not only what writing is, but what it *does*, in any specific context of use. It is only in observing and exploring the use of modes that we can make sense of which modal dimensions are playing a key part in any specific context.

NOTES

1. Of course it is also the case that notions such as 'sentence' have been widely problematised when applied to speech in sociolinguistics (although not when applied to writing). See for example Lemke 1998.
2. 'Involvement' of course has been explored in a number of ways in sociolinguistics with regard to spoken interaction, as in, for example, Tannen 2005.
3. 'Spoken language' may not always involve sound, as in lip reading; the complexity of the relationship between mode, sound, signs and movement is sharply articulated in studies of signing and Deaf communication. See for example, Lucas (ed.) 2001.
4. See Ormerod and Ivanič 2002: 68 for useful heuristic exploring types of meaning carried by physical characteristics of text.
5. Scollon and Scollon's work on place semiotics connects with Blommaert's (2005: 83) notion of 'placed resources' which emphasises that semiotic resources are tied to places in complex and problematic ways – what may be read in one place as having a particular meaning, may not be read or evaluated in the same way somewhere else.
6. For recent work focusing on sign producers' perspectives, see Papen 2012.
7. The labels used to categorise groups are those used by Scollon and Scollon 2003.

Chapter 3

Writing as verbal

INTRODUCTION

This chapter focuses on the verbal dimension to writing. This is the dimension that tends to be most emphasised in studies of writing, historically and currently, and a wide array of tools has been developed both to describe and define particular types and features of written texts. It is impossible to cover all of these in one chapter but my aim is to offer an overview of some key approaches, including reference to some ongoing debates.

The aims of this chapter are:

- to give a broad overview of three common ways of analysing texts – content, form and function
- to illustrate the way in which the social dimension to writing is often explored through different approaches to the relationship between form and function, which are discussed here in terms of layering function onto form, collapsing form and function, elevating form over function
- to illustrate some key traditions and analytical tools for analysing the verbal workings of written text, including aspects of discourse analysis, stylistics, rhetoric and contrastive rhetoric(s)
- to consider the importance attached to *typification* in studies of writing which is most strongly illustrated in the widespread use of the notion of *genre* and to explore the different meanings and uses of this notion

The focus in this chapter is on what I would describe as 'verbal heavy' texts but I also include some more obviously 'verbal light' texts to show how some key analytical notions are used across text types.

APPROACHES TO TEXT ANALYSIS: CONTENT, FORM, FUNCTION

There are many ways of analysing the verbal dimension to written texts and in this chapter I point to several key traditions, each with their own specific interests and clusters of analytical tools. However, before considering specific traditions, it may be useful to begin with three key categories, the relationship between which is at the centre of written text analysis. In broad terms, distinctions between approaches to written text analysis can be characterised in terms of whether they focus on *content* (the what of the written texts), *form* (the how) or *function* (the why or the purpose). What links all three from a socially oriented perspective is an interest in making links between the text and context, with specific contextual or social dimensions defined differently by different researchers and traditions. Much analysis from what we can broadly characterise as (socio)linguistic, rhetorical or discourse perspectives on writing is driven not so much by an attempt to get at the 'true meaning' of a text or a writer's intended meanings, so much as a concern to explore how a text works to generate meanings, and through analysis, to make the features of such workings visible.

Content analysis

An example of content analysis of written texts is work by Pratt and Pratt (1995, summarised by Huckin, 2003: 19) who analysed the content of 3,319 food, beverage and nutrition advertisements in three US magazines, *Ebony, Essence* and *Ladies Home Journal*, in relation to two specified groups of readers, categorised by the researchers as 'African-American' or 'non-African-American'. The researchers analysed the content of the advertisements along three dimensions: product categories (fruits, vegetables, desserts etc.); the form in which the product was advertised (fresh, canned, cholesterol-free etc.); and nutritional themes (high in fibre, good for general health, good for weight control etc.). An example of their quantitative analysis of the form in which food was advertised is Table 3.1. The content analysis showed that there was a significant difference in the frequency and type of promotional messages being made. For example, the magazines aimed at African-American readers had far more adverts on alcoholic beverages than did the magazines aimed at non-African-American readers and had far fewer adverts for vegetables. The purpose of this content analysis was to reach an understanding about how specific features of the texts (food types) were constructed and manipulated by the text producers in their configuration of a particular readership, marked in terms of a particular social category 'ethnicity'. The researchers' analysis explicitly links a particular aspect of the texts – key content items – with a particular aspect of social context – readers of the text, defined in terms of a pre-defined ethnic category. Of course the particular premise, or interest of the researchers in carrying out such analysis is that (print) advertisements can influence or reinforce habitual food choices made by adults, and therefore advertisements which promote unhealthy foods to particular groups of readers may be adversely affecting their health.

Another example of content analysis but one that foregrounds gender rather than ethnicity, and explores this social dimension in terms of the producers of the texts, rather than producers and intended readers, as in the example above, is work by Herring et al. on weblogs (2004. Available at http://blog.lib.umn.edu/blogosphere/

Table 3.1   Comparison of characteristics of food and of promotional statements in food, beverage and nutrition advertisements in *Ebony*, *Essence* and *LHJ* (for full details, see Pratt and Pratt 1995)

Characteristic of Food and Promotional Statements	Ebony	Essence	LHJ
Form in which food was advertised (total number)	1093	755	2264
Form in which food was advertised (in percentages)			
Baked/on platter	2.0	2.9	8.1
Fresh	2.8	1.3	7.4
Canned/bottled	63.3	64.8	24.7
Frozen	1.6	2.0	5.2
Dry	8.0	17.2	18.2
Requires constitution	4.3	5.6	7.3
Ready to eat	11.8	3.7	15.2
Low salt	0.9	0.7	2.1
Low calories	0.7	0.4	1.1
Reduced calories	0.5	0.5	1.4
Reduced fat	2.0	0.4	4.5
Low cholesterol	1.6	0.4	3.2
Cholesterol free	0.4	0.1	1.5

women_and_children.html (accessed 30 June 2011)). Their primary aim in this study was to explore gender – mapped against age group – of weblog, or blog, authors. Their interest was to explore who blog authors were, against a backdrop of media claims that 'blogging' is a predominantly male activity. In their search for indicators of the gender of authors, they used content analysis of blogs, focusing in particular on the following: names, graphical representations (if present) and relevant content of the blog entries (for example, reference to 'my husband' resulted in a 'female' gender classification). Age of blog authors was determined by information explicitly provided by the authors (for example, in profiles) or inferred from the content of the blog entries (for example, reference to attending high school resulted in a 'teen' age classification).[1]

Their analysis showed that the gender and age of authors varied according to type of blog. They identified three basic types of weblogs: *filters* – blogs with links to world events, online happenings, etc.; *personal journals* – blogs with mainly the blogger's thoughts and comments; and *k(nowledge) logs* – blogs which were 'repositories of information and observations with a typically technological focus' (Herring et al. 2004). See Figure 3.1 for examples of the first two types. (They also analysed 'mixed' blogs; see Herring et al. 2004 for further details). They found that the personal blog was by far the most common type being used by all categories of authors, although there were greater numbers of females using this type than any other group, with the largest female group being the 'teens'. Adult male authors predominated in two types of blogs – the filter and the k-log. Herring et al. argue that the personal blogs are a continuation of early paper and current online journal keeping, typically including accounts of someone's daily activity, reflections and comments (see also Chapter 6 for discussion of diaries and notebooks).

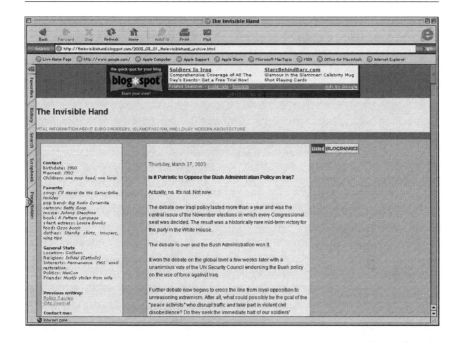

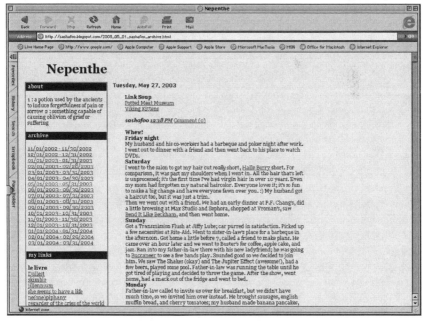

Figure 3.1   Examples of a filter blog and a personal blog (Herring et al. 2004, 2005; note the filter blog is a more recent screen shot from the same blog)

With regard to their original question in carrying out the research – is it the case that blog authors are predominantly male, as public media and discourse seem to suggest? – they show that this is in fact not the case and that if all kinds of blogs are taken into account, young and older women are using blogs as much as men. But they argue that particular kinds of blog are privileged in public discourse – the filter and k-blogs – and these are indeed dominated by male authors. Blogs considered to be less socially prestigious, personal blogs, are used by everyone but more so by female authors, with female 'teens' being the largest group. Thus, Herring et al. (2004) argue that, whilst the blogworld or blogosphere is often construed as a democratic space – open to anyone to use (as long as they have the specific resources to do so) – the values attached to specific kinds of blogs reflects a much commented upon socio-historical phenomenon, the 'Androcentric rule' (Spender 1989) that is, that what gets classified or marked as a 'female' activity tends to be marginalised or made invisible. The work of Herring et al. (2005) can thus can be viewed as part of a long tradition of exploring the relationship between genre, gender and writing and is an issue I return to in Chapter 6 (for useful bibliography, see http://www.ling.lancs.ac.uk/groups/gal/ggb/links.htm).

Any text can be analysed in terms of its content – what it says, it mentions (and what it omits, although this last is more challenging) and mapped in some way against specifically defined aspects of context: some of these aspects may be oriented more towards the text and some more towards aspects of social context. In the examples discussed above, the contextual dimension of the texts is most obvious in the focus on particular text types, or genres (something I come back to below) – advertisements and weblogs – and the social aspects of context that were foregrounded were the categories of ethnicity and gender, with an attempt to make connections between these particular contextual dimensions and the texts produced. Exactly how we make such connections between configurations of specific texts and social worlds is an ongoing debate in sociolinguistics generally and of concern across this book.

It is important to acknowledge that content (the what of a text) is a dimension to all analysis in that, whilst content analysis per se is often not explicitly mentioned as a tool or approach, content clearly plays a key part in scholars' selection of texts to be analysed, as part of larger imperatives driving their/our work (which could be specific interests such as education, health etc. or broader concerns around equality and access etc.). Content is also of interest more generally in terms of the ways in which specific rhetorical and cultural practices are shaping language practices, including writing, a key example here being the link between 'popular culture' and digital and online practices (see for example Williams 2009; see also discussions in Chapter 6 and Chapter 7). However within socially oriented approaches to writing, content analysis as a central goal has been to date less common than work explicitly seeking to explore features or forms of texts in relation to *function. Function* is a powerful notion in sociolinguistics more generally, emphasising an interest not just in what a text is but what it does in any given context, at any specific moment.

Form–functional analysis

Much analysis of writing from a sociolinguistic perspective tends to focus on how texts work to generate meanings, using a combination of what can be described as the 'how' analytic lens (form) and the 'why' analytic lens (function). The relationship between these aspects and how these are treated analytically is a point of debate within sociolinguistics and can be viewed I think as either/both a 'fruitful convergence' or a 'problematic conflation'. For the moment, I'll focus on the form–function complex as a fruitful convergence and return in Chapter 5 to consider some reasons why it can also be viewed as a problematic conflation.

A key reason why the form–function complex can be viewed as a 'fruitful convergence' is that function helps tie form into use and users, and therefore social context, a key interest in sociolinguistics.

> Many sociolinguistic studies have taken linguistic form as their starting point, for example looking at speakers' variable use of patterns of pronunciation or grammatical features. In order to interpret patterns in the incidence of linguistic forms, however, analysts need to make inferences about their meanings or functions.
>
> (Swann et al. 2004: 114)

Thus in analysis of writing, as with sociolinguistics more generally, a focus on 'form for form's sake' is not usually a goal, but a focus on form in relation to its function definitely is. And what we tend to find are different ways of working this fruitful convergence. Here I'll suggest three key ones: the layering of function onto form; the collapsing of form and function; the (temporary) elevating of form over function.

Layering function onto form

A common way of considering function is to start (analytically) with a focus on a particular form, and then seek to understand the function of that form (or cluster of forms). One example is Bazerman's study (1984) of specific syntactical features in experimental scientific articles in one physics journal over the period 1893–1980. Examples of findings from his detailed tracking of articles include a significant rise in the number and length of noun clauses in sentences, illustrated in this extract:

> *The analysis of the continuum intensity* and of *the optical thickness of the plasma column* as well as *the Schlieren measurements* showed that *plasmas with electron densities* between 5×1017 and 7×1019 cm^{-3} can be reproduced rather reproducibly.
>
> (Bazerman 1984: 176; my emphasis)

He also points to a rise in temporal and causal subordination, an example being: 'As the electric field was applied, the oscillator was simultaneously returned to within 10Hz of the shifted point of maximum slope' (Bazerman 1984: 176).

The importance attached by Bazerman to the frequency of particular formal features is in the way they contribute to the construction of meanings in this specific field of knowledge; the increased number and juxtaposition of noun clauses enables more (compact) meanings to be held in one space, just as temporal subordinate clauses enable two processes to be discussed at the same time. Thus although he found that sentence length remained the same over the period studied, the formal, and thus functional, work that was going on, changed. Simply put, the analysis shows that as the field itself developed over time, more information and greater complexity of information demanded 'greater density of expression' (Bazerman 1984: 190). This kind of close analysis of the specific formal features enables Bazerman to reach conclusions not just about the function of such features in specific texts or even a specific field, but to foreground changing knowledge-making practices over time.

Further examples of an interest in form from a functional perspective in the analysis of scientific writing can be found in the extensive corpus-based work that has been carried out. Computer-based corpus studies very successfully manage large quantities of text data and can enable researchers to reach conclusions about the function of particular formal features (see Baker 2010 for an overview). One example is work by Hyland (2002) in his analysis of self-reference (for example *I, me, my, our, we*) using a corpus of 1.3 million words in articles from a range of disciplines. Hyland not only quantified these features by looking at their distribution across different disciplinary texts, but mapped these in terms of specific functions, such as *stating a goal, explaining a procedure, expressing self-benefits* etc. (for details see Hyland 2002). And, having carried out work analysing the occurrence of such features in one corpus – published articles – Hyland was able to make comparisons with other corpora, for example, reports written by students using English as an additional language, as illustrated in Table 3.2. Hyland used his analysis across the corpora to reach conclusions about the range of functions evident in the writing of the two different groups, and argued on the basis of his analysis that less experienced writers face greater challenges in claiming authority in their academic writing.

An important point to note here is that in order to reach such conclusions, Hyland draws not only on textual analysis but also on interviews with writers. The value of combining text data and analysis with interviews is discussed by Harwood (2006) and the importance of the use of multiple methods in order to explore function is an issue I return to in Chapter 5.

Table 3.2   Personal reference in research articles and student reports (per 10,000 words) (Hyland 2002: 1099)

Field	Totals		Singular reference		Plural reference	
	Articles	Reports	Articles	Report	Articles	Reports
Science & Engineering	32.7	9.4	0.1	4.9	30.6	4.5
Business & Professional	46.9	10.5	22.2	6.7	24.7	3.8
Overall	41.2	10.1	14.4	6.1	26.8	4.1

The layering of function onto form in sociolinguistically oriented studies of written texts occurs not only at the level of micro features of texts but also at more meso or macro levels (see Table 3.3 for overview). Thus, at the meso level, attention to function is evident in the familiar categories *Introduction, Discussion, Conclusion*, which are treated as both formal or structural elements – identifiable as specific sections or units of a text – and functional – to introduce, to discuss etc. Another example of this layering of function onto form, and staying with the focus here on academic writing, is evident in Swales's widely used 'move analysis' of introductions to research articles (Swales 1990, 2004). The functional emphasis is most evident in the acronym CARS – Create a research space – that Swales coined to capture the key moves made in research article introductions. Move is both a formal category and a functional category here, that is something that can be identified in the form of the text (although there may be debates about the boundaries of these as identifiable units) and in terms of specific functions. Furthermore, move analysis also presupposes a larger unit of analysis, that of the article itself and its structure, IMRD (introduction, methods, results, discussion) which again is marked formally (through headings, layout, cohesion markers etc.) and functionally, as indicated by the section labelling (methods etc.).

Figure 3.2   Move analysis (Swales 2004: 230)

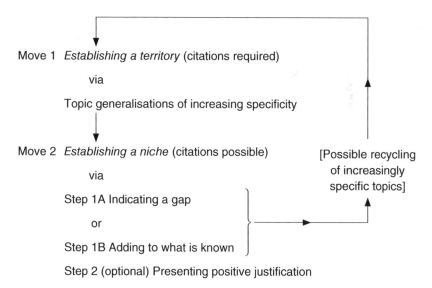

The importance of explicitly framing analytical units of texts as both formal and functional is captured by Swales in his reference to the 'rhetorical work that needs to be done in order to create a research space' (Swales 1990: 142). As I briefly discuss below, 'rhetoric(al)' is a term widely used to signal this form/functional link in analysing written texts but signals not only an intra-textual interest but also a focus on how the text is likely to impact on readers and users. I return to the issue of such impact, through the notion of 'uptake', in Chapters 5 and 6.

The link between form and function is also evident in other key ways of analysing features across written texts. 'Register' is used to refer to language variation according to the context in which language is used with a key distinction often made between formal and informal registers but it is also used to signal differences in terms of particular domains of use and practice, for example, specialist terminology and phrasing used in law, medicine etc. (see Box 3.1.). Whilst register is often used to refer to textual or formal elements, premised upon assumed notions of types of language use, it is also sometimes used to signal a more interactive and active process, and thus links with more dynamic notions of style and styling (see Agha 2003; Blommaert and Rampton 2011).

Box 3.1

Register – common uses
1. Used in sociolinguistics to signal variation of language in relation to context, as compared with variation in relation to use, such as dialect
2. Used in a general way to refer to level of formality in language use
3. Used to refer to a collection of features relating to specific area of experience or knowledge, for example scientific register ('varieties defined by their situation characteristics': Biber et al. 1998)
4. Used in Systemic Functional Linguistics to refer to the contextual variables involved in any text constituted by *field* (activity), *tenor* (roles and relationships between participants), or *mode* (communication channel or mode used) (Halliday 1978).

Enregisterment
Used to refer to processes by which registers come into being, a process 'through which a linguistic repertoire becomes differentiable within a language as a socially recognized register of forms' (Agha 2003: 231)

Other notions which are used to articulate how texts are formally and functionally knitted together are *coherence* and *cohesion*. Whereas the term *coherence* is usually used to refer to the meaningfulness of the text as a whole, *cohesion* is usually reserved for the more formal analysis of how texts are linked internally. Foundational work in this latter area is that by Halliday and Hasan (1976, 1985) whose interest was in developing a system for identifying 'texture', that is how a text knits together (see Figure 3.3).

Figure 3.3   Examples of cohesive ties (from Halliday and Hasan 1976; see for full discussion)

Reference – Example: Three blind mice. See how *they* run.

Substitution – Example: My axe is too blunt. I must get a sharper *one*.

Ellipsis – Example: Four other Oysters followed them, and yet another *four*.

Conjunction –They fought a battle. *Afterwards* it snowed.

Lexical cohesion – Alice *rubbed* her eyes, and looked again. She couldn't make out what had happened at all – *Rub* as she would, she could make nothing more of it.

There is considerable debate about the analytical desirability or validity of separating cohesion from coherence and the importance of combining a concern with how a text formally functions, with a more context sensitive interest. This is illustrated in an extract from a newspaper and comment by Hewings and North (2010).

Figure 3.4   Exploring cohesion and coherence: data extract and analysis (Hewings and North 2010: 43)

Extract
I love coaching but if you ain't got good players [. . .] Kanu was a great free transfer, I thought; Sol Campbell was. They cost good wages but anyone else could have taken them and I didn't see anyone else queuing up. People told me Campbell was finished but I didn't think so
                         ('Hair-raising goal for O'Neil', *The Times*, 15 January 2007)

Analysis
The different parts of this text are linked together by cohesive devices such as '*They* cost good wages' and 'I don't think *so*'. They also hang together in terms of the coherent meaning relationships between different clauses; 'Kanu' and 'Sol Campbell', for instance, are mentioned as examples of the 'good players' referred to in the first sentence, while the whole extract works together to suggest the speaker's good judgement as a football manger [. . .] But interpreting such relationships depends on knowledge of the context in which the text was produced (in this case, a newspaper interview of a football manager) and beyond that, of relevant extralinguistic knowledge (for example, that Kanu and Campbell are footballers) and beyond that again, of the cultural practices associated with English football and sports reporting.

The problematic nature of the relationship between cohesion and coherence and the kinds of tools that can be used to get at these is brought into sharp relief once we consider multimodal or digital texts. For example, how do analysts make sense of the cohesion at work in relatively simple blog pages? (For an example of a blog page see Chapter 7.) We need to consider not just how the verbal elements of the text formally cohere but also how features of the layout, colour, headings, links, images and elements such as YouTube clips cohere overall (see Schiller 2008, Appendix A for a useful list of questions for exploring cohesion in webpages). One way of thinking about this is in terms of 'completeness', which is to do with both the textual features and the way in which these get recognised and used:

The text (or the semiotic unity), the largest level entity, is recognized – from the maker's as much as from the viewer's/hearer's/reader's perspective – by a sense of its 'completeness'; in meaning, in the social and communicational environment in which it is made – the sense of its completeness derives from the 'completeness' of the social event/activity [. . .]

(Kress 2010: 147)

Problems in attempting to distinguish between coherence and cohesion on intratextual and extra-textual grounds (i.e. what the reader/looker does) are of increasing interest in relation to the much larger question of how to define the boundaries of a written text. This is an obvious issue with regard to digital texts, such as web pages, as these are linked to many other web spaces and ultimately the entire worldwide web, but similar issues arise with regard to any text. As I discuss in Chapter 5, notions such as 'text trajectories' or 'text chains' might prove to be useful here, offering a warrant for boundedness on the basis not of individual texts but on the relations between texts, or whole chains of texts, and the work they do in specific social contexts.

Collapsing the form function dichotomy

Thus far I have talked as if form and function are always treated as if they are different phenomena or at least distinct categories, and indicated that description and analysis seem often to move from form to function or hover between an interest in function and form. However, it's important to remember that in some systems of linguistic analysis and theory, this distinction between form and function is explicitly collapsed. This is the case with systemic functional linguistics (SFL), most notably associated with M. A. K. Halliday, and which, as the name suggests, puts function at the centre of its theory: it is based on the premise that language is functional, a resource evolved to meet human needs, and that any system seeking to label and categorise language needs to put function – rather than form as distinct from function – at its core (for summary see Matthiessen and Halliday 1997; for useful SFL web resource, see http://www.isfla.org/Systemics/index.html).

In order to illustrate briefly how SF linguists construct a functional description of language, consider the terms used in the parsing of some sentences in an extract of a student's writing by Moore (2010) in Figure 3.5.

An obvious question that might be asked is why develop what is clearly a complex and – for many people – a 'new' system for labelling bits of language? What does it do that a traditional grammar and its labels can't? One central reason is that the theoretical goal of SFL is to build a description of language that reflects its functional imperative (rather than impose a system that emphasises form only). A more practical reason behind an SFL approach is to develop ways of describing language that can be used productively in pedagogic contexts.

To illustrate these points, I will continue with the example from work by Moore, referred to above, who discusses how the SFL language of description can help

Figure 3.5   Parsing of sample sentences using SFL framework
(Moore 2010: 56)

PARTICIPANT	PROCESS	PARTICIPANT
Type 1: Material processes		
Actor	**Material**	**Goal**
Britain	*broke*	*its alliance (with Japan)*
Monet	*used*	*a blush of atmospheric colour*
Type 2: Mental processes		
Senser	**Mental**	**Phenomenon**
I	*will analyse*	*the events (leading to the formation of the alliance)*
One	*begins dividing*	*the composition (into three levels)*
Type 3: Verbal processes		
Sayer	**Verbal**	**Verbiage**
Historians	*have offered*	*very divergent interpretations (on this issue)*
Type 4: Relational processes		
Carrier	**Relational**	**Attribute**
The images	*are*	*inviting*
These changes (in women's position)	*are*	*very important*
Type 5: Existential processes		
Subject 'dummy'	**Existential**	**Existent**
There	*is*	*a strong geometric element (in the work)*

explain to students some of the problems they face in their academic writing. In one instance, for example, he shows how a focus on the specific types of material *processes* as categorised in an SFL approach – material, mental, verbal, relational, existential – (rather than for example a focus on the one formal label of *verb*) helped make visible the ways in which knowledge is constructed in one specific university discipline, history. The analytical framework enabled Moore, as the teacher, to explore with

Figure 3.6   A souvenir label (Pietikäinen and Helen Kelly-Holmes 2011: 340; full analysis 340–51)

the student how her use of processes in her writing contrasted with those expected in this discipline, and furthermore, to show how the study of history at university level might be usefully conceived not as an unproblematical laying out of historical events (material processes) but more as a consideration of the way different scholars have tended to view these events (mental and verbal processes) (see Coffin 2006 for detailed analysis of discourse of history from an SFL perspective). The notion of function illustrated here is at a micro level – at the level of particular elements in a sentence and looking at what they are doing grammatically-semantically. This central interest in function at a micro level (single item, clause) is linked in SFL to a more macro level category, that of genre, which I return to below (for overview, see Martin 2010).

Elevating form over function

In what might seem like an opposing approach to the collapsing of the form/function dichotomy, approaches clustering around the labels 'poetic', 'literary', 'creative' and 'playful' can be viewed as elevating form over function, that is as paying particular attention to the forms of language used. This links with some multimodal approaches to texts, where, given that a goal of analysis is to make all aspects of semiotic form visible, form (used here in broad terms to encompass multimodal and material elements, as discussed in Chapter 2) is inevitably foregrounded. Consider the souvenir label attached to a ceramic in a museum shop in Finland in

Figure 3.6 and the following extract from the researcher's analysis (Pietikäinen and Kelly-Holmes 2011).

> The language of the label is primarily English, the brand *Dragonia* being a unique piece of language play designed to create a differentiated product (cf. Moore 2003). It is also a case of language mixing and creativity: the English word 'dragon' is fused with a Finnish suffix – 'ia', meaning the place or the house of the Dragon. The person's Finnish name and their title 'ceramicist' work as indexes of authenticity [. . .] While the use of English here narrates the product into a souvenir and guarantees its mobility, the visual, indexing the art of 'primitive' cave-type or Shamanic drawings, offers an additional authenticating support to the souvenir [. . .]

The analytical commentary illustrates the importance of focusing on the 'poetic function' of language (Jakobson 1960; see also Chapter 7), that is the way language is used to draw attention to itself, an approach that is most commonly adopted in studies of writings construed as 'literary' or 'creative'. As the above commentary illustrates, this attention to form is also increasingly evident in everyday or non-literary writing and is accompanied by an attention to aspects often ignored in the more rationalistically or referentially oriented analytical lens of (socio)linguistics, such as 'play' (as in the analysis of the souvenir label), 'fun', 'pleasure' and in general the aesthetics of everyday written communication.

A key example of attention to a form traditionally conceptualised as 'literary' or 'creative' but considered central to everyday spoken and written language is that of metaphor. The significance of the use of metaphor in everyday use of language (and thought) was emphasised in work by Lakoff and Johnson (1980) and has been developed and extended in a number of ways in spoken interaction in many contexts (see for example the work of Cameron 2010).

With regard to writing, in a study of death row penfriend letters between 162 individuals, including fifty-nine prisoners on death row, Maybin analyses the nature of the interaction between correspondents paying particular attention to the use of metaphor, as illustrated below in her discussion of letters between Sam and Karen:

Figure 3.7   Extracts from letter and analysis (Maybin 2011:137)
          (Numbers refer to letters in original texts)

> Sam frequently used metaphor e.g. 'all my life I've ran against the wind so this struggle is nothing new to me' (3), 'in my mind I can hear your voice' (5). Karen also produced her own metaphors, especially as the correspondence got going e.g. 'you wouldn't let yourself be "bought"' (5) [. . .] She also, on two occasions, quoted Sam's metaphors back to him (the only occasions in which she quoted any language from his letters)
>
> [. . .] In his fifth letter, Sam commented 'it hurt me because they don't seem to care, or is it they forget how to care after so many years of pain'. Karen

responded: 'I suspect it's because it is one of their few pleasures after, as you say, "so many years of pain"'.

(Maybin 2011: 137)

Of course, in socially oriented studies of such devices as illustrated here, it is probably more accurate to say that form gets *temporarily* elevated over function, and that an interest in function does not disappear. Thus, with regard to the souvenir label above, the analysis enables the researchers to reach conclusions about how a range of semiotic resources – including image and languages – work at construing a particular value, 'authenticity'. And Maybin's work on correspondence emphasises the way in which resources such as metaphor serve particular purposes in written dialogic exchange:

> The use of quotation and metaphor across these three letters generates a rich range of intertextual resources for interactional work and facilitates the discussion of difficult topics like imprisonment, justice and death.
>
> (Maybin 2011: 136)

The importance of intertextuality is returned to in Chapter 5.

Analytical attention to users' interest in form is increasingly being signalled in studies of everyday language use through reference to 'creativity' (see Swann et al. 2011), a term used above in the analysis of the souvenir label. Examples of such creativity, often multilingual, abound – as with the souvenir label above – and can be found in daily newspaper cartoons (hard copy or electronic), as in for example a recent cartoon showing a dejected-looking regional Spanish football team with the headline S.A.D. where D was added to create an English word *sad* from the S.A. (Sociedad Anónima = Ltd). A further good example of everyday creativity on a large scale is in text messaging, a communicative practice that has grown hugely since 2000.[2] Tagg (2011), drawing on a corpus-based study of some 11,000 text messages, argues, for example, that (mis)spellings such as *wot, u, wud*, are not errors but choices reflecting an interest in the kind of language-play long since common in advertising – such as *Beanz Meanz Heinz*. Defining creativity as 'the manipulation of language form to achieve a certain effect' (Tagg 2011: 228), Tagg gives examples of the kind of manipulation she found. Repetition was one (syntactic parallelism, repetition of lexical items) as illustrated in the two examples in Figure 3.8.

Figure 3.8   The manipulation of form in text messaging (Tagg 2011: 229)

Example 1
Am watching house-very entertaining – am getting the whole hugh laurie thing **– even with the stick – indeed especially with the stick.**

Example 2
T01: All done? All handed in? Celebrations in full swing yet?
T02: All done, all handed in. Don't know if mega shop in asda counts as a **celebration** but that's what I'm doing!

Two important points are made by Tagg: firstly, that users are making choices about the specific forms they are using, drawing on their available resources; secondly, that the medium (used here to signal the specific technology) mediates choices around form and that users manage their choices according to what the medium affords. Thus for example, repetition in the first example in Figure 3.8 enables the writer to indicate a clear stance (positive evaluation of a TV programme and in particular of the walking stick) despite the specific material constraints of this medium (Tagg 2011: 229); repetition in the second example enables successful turn-taking across text messages, by enabling the writer to signal that she is 'responding fully' (Tagg 2011: 229).

As the discussion in the previous section illustrates, all types of socially oriented analyses of written texts involve grappling in some way with the relationship between form and function, and also, although often not explicitly mentioned, content. In the following section I want to continue with a focus on approaches to verbal text analysis but turn my attention to some particularly influential traditions of analysis of verbal written texts, and also use these to illustrate some of the unresolved tensions (or challenges), in particular the troublesome notion of *genre*.

TRADITIONS OF WRITTEN TEXT ANALYSIS

Critical discourse analysis

Discourse is used to signal a range of approaches to language, including writing, and if we adopt the first definition in Box 3.2 most of the work discussed in this chapter could be described as 'discourse analysis'. However, a key distinction in discourse analytical approaches to written texts can be made between those approaches which stay close to texts, thus keeping the functional interest closer to form, and those approaches which can be described as working outwards towards the social functions of the text, often by drawing on social theory (the latter being evident in definitions 3 and 4 in Box 3.2).

There are many researchers working within this latter tradition who, building in particular on the work of Fairclough (e.g. 1992, 2001) explicitly seek to combine close linguistic analysis with social analysis. Fairclough explicitly draws on the work of social theorists, notably Foucault (1972) to develop what he calls TODA, Text Oriented Discourse Analysis. Within this approach, the goal is to pay attention to micro level features of the text whilst also connecting these to more interpretive and explanatory macro social categories to look at 'orders of discourse' (Fairclough 1992, Chapter 3. See Box 3.2). This approach has often been used in the analysis of written or scripted texts, such as media reports, political speeches and advertisements and here I'll consider two examples. The first, in Figure 3.9, is a brief example of the kind of analysis that is carried out within this tradition. Figure 3.9 is an extract from a brochure from a Hungarian chemical waste company (for full details see Gille 2000, Fairclough 2006) followed by an extract from Fairclough's analysis.

Box 3.2 Discourse

1. A stretch of language longer than a single sentence or utterance
2. A type of language used in a particular context (in much the same way as register – see Box 3.1)
3. A way of representing and being in the world
4. A way of structuring and representing knowledge, values and ideologies (most influenced by the work of Foucault, e.g. 1972)

Note: 3 and 4 often overlap; 1 and 2 are often subsumed under 3 and 4, for example a type of language used in a particular context may be analysed in terms of a particular way of structuring knowledge and identity.

Orders of discourse: A Foucauldian notion used by Fairclough (1992: 43) to refer to 'the totality of discursive practices within an institution or society, and the relationships between them'.

(modified version of Swann et al. 2004: 83)

Figure 3.9   Extract from waste company brochure and analysis (Gille 2000: 252–3 – English translation reproduced in Fairclough 2006: 127–9)

Extract
Hungary, like her Eastern neighbours, was characterised by the dumping of the hazardous by-products of industry, that is by 'sweeping the problem under the rug' due to the incorrect industrial policy of the past decades, while in Western European countries with a developed industry and with an ever higher concern about the environment the most widely accepted solution has been the utilisation of industrial wastes by incineration, which is already applied in numerous densely populated areas of Western Europe (Switzerland, the Ruhr, the vicinity of Lyon, Strasbourg, etc.).

Analysis
The second paragraph consists of a single complex sentence divided into two contrastively related parts: the temporal conjunction 'while' combines the sense of 'at the same time as' and the sense of 'on the other hand'. This is where the opposition between East (first part of the sentence) and West (second part of the sentence) is textured or textually constituted. The opposition is between what is represented as the failed and denigrated practice of 'dumping' and the successful and virtuous practice of 'incineration'. As this formulation suggests, *evaluation* is a significant feature of this paragraph (Fairclough 2003: 171–90). The part of the sentence that describes waste-disposal in the East includes several expressions which *connote* ('dumping', 'sweeping the problem under the rug') or denote ('incorrect') negative values.

The analysis draws attention to the ways in which micro features of the text serve to instantiate specific discourses (for example around 'East' and 'West') and how both are anchored to a series of value judgements and evaluations. Similar connections are made in the second example in Figure 3.10, an advertisement from *The Big Issue in the North*, a weekly magazine sold in the streets by homeless people in the UK.[3] The aim of the magazine is to 'offer homeless and vulnerably housed people the opportunity to earn a legitimate income' (http://www.bigissue.co.uk/bigissue. html (accessed 9 November 2011)) and similar magazines are sold on the streets in many parts of the world in many languages. Chouliaraki and Fairclough (1999) identify the specific discourses at work in this particular text and argue that these are illustrative of discourse practices at the beginning of the twenty-first century. They identify the following as being evident in this text: a 'charity discourse', an obvious example of which is the cut-off slip at the bottom of the text where the reader is asked to make a financial donation and the verbal appeal: 'Please support our Christmas Appeal and help us help vendors leave the streets for good'; an 'advertising discourse', where the reader is addressed directly through the verbal language including ***we*** *could try to guilt trip* ***you*** and the image of the young man, whose gaze is directed at the reader; an 'academic social science discourse', which is identified in the following phrases, *challenge stereotypes, sense of self-worth, culture of long-term homelessness* and in the use of nominalisations, which are common in academic discourse, such as *homelessness* and *self-worth*; an 'everyday discourse', *earning a living, find homes, jobs*; a 'political or socially engaged discourse' such as *The Big Issue exists to challenge stereotypes and to help homeless people reclaim their sense of self-worth and dignity by earning a living – all year round.*

Chouliaraki and Fairclough use their analysis of this particular text to make several general points about discourse practices in late modern society. First, they argue that the mixing of discourses in one text, 'hybridity', is a dominant feature of language use and such hybridity means that it is difficult to fix meanings in texts in any straightforward way or to argue that one particular meaning is being advanced in a text. So in this example it is not easy to argue that the text is doing one particular thing – making a charitable appeal – because it is also making a political statement. The hybridity exemplified in this text signals, Chouliaraki and Fairclough argue, significant tensions at the heart of society, not least tensions between consumerism and political action. Second, they point to what they refer to as 'the commodification' of language. By this they mean the ways in which language has itself become a commodity that is used to sell products. In this respect, the aesthetic design of the text is all-important. Third, Chouliaraki and Fairclough point to what they refer to as the 'reflexivity' in discourse practices. This refers to explicit commentary on the use of language and the production of texts. An example they give from this text is the statement 'we could try to guilt trip you', which is an explicit reference to the production of the text itself. Chouliaraki and Fairclough argue that such 'heightened reflexivity' (explicit attention to discourse practices) is a feature of commodification, that is, useful for selling goods, as well as providing an opportunity for greater individual control over discourse practices.

Figure 3.10   The Big Issue Christmas Appeal (in Chouliaraki and Fairclough 1999: 11)

Drawing conclusions about discourse practices based on close attention to individual texts as illustrated above is common in CDA, but there are also examples of quantitative methodologies using computer-based corpus analysis. For example, in order to study the discoursal representation in the media of Islam and Muslims in a number of British and US newspapers, Baker (2010) compared a number of corpora; the first two were sub-corpora of UK newspaper articles which appeared a few years prior to the 9/11 attacks on the Twin Towers and of articles appearing a few years later; the second two were similar sub-corpora – before and after the 9/11 attack – but using US newspaper articles. Baker analysed the keywords in the sub-corpora and on the basis of his findings (see Figure 3.11) argues that 'a "moral panic" had developed around Muslims in relation to terrorism' (Baker 2010: 135).

Rhetoric and new rhetoric

In tracking the development of specific approaches and analytical tools for analysing texts (spoken and written, prestigious and everyday) the work of what is usually referred to as 'classical rhetoric', that is work in the Greek tradition (e.g. Aristotle) and Latin traditions (e.g. Cicero), is widely acknowledged as significant and continues to shape many of the ways we think and talk about written texts. Some notions and frameworks will be familiar to those who have never studied work in classical rhetoric. These include, for example, the idea that language can be broadly distinguished between different types or forms of discourse: four classical divisions are *argumentation, exposition, description* and *narration* which have been picked up in more recent times in, for example, Kinneavy's classification of language types: *expressive, referential, persuasive, literary* (Kinneavy 1971 and discussed in Swales 1990: 42). These categories carry through to many common ways of classifying texts, parts of texts or types of texts, a key example being the distinction often made between 'argument' and 'narrative' (see Box 3.3). More prosaically, we continue to be influenced by classical thinking in the way we go about deciding whether any text can in fact count as a text, as in for example Aristotle's three-part structure of a *beginning*, a *middle* and an *end*. Other tools may be less familiar although their influence will probably be recognisable in some current approaches, albeit somewhat reconfigured: for example, the notion of 'five canons of rhetoric' – *inventio, dispositio, elocutio, memoria* and *pronuntiatio* – continues to be evident in the way we approach writing: process and design (inventio), style (elocutio) and performance (pronuntiatio) (see Corbett and Connors 1999 for overview of classical rhetoric). Similarly, notions such as *topoi* (topic/content), *modes* (for example, narrative, satire, allegory), *forms of argumentation* and *style* (middle, high, low) continue to be a focus in analysis of texts (for useful discussion, see Threadgold 2001). Other classical analytical tools and labels include *tropes* and *schemes*, the former referring to lexical or semantic deviation of some kind, for example in the use of metaphor, and the latter to the foregrounding of form in some way, for example through the repetition of a phrase (for more on foregrounding and deviation see Box 3.4). These 'parts' or 'figures of speech' have been central to the study and analysis of literary texts

Figure 3.11   Keywords indicative of moral panic regarding Islam in British and American press reporting after 9/11 (Baker 2010: 136)

Keywords: words that occur with a significantly high frequency in any one corpus (significance usually calculated by comparison with a reference corpus – see Baker 2010: 26 for how calculated).

Moral panic category	British keywords after 9/11	American keywords after 9/11
Consequence	*anger, angry, bad, bombing, bombings, conflict, crime, dead, death, destruction, died, evil, fear, fears, injured, kill, killed, killing, murder, terror, threat, victims, violence, wounded, wrong*	*attacks, sept*
Corrective action	*arrested, fight, fighting, invasion, jail, justice, moderate, occupation, police, revenge, troops*	*American, Americans, forces, intelligence, marine, marines, military, officials, war on terror*
Desired outcome	*best, better, freedom, good, peace, support*	
Moral behaviour	*America, American, Britain, British*	*Bush, pentagon, United States, US*
Object of offence	*atrocities, attack, attacks, bomb, bombs, criminal, extremism, failed, hatred, illegal, jihad, radical, regime, terrible, terrorism, weapons*	*terrorism*
Scapegoat*	*Arab, suicide bombers, enemy, extremists, immigrants, Iran, Iraq, Iraqi, Islam, mosque, Muslim, Muslims, Pakistan, Palestinian, religious, terrorists*	*Afghan, Afghanistan, al Qaeda, bin Laden, Hussein, Hussein's, insurgents, Iraq, Iraq's, Iraqi, Iraqis, Saddam, Shiite, Shiites, Sunni, Taliban, terrorist, terrorists*
Rhetoric	*question, need, must, why*	

* Note that the Scapegoat category does not imply people or groups who are 'blameless', but those who are often assigned a disproportional amount of attention for a perceived problem.

with the development of lists and taxonomies being of greater interest at particular moments in time; for example, during the European Renaissance period, Peacham (1557) identified almost 200 types of figures of speech in English (discussed in Wales 2001: 153).

A defining characteristic of rhetoric is an interest in how texts (spoken and written) persuade, or what we can gloss in broad terms as a concern with the effect that texts have on others. The pedagogical take-up of this concern from classical rhetoric has tended (historically and currently) to restrict the frame of reference to textual features but a focus on persuasion necessarily involves paying attention to phenomena beyond the text, most obviously to readers and listeners, and an interest in what texts are doing in a particular context, why and how.[4] A move away from text-bound approaches towards more contextual accounts is often referred to as 'New Rhetoric', a tradition located mainly in the US (see Freedman and Medway 1994; Petraglia 1995), a key work in this field being that of Miller, whose explicitly action-marked Aristotelian definition of genre is widely cited: 'A rhetorically sound definition of genre must be centred not on the substance or the form of discourse but on the action it is used to accomplish' (Miller 1984: 152).

This framing of genre as social action has led to approaches that seek to offer more contextualised accounts of what texts achieve, by tracking how texts get used and drawing on additional notions such as 'genre suite' (for example Berkenkotter et al. 2011, which is discussed in detail in Chapter 5), and approaches that aim to locate texts as part of 'activity systems' (for example Russell 1997) which I refer to again below and discuss in more detail in Chapter 7. I return to the question of genre in the final section of this chapter.

Box 3.3 Key features of argument and narrative

Key features of argument: Focus on claim, evidence, appeals, warrants. Structured by claim, evidence and overarching argument

Example of key analytic frame used: Toulmin 1958: Used widely in analysis of written academic discourse (e.g. Andrews 2009) and in wide range of contexts (Lunsford and Ruszkiewicz 1999)

Key features of narrative: Focus on representation of events, action, description of people, places. Structured by chronology both as represented at the surface level of a text and at a deeper level, that is, other possible sequences of events (the former referred to as *sjuzet* and the latter as *fabula* by analysts known as the Russian formalists, for example Shklovsky 1925)

Example of key analytical frame used: Labov 1972: Orientation, Complicating Action, Evaluation, Abstract, Resolution, Coda. Widely used in analysis of spoken discourse but also of written texts (e.g. newspaper articles) Bell 2007; see also Chapter 5

Stylistics

Drawing boundaries between different approaches obviously oversimplifies the ways in which researchers engage with traditions of inquiry and analyses of specific texts. And in some work on everyday writing there are no clear boundaries between 'rhetoric' and 'stylistics'. For example, the work of Cook on food labels explicitly uses notions from both traditions to explore how labels seek to persuade: rhetoric, through attention to ethos, pathos, logos; and stylistics, through attention to linguistic devices. An example of this kind of data and Cook's analysis is in Figure 3.12.

Figure 3.12   Food label and analysis (Cook 2010: 139)

Extracts
The packet is pastel grey with line drawings of happy pigs among oak leaves and acorns. On the front, we read:

> Waitrose organic Chipolatas are made from selected cuts of belly and shoulder of pork from organically reared, English pigs. The pork is coarsely chopped and blended with herbs and spices to produce succulent and full flavoured chipolatas. Our organic pigs are reared outside with freedom to root and roam on selected farms in Norfolk and Lincolnshire.

and on the back

> James Keith supplies Waitrose exclusively, with pigs from his farm in Norfolk. The pigs are reared outdoors throughout their lives in small family groups and fed on a balanced cereal diet with vitamins and minerals. Warm shelters and straw bedding protect them from winter, while mud baths keep them cool in summer. James' expertise, care and commitment to the more extensive nature of organic farming ensures we deliver consistently high quality and traceable sausages.

Analysis
Though this is factual (and correct) information, it is phrased and presented in a way to appeal to readers' emotions, with intimations of exclusivity (*selected* (twice), *exclusively*), culinary expertise (*coarsely chopped and blended*), self-indulgence (*succulent and full flavoured*), nationalism (*English, Norfolk, Lincolnshire*). The language is extravagant, with alliterative phrasing (*full flavoured, root and roam, care and commitment*) and sensual tactile imagery (*mud baths, warm shelters*). In addition, the accountability of the supermarket (*we deliver consistently high quality and traceable sausages*) is complemented by the personal touch of the small business run by a named individual in which animals are treated almost as humans (*family groups, bedding* and *baths*). In addition, the narrative alternates between impersonal third person (*Waitrose organic Chipolatas are made from*) and more intimate first person (*our organic pigs, we deliver*) as though the reader were engaged face to face

in a friendly chat with the retailer, as they might be in a local shop or market stall. The whole creates a friendly but powerful message, a bucolic image of a rural idyll, calculated to appeal to an urban market.

However, as is illustrated in Cook's predominantly text-stylistic analysis in Figure 3.12, if rhetoric signals an interest in looking outwards to purposes beyond the text, stylistics seems to draw back to the text. There is a range of definitions of stylistics (see Wales 2001 for useful overview) and its origins, including its links with classical rhetoric, through the branch of rhetoric referred to as *elocutio*; in broad terms, stylistics is the study of the significance of form and a key current approach is the study of 'linguistic features which are stylistically relevant' (Short 1996: 18). Because of its main focus on 'literary' texts, the kinds of analytic categories and labelling systems developed reflect the kinds of language that many literary texts use but also, as importantly, the ways in which writers and readers are presumed to engage with the production and reception/engagement with such texts (this is an issue I return to in Chapter 7). Key notions, *foregrounding* and *backgrounding*, which are understood as having psychological effect – i.e. how the writer and reader produce, appreciate, interpret and engage with texts – are strongly linked with a key textual or linguistic category, *deviation* – that is specific features of a text that are surprising or unusual in some way (see Box 3.4). The underlying premise for the development of these kinds of categories is that (literary) writers are actively seeking to craft language in ways which the reader may not be anticipating and to use and craft language in interesting and novel ('deviant') ways. Consider the brief extracts in Figure 3.13 of a poem and an analysis and the attention the analytical comment pays to specific forms.

Figure 3.13   Extract of poem and stylistic analysis (Short 1996: 62, 67)

Extract
[. . .]while a fist of cold
Squeezes the fire at the core of the world,

Squeezes the fire at the core of the heart,
And now it is about to start

(Ted Hughes, 'October Dawn')

Analysis
The last stanza is [. . .] foregrounded for a number of reasons. Its first line is the second part of a very marked two-part parallelism, its second line is the last of the poem (and therefore inevitably attracts some degree of foregrounding), and this line is also the climactic end of a series of lines related together by adverbial linkers (First . . . Soon . . . Then . . . And now . . .). But the content of the poem's last line hardly seems to deserve all this foregrounding, as it says nothing that we cannot already have deduced from the rest of the poem. As a consequence I feel somewhat let down at the end of the poem, experiencing

an effect often called *bathos*. Perhaps you can find a sensible justification for the foregrounding. In that case you will have done better than I have interpretatively, and at the same time will have helped to make 'October Dawn' an even better poem that it already appears to be.

Short's analysis indicates a view of stylistics which is concerned with exploring the link between linguistic form and meaning, understood here as interpretation of the text. Within this approach, what constitutes 'deviation' and whether this gets positively or negatively evaluated depends not least on the reader (and it's important to acknowledge that this is an introductory text and the 'you' being addressed is likely to be students of stylistics and literature). For he points to both the significance of intra- and extra-textual dimensions and signals an interest in the way in which 'real' readers rather than just 'expert' (i.e. scholarly) readers engage with texts (this is an area of increasing interest, see for example Lillis 2006, Allington and Swann 2009, Swann and Allington 2009). The general relevance of stylistics to a discussion of socially oriented approaches to writing is that, as the name implies, particular attention is attached to style or form, and particular significance is attached to acknowledging creative and aesthetic dimensions.

As already discussed, attention to 'style' or 'form' is increasingly evident in attention being paid to form in non-literary writing, by users and by analysts, as illustrated in the discussions above (for example the discourse of *The Big Issue*, the form of a souvenir label, metaphor in letters, play in a souvenir label). There is

---

Box 3.4

Stylistics
Definition: Stylistics is the study of style. Style can be broadly defined as 'perceived distinctive manner of expression'; different styles are associated with different domains or contexts of use; distinctions between style can be analysed in terms of 'the set or sum of linguistic features that seem to be characteristic' (see Wales 2001: 370–2 for further elaboration and definitions)

Key notions
Foregrounding: The effect of some aspect of a text being emphasised and pushed to the fore

Backgrounding: The effect of some aspect of the text being made less visible or significant

Linguistic deviation: Uses of language that seem to differ or deviate from 'normal' usage and thus draw attention to or foreground that language. Example from literary writing: 'Come we burn daylight, ho!' Romeo and Juliet, discussed in Short (1996). Example from television advertising: 'Lorries go, Drills go, Lambs go, Caterpillars go, Cargo, P & O' (see Cook 2001: 143)

evidence therefore of an interest in the formal and aesthetic dimensions to writing as a semiotic practice, alongside an interest in the more functional dimension to language use (how and why it gets used) – providing evidence therefore for Chouliaraki and Fairclough's claim of a 'heightened reflexivity' in language use in contemporary society (I return to the poetic–aesthetic frame for exploring writing in Chapter 7).

Contrastive rhetorics

As the name suggests, work in contrastive rhetorics (I'm explicitly using the plural here which I will explain below) involves a focus on comparing two or multiple traditions of meaning making in writing. Contrastive Rhetoric (CR– the singular is the more widely-used form) is a well-established, if contested, field which seeks to compare the ways in which linguistic and rhetorical features are used to construct and represent meaning in written texts, in two or more languages, or in the same language by writers from different language backgrounds (for example of latter, see Connor et al. 1995 comparison of job applications, in English, by Flemish and US students). Carrying out empirical analyses of differences at the level of texts is central to this work; much work has focused on academic writing in different languages (for example Connor and Kaplan 1987, Hinds 1990, Taylor and Chen 1991) and increasingly at disciplinary discourse level (for example, Fløttum et al. 2006, Lorés-Sanz et al. 2010). Foundational work in CR involves comparisons of texts based on highly rigid notions of different languages (not unusual in linguistics generally) i.e. 'English', 'Japanese', 'Swahili' which in turn are usually configured as 'cultures', often based on nation state categorisations. This link between clearly demarcated languages and cultures is most strongly evident in Kaplan's widely cited early work (1966) in which he reaches conclusions not only about the linguistic/rhetorical differences between texts but uses these to justify claims about differences in cultural thought patterns. His (in)famous 'doodles' include the representation of English rhetoric as a straight line, Oriental languages as a spiral, Arabic as a series of zig-zags. Whilst these representations have been highly criticised, the assumptions about the boundedness of languages and their relationship to particular culturally (nationally) marked ways of doing things are still pervasive in current CR work, as Kubota illustrates in her overview of the field (Kubota 2010). Furthermore, as Kubota points out, much discussion in CR has *English* as its (implicit) point of reference, often driven by pedagogical concerns about how to support writers using English as a second/additional language. 'Contrastive rhetoric research often takes for granted prescriptive rhetorical conventions in English' (Kubota 2010: 276). This means that claims are often made about rhetorical features of texts (and language and cultures) based on assumptions about conventions and expectations that do not in fact map onto descriptions of actual usage and practice. Kubota gives as an example the emphasis in the US on the teaching of the '5 paragraph theme' to students using English as an additional language, whilst there is little evidence that this is the rhetorical form used and valued in school or university writing.

In contrast with this CR tradition, a range of approaches is developing which emphasises the fuzzier edges to languages and cultures and which I am glossing here in the plural term as 'contrastive rhetorics'. Whilst CR is more or less explicitly premised on the assumption that writing should be examined in terms of one language, a standard version of that language and through a lens of appropriacy and correctness/error, CRs starts from the premise that most people in the world live and move through complex configurations of linguistic repertoires and resources and that all of these are (and should be allowed to be) drawn on when producing written texts. Whilst multilingualism at a text analytical level is a long-standing interest in the sociolinguistics of speaking, as in studies of code mixing and switching, less attention has been paid to such mixing in studies of written language. However this interest is growing, as indicated by, for example, current work on 'meshing'[5] (Canagarajah 2011) and an example of this is in the brief extract from an academic text written by Smitherman in Figure 3.14.

Figure 3.14   Extract from *Talkin That Talk* (Smitherman 2000: 346)

> In the current controversy surrounding the Black Idiom (as well as other so-called 'minority' dialects) linguists/educators/English teachers/and juts plain folk bees comin from one of three bags: (1) eradicationist; (2) bi-dialectalist; (3) legitimizer. These positions have undergirding them not simply linguistic issues but important socio-political concerns. (I mean, where is yo head?) While Ima rap specifically bout the Black Thang, with minor modifications, what Ima say can apply to most 'divergent dialects'. (Now I ain gon cite no specific folk since this piece ain bout name-calling.) [. . .]

'Translinguality' (Horner et al. 2011) is a term being used to refer to a shift away from singular and bounded notions of language use towards recognising the range of resources that people use in constructing written texts:

> This approach sees difference in language not as a barrier to overcome or as a problem to manage, but as a resource for producing meaning in writing, speaking, reading, and listening.
>
> (Horner et al. 2011)

In such discussions the emphasis tends to be on how teachers may adopt this translingual stance (see Lu 1994), but the same questions arise for researchers and analysts. What does a translingual stance mean for the analysis of written texts? Most obviously, mixing and meshing would not be seen as error but as 'normal' usage, implicitly or explicitly chosen by users (see Chapter 6).

TYPIFICATION AND GENRE

In analysing language, the idea of looking for similarities and differences – whether at the level of language more generally, or at the level of specific uses of language

Table 3.3   Overview of examples of commonly used analytical tools for analysing the verbal dimension to written texts

Micro text level analysis	**Examples** Specific *textual feature*, lexical, functional or grammatical
	Specific *structural unit* or relation between units, for example, sentence, clause, phrase, theme/rheme
	Specific grammatical units, for example, parts of speech (noun, verb, adjective, material process, etc.)
	Specific stylistic units, for example, simile, metaphor, alliteration
	Punctuation
Meso text level analysis *Relations between parts of texts*	**Examples** Paragraphs, verses, scenes
	Stages
	Parts
	Beginning/middle/end (Introduction/conclusion)
	Structure (of particular texts, for example, academic articles IMRD, problem solution)
	Moves (Swales)
	Cohesion (for example, Hasan)
Macro text level analysis	**Examples** *Language* Used to refer to a boundaried cluster of verbal resources, usually marked by a geopolitical label e.g. 'English', 'Chinese'
	Genre Used to refer to types of texts in some way (as abstract notion, to signal clusters of texts which are related; as empirical notion, using labels which have become conventionally acceptable such as reports, articles, novels, poems; and/or categories of rhetorical aspects – discussion, description, analysis etc.)
	Rhetoric Key examples, argument, narrative
	Discourse(s) Ways in which meanings are constructed through language with emphasis on power and ideologies
	Register Variety of text(s) and features according to context of use

– and the idea of there being 'types' is very strong. Such typification is captured in the notion of 'genre' which, whilst widely used in relation to spoken language, has a long history when describing and classifying literary texts, and has grown in use with regard to a much wider array of everyday writing (see Box 3.5 for definitions).

Box 3.5 Genre

1. Used in literary studies to refer to different types of institutionally recognisable literary texts such as poetry, novels, plays
2. Used in studies of writing to refer to clusters of texts grouped according to their function or purpose, such as essays, letters, forms, academic articles
3. Used in SFL as one of three levels of analysis of communication, the others being register and lexicogrammar (e.g. Martin 2010)
4. Used to refer to socially and culturally patterned ways of engaging in activity (for example Russell 1997; Bazerman et al. 2009; Miller 1984).

Genre is in widespread use albeit with different emphases. In the study of non-literary texts, a key distinction is often made between the use of genre to refer to types of *texts* or types of *activity*, with such distinctions reflecting and being attributed to different research traditions. For example, SFL is often described as adopting a text-oriented approach to genre, in contrast with New Rhetoric which may be described as adopting an activity approach. An example of the former is where categories of genre, particularly when applied to pedagogical settings, involve the labelling of text types and subtypes, such as narrative and argument (and different types of these) and micro- or sub-genres such as recount, procedure, factual report.[7] With regard to New Rhetoric, Miller's emphasis on genre as action, discussed above, is often cited.

However, even in those approaches and traditions where genre as action is foregrounded (including some accounts of genre in SFL)[8] in researchers' analysis it is often the text that becomes the focal point. Thus whilst genre is often used at a theoretical level to signal that types of writing reflect, enact and signal types of sociohistorically-derived activity, what we find is that additional frameworks and terms and notions are employed in order to get at such activity. One example is the use of activity theory alongside genre (for example Russell 1997); here genre is used as a typified *activity* rather than a text type, where the emphasis is on the activity (for example the doing of research) which involves engaging in a range of 'text-types', such as notes, lab reports, scientific articles (for diagram and further discussion see Chapter 7). In sociodiscursive and social practice accounts, a distinction is often made between 'text type', 'genre', 'discourse' and 'practice' (or discursive practice), whereby a text type may be seen as an example or instantiation of a genre – a student's essay for assessment as an instance of a particular type of writing in higher education, essayist literacy, with essayist literacy construed as a particular discourse practice – a way of knowing, being and doing in the world (see for discussion Scollon and Scollon 1981; see also Chapters 4 and 6 for further discussion). It is possible to discern different starting points in data collection, observation and analysis: basically starting from activity/action towards texts, or starting from texts outwards towards activity. However, across all approaches there tends to be slippage in analytical practice towards genre as text analysis. There is no easy solution to this tension; in my own research because of my interest in how texts are connected with situated activity, I find *practice* a more useful notion than genre, a preference signalled by some other writing researchers (for example Reuter and Lahanier-Reuter 2007; and I focus on the notion of practice in Chapter 4). A further question to consider about genre is to ask whether it is being used to describe an empirically observable phenomenon – whether text and/or action – or whether it is used to refer to something more abstract, something that serves as a powerful heuristic, that is as a tool for exploring and raising questions about actual texts or action.

The notion of genre is therefore complex at a number of levels and complicated by slippages in academic usages between the different dimensions. Some of these tensions and slippages are outlined in Box 3.6.[9] In Chapter 5, I return to the notion of genre and how – when used as a way of explicitly capturing the clustering and trajectories of texts – it can usefully disrupt the ways in which genre is often tied to text and rather tie text analysis more tightly into analysis of practice.

Box 3.6 Different ways of working with genre

- As text type or as activity
- As predefined notion of specific genre(s) or genre yet to be identified
- As predominantly stable or predominantly dynamic
- Using the analyst's categorisation of genre or users' categorisation
- To index an empirical fact/existence or to index an abstract notion/heuristic/ideology/metaphor

---

CONCLUSION

Exploring the verbal dimension to writing involves paying attention to three key aspects – content, form and function. Content tends to get backgrounded in sociolinguistic analysis but it's clear that the content of texts is often central to researchers' focus of inquiry, and, as I discuss in Chapters 6 and 7, content is becoming increasingly central to debates about digital and online technologies in terms of the link between popular culture and production practices (including writing). However, in what I have characterised as sociolinguistic approaches to writing, the concern tends to be with how texts work to generate meaning, and here the relationship between form and function is of central interest. As discussed, function is an important notion because it is the means by which form is anchored to social context, although there is a range of ways in which this is done. I have talked of there being three, in broad terms: layering function onto form; collapsing the form/function dichotomy; and elevating form over function. These different approaches are reflected in many ways in specific academic traditions of inquiry, which in turn are overlain with other interests; thus for example a key analytical goal in CDA is to connect form and function through a notion of discourse, in order to map discourse practice against social practice. In contrast, stylistics seeks to connect form with function but lingers with form, and this lingering is part of an evaluative orientation to texts in which form and attention to form is valued, as well as notions such as enjoyment and pleasure, both in production and (analytic) reception. The extent to which different approaches make function a predominantly textually-based category varies, but there is inevitably a tendency in all textually-oriented studies to understand function in terms of what the text seems to be doing. Some traditions explicitly signal an interest beyond the text – for example the notion of 'rhetorical purpose' indexes a purpose/human agency dimension – which connects with practice orientations to writing that are discussed in Chapters 4 and 5.

In terms of level of textual analysis, distinctions can be made between micro, meso and macro analysis, the micro involving a focus on specific and apparently small features of a text – of course small doesn't mean inconsequential – the meso seeking to focus on a larger section of the text or indeed the text as a whole and the macro – larger categories such as 'genre', 'language' and 'discourse', which influence how we engage with the object we are looking at and indeed the previous two levels of categories. Another key distinction between approaches can be made on the basis of whether the analytical focus is on single texts or types of texts (usually in order to identify patterns across these types) and approaches which seek to explore specific texts in relation to other texts, in terms of 'text chains' or 'ecologies'. I will illustrate examples of these latter approaches in Chapter 5.

As this chapter has illustrated, we are not short of tools for analysing the verbal dimension to written texts; the challenge is how we might best make use of these in writing research and, where necessary, develop new ones. What is important is that in adopting a particular approach, we are reflexive about what such an approach both makes visible and obscures. Different academic traditions offer different frames of reference, and we can usefully draw on these in analysing verbal dimensions to writing. How different traditions may structure our approaches to writing as a semiotic object and practice is an issue I return to in Chapter 7.

NOTES

1. Reading off these categories from text data alone is of course problematic. In their analysis Herring et al. state 'reference to "my husband" resulted in a "female" gender classification, assuming other indicators were consistent'.
2. A range of terms is in current use, such as texting, SMS, TMS.
3. This commentary is a shortened and slightly revised version of Lillis and Mckinney 2003: 13.
4. Rhetoric as a field continues to play a key, albeit highly contested, role in writing research and pedagogy in some parts of the world, notably the US. For interesting discussions of some of the debates, see Petraglia 1995; Berlin 1996; Crowley 1998.
5. 'Meshing' signals a specific orientation to the notion of 'language' use, challenging the idea that users need to choose one code over another, see Young 2007. Canagarajah (2011: 403) distinguishes meshing from codeswitching as follows. 'Whereas codeswitching treats language alternation as involving bilingual competence and switches between two different systems, codemeshing treats the languages as part of a single integrated system.'
6. See also Box 4.5 on 'languaging'.
7. As this section of the chapter seeks to illustrate, 'genre' is a label that is used in many ways. Thus in more textually oriented and taxonomic approaches to genre, we find terms such as

'subgenre' or 'mini-genres' e.g. see Lemke 1998 for reference to mini-genres of scientific research articles which include elements such as figures, captions, reference lists.

8. A much-quoted definition of genre from Martin is as follows: 'A genre is a staged goal-oriented, purposeful activity in which speakers engage as members of our culture' (Martin 1984: 25). Examples of genres as staged activities are making a dental appointment, buying vegetables, telling a story, writing an essay, applying for a job, writing a letter to the editor, inviting someone to dinner.

9. Swales 2009 provides an interesting overview and account of the range of powerful metaphors of genre currently being used in the study of writing.

Chapter 4

Writing as everyday practice

The question of what is 'ordinary' or 'everyday' involves more than simply the data we select but crucially depends on how we analyze and frame them.
(Briggs 1997: 454, cited in Blommaert 2005: 51)

INTRODUCTION

This chapter marks a shift away from analysing writing as a verbal text, discussed in Chapter 3, towards a focus on the way writing is embedded within activities of everyday life. The chapter outlines what it means to adopt a 'social practice' approach to writing – which includes providing a lens for making the everyday nature of writing visible – and illustrates some of the key analytical tools currently used in this approach to writing.

The aims of this chapter are:

- to consider what counts as 'writing', nested within a discussion of what counts as 'literacy'
- to illustrate some of the ways in which writing is an everyday practice
- to outline some of the analytical tools developed for exploring writing as a social practice
- to consider the significant growth of writers/writing at this historical moment and the ways in which old and new writing technologies are being used together for particular purposes
- to consider ways in which writing is a differentially evaluated resource across different domains, using the example of a key social institution, that of formal schooling.

The chapter introduces frameworks and analytical tools which are further illustrated and explored in Chapters 5, 6 and 7.

WHAT COUNTS AS LITERACY? WHAT COUNTS AS WRITING?

Given that a central argument in this book is that writing should hold a key place in sociolinguistics because in many ways it is as 'ordinary' as spoken language, it is worth stopping to consider the ubiquity of writing and literacy more generally. Historical landmarks signalling the growth and use of literacy usually foreground technological and/or profound social changes, with the following often specifically mentioned: the invention of the printing press (Havelock 1976); the rise of the 'modern' city (Beroujon 2010; Colloque de la casa de Velázquez 1981); indus-trialisation and the rise of working-class organisations, such as WEA (Workers Educational Association) in the UK (for example, Williams and White 1988); com-pulsory state level as well as religious schooling (Laqueur 1976, in Cook-Gumperz 2006); relatively cheap postal systems (How 2003); the rise of the internet and growth in new technologies, an issue I return to below; the shift from labour, land or industrial production towards a 'knowledge based economy' (Brandt 2009). Accounts of significant landmarks in the rise in literacy from postcolonial or global 'periphery' (or 'non-centre') contexts[1] also foreground these dimensions but in addi-tion emphasise the impact of colonial practices, such as the influence of missionary workers on particular ways of inscribing local oral languages and semiotic practices (see Lewis 2001), and the differential values attached to 'non-centre' or Western ways of inscription (see discussion in Blommaert 2008: 117; Williams 2006) includ-ing the visual in writing practices (see Menezes de Souza 2003, Baca and Villanueva 2010 discussed in Chapter 2). It is calculated that from the mid-nineteenth to the early twenty-first century the number of people reading and writing globally rose from 10 per cent to 80 per cent and that the current global adult 'literacy rate' is 83 per cent, with a male literacy rate of 88 per cent and a female literacy rate of 79 per cent. Such figures suggest that by far most of the world can be described as engaging in some kind of reading and writing (UNESCO 2006, 2011).[2]

If historical overviews and statistical surveys point to the increase in reading and writing activity globally, research in New Literacy Studies (NLS) provides empirical (mainly contemporaneous) accounts of the range of everyday literacy activities in which people engage. Contrary to many survey approaches founded upon particu-lar, narrow definitions of literacy (for critique, see Hamilton and Barton 2000) and assumptions about what kinds of writing actually (should) count as 'writing' – most obviously, socially privileged texts such as literary, legal or religious texts – NLS starts from the premise that there is a need to explore what kinds of writing (literacy) are going on, where, how and why. In much the same way that sociolinguistics has championed the notion that everyday speech is worthy of academic study, NLS has made everyday or 'ordinary' writing (and reading) a worthy topic of investiga-tion and thus gone some considerable way to reconfiguring what we understand by 'literacy'.

Writing as ordinary

Some examples of the ordinary writing in which many people are involved on a routine basis are outlined in Figure 4.1. Based on their ethnography of literacy practices in north-west England, Barton and Hamilton (1998) identified six areas of everyday practices where writing and reading were central: organising life; personal communication; private leisure; documenting life; sense making; social participation. The categories are not intended to be completely distinct – they do of course overlap – but to give a strong sense of the range of writing practices that are embedded in everyday life. Some of these types of writing are considered by users to have a purely transactional purpose; for example leaving a note to tell someone what time you will be back or completing a form with information about previous schooling experiences and qualifications. Others clearly have a creative or aesthetic purpose, such as writing poetry, keeping a reflective diary.

The ordinariness of writing (and reading) activities is emphasised across New Literary Studies (NLS) work: some of the specific meanings and values attached to this notion of 'ordinary' in relation to literacy more generally, and writing specifically, are outlined in Box 4.1.

Box 4.1 Ordinary writing

- Writing is *ordinary* in that it is part of everyday life and routines
- Writing is *ordinary* in that it is ubiquitous
- Some *ordinary* writing may be transitory in the sense of discardable (Sinor 2002)
- The *ordinary* nature of some writing makes it invisible even whilst it may be central to everyday life. Like all ordinary communication, therefore empirical and theoretical tools are needed in order to make the nature and consequences of writing visible.

In mapping people's everyday practices, some writers, like Barton and Hamilton make a distinction between 'vernacular' (and link this with 'ordinary', 1998: 251) and 'dominant' literacy practices on the basis of the domain of practice and, importantly, the locus of control and regulation over such practices. I return to the question of control in Chapter 6 but for the purposes of the discussion here, I want simply to emphasise that whatever the specific nature of such practices, they are all 'everyday' writing in the sense of being routinely embedded in people's lives (although exactly which specific practices in whose lives is always a question for exploration). Across the book, examples of these various kinds of everyday writing are illustrated and discussed.

Figure 4.1   Writing as everyday practice (based on Barton and Hamilton 1998: Chapters 1 and 14)*

A	Driven by peoples' everyday needs and interests	Examples
1	Organising life	Diaries, calendars, address books, records of finances
2	Personal communication	Letters, emails, notes, texting
3	Private leisure	Writing poetry, stories, social networking sites, making videos
4	Documenting life	Records of events, photo albums, flikr, recipe books, diaries, life histories, family histories
5	Sense making	Personal/reflective diaries, research relating to specific problem (i.e. legal, health), informal learning
6	Social participation	Campaigning and community activity newsletters, webpages, emails, texting, graffiti
B	Driven by institutional demands and regulations	Examples
7	Governance (local, national state/ transnational)	Form filling (tax, letters/ applications for citizenship, passports etc.) e and hard copy
8	Work (organisation/regulation)	Notes, letters, memos, form filling, record keeping e and hard copy, emails
9	Education/training,	'Schooled' writing practices (essays, reports, dissertations, theses) assessment forms
10	Religion, health/ medicine, law	Letters, newsletters, forms, emails, texting, weblogs

* I've inserted examples of what Barton and Hamilton refer to as 'dominant' rather than 'vernacular' literacy practices here and also added in examples of online and mobile technologies that have become common in many parts of the UK since their research was carried out in 1998. See also Barton 2010.

A SOCIAL PRACTICE PERSPECTIVE

Considerable research has been carried out since the 1970s in different parts of the world, often under the heading of NLS, setting out to describe, explain and interpret the everyday reading and writing practices in which people engage. At the heart of this work is the notion of 'practice'. Whilst used with varying emphases in different works (see also Figure 4. 2) 'practice' signals two key principles: an empirical commitment to observe and explore what, where and how people read and write, including their perspectives on what they do, as well as their values and interests; a theoretical interest in seeking explanations for the nature and consequences of what people do, including a focus on issues of power and agency drawing on notions from sociological and critical discourse theories. Both principles challenge the idea that 'literacy' (or writing) is one unified phenomenon with one set of outcomes, a position encapsulated in the highly influential distinction made by Street between an *autonomous* and an *ideological* model of literacy (Street 1984, 2003). Whilst literacy tends to be looked at through the lens of an 'autonomous' model, both in everyday discourse and many academic fields, Street argues that literacy – and our specific focus here, writing – is never one thing, with one pre-identifiable set of consequences for individuals or groups (see Box 4.2). We cannot take 'writing' – what it is and what it means to do writing – as a given. That there are specific functions or purposes in any instance of writing is clear; however what these functions are cannot be solely assumed on the basis of prior assumptions about particular texts and genres: hence the considerable effort in NLS in observing and exploring what people are doing with reading and writing across contexts and domains of social life.

Box 4.2 Autonomous and ideological models of literacy
(Street 1984, 2003)

Autonomous model of literacy: The view that literacy in itself has consequences irrespective or autonomous of context.

Ideological model of literacy: The view that literacy not only varies with social context and with cultural norms and discourses regarding, for instance, identity, gender and belief, but that its uses and meanings are always embedded in relations of power. Literacy in this sense always involves debates over meanings and struggles for control of the literacy agenda.

At an empirical level, therefore, a key focus has been on identifying and describing the range of practices in which people engage, with different dimensions of context being foregrounded. In some widely cited work, the key focus is on the range of practices in which specific *communities* engage, with community being configured along dimensions of geographical location/culture/linguistic background/social class/gender (see Chapter 5 for discussion of community). Such work includes

Heath's (1983) widely cited research comparing the everyday practices of people in three communities in the US, defined as 'mainstream', 'Roadville' and 'Trackton' – corresponding to white middle-class, black working-class and white working-class communities (see below for further discussion); the literacy practices of villagers in Iran, identifying in particular two literacies, a 'commercial' and a 'traditional' (Street 1984); the literacy practices of the Vai in West Africa, pointing to three distinct traditions and practices – Koranic, Western and indigenous (Scribner and Cole 1981); as already mentioned, the literacy practices of a community in one area of the north of England (Barton and Hamilton 1998); the everyday literacy practices of minority multilingual communities (Baynham 1995; Saxena 1991); women's practices in Nepal (Robinson-Pant 2001); adult literacy practices in community-based activity in South Africa (Kell 1996, 2010); the literacy practices of younger and older people in West Africa (Blommaert 2008). Whilst these studies foreground communities in their exploration of literacy practices, in other studies it is the specific *domain of activity* that receives particular attention; for example, literacy in prison (Wilson 2000, 2003), farming (Jones 2000; Mbodj-Pouye 2010), public scribing in Mexico (Kalman 1999), medical and health care literacy practices (Papen 2010; Berkenkotter et al. 2011), the making and placing of subway signs (Denis and Pontille 2009), administrative and legislative practices (Walsh 2009), academic literacy practices of students and scholars (Lea and Street 1998; Lillis and Scott 2007; Lillis and Curry 2010).

Across this work there is a keen interest in the modes, materialities and technologies of the literacy practices in which people engage. Given the growth in the use of online and mobile technologies, there is considerable interest currently in exploring the literacy practices associated with and afforded by such technologies, including a focus on who is using which specific technologies and for what purposes (see for example, Barton 2010 on the use of Flickr; Black 2005, 2006 on online fan fiction; Lee 2007 on instant messaging; Williams 2009 on young people's use of online practices; Lea and Jones 2011 on undergraduates' use of technologies in and outside of the formal curriculum). In this and subsequent chapters I illustrate the considerable amount of writing nested in all areas of social activity, and below discuss an example of the use of 'old' and 'new' technologies in a specific context (see also Chapter 6 for discussion of research on digital technologies in relation to identity work).

This drive to explore empirically what people do, where, how and why, and with what consequences, is at the centre of New Literacy Studies; in order to carry out such research, both empirical and theoretical tools have been developed, and continue to be developed, as I now discuss.

Theoretical and empirical tools for exploring writing as social practice

The interest in, and attention to, ordinary writing that people do in their lives – and the meanings attached to such writing – reflects the 'ethnographic pull' in sociolinguistics, discussed in Chapter 1. As in ethnographic approaches to spoken language, what this means at the empirical level is that *writing* – used to mean what, where and how people produce, respond to and engage with written texts –is the primary framework. This ethnographic pull involves a particular 'ontology of language' which is that:

> There is no way in which language can be 'context-less' in this anthropological tradition in ethnography. To language, there is always a particular function, a concrete shape, a specific mode of operation, and an identifiable set of relations between singular acts of language and wider patterns of resources and their functions.

> (Blommaert 2006: 4)

This ontological position, particularly with regard to the impossibility of 'context-less' writing means at an empirical level that careful attention needs to be paid to observing and making sense of the contexts in which reading and writing activities take place and people's perspectives on these. A key challenge therefore has been to develop observational and analytical tools that can facilitate this attention to immediate context and many of the tools developed in the 'ethnography of communication' (Gumperz and Hymes 1972; see Chapter 1) used in sociolinguistics to study spoken interaction have been taken up in the study of literacy, as indicated in Figure 4.2. Some of these tools for empirical description seem to be quite straightforward: for example, answering the question of who is writing what and in which situation/context (participants, texts, events) seems to be something we can get at quite easily through, for example, different forms of observation.

Certainly the usefulness of such methodological tools has been borne out by much literacy research, as illustrated in the chapters across this book (see for example, Chapter 5 for the use of networks and communities, or Chapter 6 for the use of roles). For examples of the use of log/journals for documenting and tracking 'everyday' writing and literacy practices, consider Figures 4.3 and 4.4. The clock face in Figure 4.3 was completed by a young person asked to log her everyday literacy practices; such logging enables the researcher to learn about many of the aspects of 'events/Practices 1' listed in Figure 4.2, that is, the activities, such as the particular artefacts used, domains of activity and some details of the participants and communities involved. This attention to the details of one person's practices was part of a much larger study aiming to find out about the kinds of literacy practices in which people attending further education colleges in the UK currently engage (Ivanič et al. 2009). Figure 4.4 shows extracts from a journal kept by a social worker as part of a larger study seeking to explore the kinds of writing that social workers do and the challenges that such writing poses. In this instance, the social workers were provided with a template by researchers to encourage them to indicate what kinds of writing they engaged in, where and when, using which kinds of materials and technologies, and to indicate whether writing was an (un)interrupted activity. The journal again reflects an attempt to get at some of the key aspects listed in Figure 4.2. On the basis of such data, it's possible to learn about individual practices but also patterns across groups and domains of activity and, furthermore, to explore the nature and

Figure 4.2   Key tools used for exploring writing as social practice
(from Barton and Hamilton 1998, 2000; Baynham 1995; Street
1984)[3]

Key organising notions	Description	Empirical tools (examples)
Events/ Practices (1)	**Activities** where literacy has a role, such as writing letters, reading newspapers, responding to emails and are made up of key elements including participants, settings, artefacts and activities.	**Observation**, physical co-presence (being present when people are writing, and using tools such as audio/video recording, field notes) or virtual (through engagement in online observation)
	Participants, the people who are involved in reading and/or writing and/or interacting around written texts	**Collections of written texts**
	Settings, the immediate setting in which an event is happening	**Talk around texts**
	Artefacts, the tools and technologies being used, drawn on	**Interviews**
	Activities, the actions in which participants are engaged.	
Practice (2)	Participants' perspectives and meanings	**Generation of diaries, logs, journals**
Domains	Places (e.g. the home, workplace) and spaces (e.g. formal, informal, non/ hierarchical) where activities occur	**Generation of diagrams**
Networks	To describe the links between people, events and the movement of texts	**Collections and productions of images (photos, drawings)**
Roles	To describe the different repeated and routine activities or positions that individuals engage with and adopt	
		Documentary data
Communities	To refer to the geographical, linguistic, political or cultural groups with which people move or identify themselves	**Questionnaires**
Practices (3)	To refer to theorisations of the meanings and values attached to literacy within particular social and cultural contexts, involving categories such as:	
	Habitus, referring to routinised practices which are embodied and socially structured	
	Agency, referring to individual control/ action/opportunity	
	Ideologies, referring to world views/ systems of ideas shaping perspectives on writing	
	Power, referring to material and ideological control over the use and evaluation of material and semiotic resources	

consequences of such activity in particular social domains. In the case of the college related study, the researchers were able to identify not only the range and amount of literacy practices people took part in both inside and outside of formal education but to identify key characteristics of these practices and the ways these differed. For example, they found that many literacy practices outside of college were shared activities (often physical or virtual collaborations with others), were self-determined (that is involving choice of activity, time and place), involved multi-media (a variety and a combination of paper and electronic media) and were multi-modal (including a variety of language, symbols, pictures, colour and sound) (for full discussion see Ivanič et al. 2009). In the case of the social work study, a key finding was that whilst writing reports and case notes is seen as a core part of social work, there is in fact little time for writing and, as importantly, little uninterrupted time for the writing of complex and highly consequential documents.

Accounts derived through the use of different methodological tools, such as those illustrated in Figures 4.3 and 4.4, can build towards explaining or theorising what is involved and at stake in writing in particular domains, focusing attention on issues such as: the specific social and material conditions under which writing takes place; the extent and ways in which particular technologies are constraining or facilitating actions and interests; the particular forms of writing that are valued; the extent to which writers have control over their writing; the systems of evaluation in place for determining what constitutes successful writing; the nature and scale

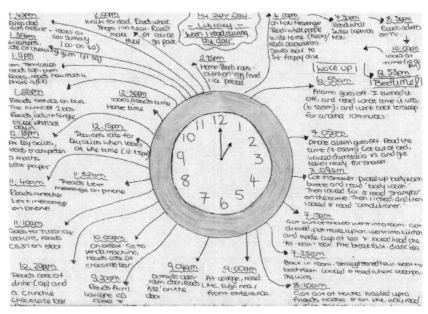

Figure 4.3   A clock face activity to track everyday literacy practices (Ivanič et al. 2009: 28)

Figure 4.4   Keeping a journal to document writing in everyday social work practice (Lillis and Rai 2012: 6)

Approx time	Place (office, home, car etc.)	Medium (handwritten notes in note book, email, IT system etc.)	Type of text (case notes, email, minutes of meeting)	Notes on text (who was involved, stage text is at – draft)
21.38 approx. 10–15 mins (U)	Home	IT system	Case notes HE	Young person and carer
22.07 approx. 30 mins (U)	Home	IT system	Referral HE	Birth mother, family support worker, manager and social worker. It took me days to get the correct referral form so that the referral could be made. I sent many emails and made three telephone calls before tracking down the correct form. I had in fact completed an incorrect form and had to redo it.
22.49 approx. 1 hour (U)	Home	IT system	Placement with parent Agreement HE	Discussion with judge in court and guardian. Discussion with birth mother and her sister in Ireland. Discussion with my manager and senior managers
23.51 3 mins (U)	Home	IT system	Telephone conversation Case note HE	Discussion with birth mother's relative. Agreement sought.

Note: U= uninterrupted

of the consequences of any writing for all involved, including writers, readers and potential users.

In general terms, the categories in Figure 4.2 such as participants, artefacts, domains have proved useful in directing researchers' attention towards things beyond the written text as (verbal) product and in helping to contextualise writing production in a number of ways. At the same time, criticisms and concerns have been raised about such tools. A key issue here is the question of boundaries and boundedness relating to both texts and practices: How do we define, characterise and observe an event, a community, a network? Whose perspective is taken account of in making such definitions, for example, the researcher's and/or (one of) the participants'? The same question arises with regard to writing: How do we define what counts as writing? How do we define the boundaries of an instance of writing? Is it on material/artefactual grounds, for example, is it one piece of paper, one book, one web page? Or is it in relation to time, that is at one moment in a particular text's history or 'entextualistion' (see Chapter 5)? There are no easy answers to such questions and, of course, the usefulness of any analytical tool or notion will depend on the specific research questions being explored. But it is important to recognise the potential limitations with categories that may construe too fixed and rigid an account of writing particularly in research seeking to track how texts 'travel' (Blommaert 2005). I turn to other notions currently being used, such as 'text histories', in Chapter 5.

A further key challenge is how to link empirical observation with participants' understandings and perspectives as well as with analysts' description and theorisation of both of these. The importance of this link for writing and literacy research – and an attempt to label these connections – is, as already discussed, captured in the use of the term 'practice' which, it can be argued, is both usefully and problematically elastic. Methodologically, some researchers use 'event' for what is observable and 'practice' for what is possible to infer about broader patterns of social and cultural ways of doing writing (for example Barton and Hamilton 1998, 2000), and in exploring both dimensions, participants' perspectives are considered crucial. Some researchers use practices to refer to all three dimensions (for example Baynham 1995; Street 1984, 2003; Lillis and Curry 2010). Thus, as indicated in Figure 4.2, practice is used in at least three ways: akin to 'event', to refer to and describe what people do/are doing; to refer to people's perspectives on these events/activities; to refer to theorisations of what people are doing and why, drawing on notions from social theory more widely, some examples of which are included in Figure 4.2 under 'Practices 3': *habitus, power, ideologies* (these are picked up at different points in the book – for habitus and agency see Chapter 6). These different meanings attached to practice and the implicit (I would argue, productive) tensions surrounding what is being foregrounded reflect researchers' ongoing attempts to link empirical accounts and observations with theorisations of what it means to do writing.[4] This tension is in part reflected in the interplay between *emic* and *etic* lenses in ethnography; emic is used to refer to insiders' understandings (for example what college students or social workers know and think about writing) and etic is used to refer to outsiders' understandings, notably the researcher's who may be drawing on a range of academic knowledge from outside of the immediate phenomenon being explored. Emic and etic are sometimes construed as a dichotomy, yet as Kell, an ethnographer of adult literacy, discusses they can more usually be viewed as always in dynamic tension (see Box 4.3). Most obviously, as the researcher becomes more immersed in the lifeworlds of participants, she may get to understand or experience emic perspectives; at the same time, she may find that in the process of approximating insiders' perspectives, she is sharpening and reconfiguring her etic understandings.

Box 4.3 *Emic* **and** *etic* **in ethnography** (from Kell 2010: 224)

Sometimes presented as if these were a dichotomy
Emic: Outside/outsider perspectives, descriptions, discourses
Etic: Inside/insider perspectives, descriptions, discourses

But emic/etic involves a dialectical relationship
Etic 1: A frame of reference with which an analyst or observer approaches data

$\updownarrow$

Emic: The discovery of valid relations internal to what is being studied

$\updownarrow$

Etic 2: A reconsideration of the initial frame of reference in the light of new understandings

---

WHO ARE WRITERS? THE CURRENT GROWTH IN WRITING ACTIVITY

If we adopt the broad NLS definition of writing to include writing of all types, we can see that the amount of writing currently going on is considerable. And there is every indication that this is on the increase. Of course, as already discussed, any answer to the questions, such as who are writers and, where and how much writing is going on will depend on what gets labelled as writing. Some types of brief or routinised writing are often not considered as 'writing' by producers (or indeed language/writing researchers). For example, somebody may think of himself as 'doing writing' or as a 'writer' if he is a member of one of the many 'creative writing' groups there are in the UK (for some estimates, http://www.nawg.co.uk/ (accessed 20 Dec. 2010)) but the same person may not think of himself as a writer or doing writing when he is inputting data in a computer system as part of his daily banking job, or when using Facebook or texting. One of the most obvious ways in which writing is made more or less visible is through the particular kinds of labelling attached to different kinds of activity, some of which are used in both everyday talk and academic discussion. Thus the following list can be considered examples of activity where writing is central but where writing is made more or less visible in labelling the activity: from the more visible, such as *writing, authoring, reporting, editing, scribing, producing, recording* to the less visible such as *designing, emailing, inputting, blogging, texting, recording, tweeting, working*.

Whilst the growth in literacy historically and geographically is indicated in available figures, some research specifically emphasises growth spurts in writing. A good example is the explosion in the use of postcards in Britain at the turn of the twentieth century, which was made possible by the establishment of the British Post Office and the cheapness of cards and postage (How 2003). Such cards were referred to as the 'letters of the poor' and after their introduction in the late nineteenth century it's calculated that some 6 billion postcards were mailed between 1901 and 1910 (for detailed discussion of Edwardian postcards see Gillen and Hall 2010).

The most obvious example of a current spurt in writing activity arises from the use of mobile and online technologies. Evidence specifically focusing on what we can describe as the more verbal-heavy texts is provided by Pelli and Bigelow who talk of a 'writing revolution' in their work on public authoring. They define public authoring in terms of published books, blogs, Facebook and Twitter.

> We found that the number of published authors per year increased nearly tenfold every century for six centuries. By 2000, there were 1 million book authors per year. One million authors is a lot, but they are only a tiny fraction, 0.01 percent, of the nearly 7 billion people on Earth. Since 1400, book authorship has grown nearly tenfold in each century. Currently, authorship, including books and new media, is growing nearly tenfold each year. That's 100 times faster. Authors, once a select minority, will soon be a majority.
>
> (Pelli and Bigelow 2009a)

It is important to note here that in their plotting of the growth in writing, Pelli and Bigelow use the term 'author': 'author' tends to be used to refer only to those people who are writers of texts which are published and have official, legal or socially prestigious status. Their use of the term includes not only those conventionally accorded 'author' status, but also writers/ings on Facebook and Twitter. A further

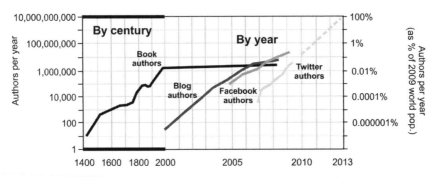

Figure 4.5   A history of authorship (Pelli and Bigelow 2009a, b)

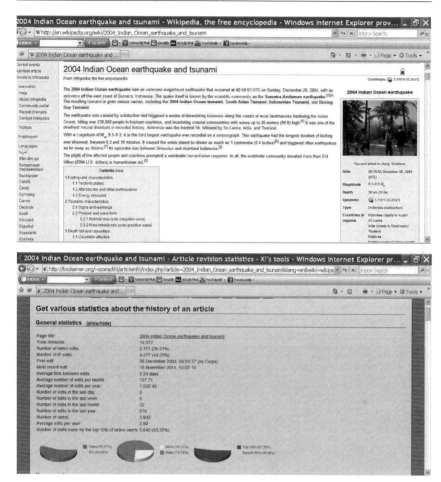

Figure 4.6   Screen shots of Wikipedia entry on Indian Ocean tsunami and statistics on edits, available at http://en.wikipedia.org/wiki/2004_ Indian_Ocean_earthquake_and_tsunami and http://toolserver. org/~soxred93/articleinfo/index.php?article=2004_Indian_Ocean_ earthquake_and_tsunami&lang=en&wiki=wikipedia (accessed 15 Sept. 2011)

dimension is that in new media contexts 'authoring' is explicitly multiple (of course much text production in general is by multiple authors, as is illustrated in Chapter 5). Richardson (2006) focusing on the creation of wikis after a tsunami killed 175,000 people in 2004, noted that the first Wikipedia entry of seventy-six words was created nine hours after the event; one day later and more than 400 edits later, the entry had grown to 3,000 words and included photos. Six months later, more than 7,000 changes had been made with the entry at 7,200 words long (Richardson

2006: 61). If we look at the statistics on this wiki we can see that by 2011 there had been 10,572 edits (see Jones 2008 for discussion of revision practices on Wikipedia).

The claim that we are witnessing a growth in production (over consumption) via digital technologies is made by many commentators: Kress (2010: 22) talks of a general shift from consumption to production, citing the large numbers of people taking part in technologically mediated innovations such as YouTube – where in 2008 a daily uploading of 60,000 videos was logged, and current figures are given as thirty-five hours of video being uploaded per minute, many created/'mashed' by users themselves (http://searchenginewatch.com/article/2073962/New-YouTube-Statistics (accessed 2 Feb. 2012)). Whilst in this site it is the visual (video) that dominates, verbal written language is often also strongly evident, sometimes embedded in the images (as in subtitles and glosses), alongside images and also as part of comments about videos, as is illustrated later in this chapter and in Chapter 6.

Several points are important to bear in mind here in terms of the amount of writing activity going on and where this is happening in the world. The first is that writing using older technologies (pens, paper) continues daily, in the form, for example, of notebooks and journals, but these latter seem to be a particularly significant practice in some poorer parts of the world (for use of notebooks, see Chapter 6; for examples of accounts of 'everyday' writing in twentieth-century Africa, see Barber 2006; Blommaert 2008). Secondly, new technologies are multiple (both in what they are/do and in terms of costs) and are being taken up differently globally, so that whilst particular practices, for example like YouTube, are proliferating particularly in the global 'centre', other technologies, notably text messaging via mobile phones are growing significantly all over the world, not least because they are comparatively inexpensive. Deumert and Masinyana (2008) point not only to the already strong but growing use of text messaging in Africa but also to the way in which this specific technology seems to be sustaining multilingual literacy practices, in this case isiXhosa alongside English in South Africa (see also Vold Lexander 2011). A third point here is that 'new' technologies are, of course, being used alongside and interspersed with 'old' technologies of writing, as I illustrate later in this chapter. Contrary to much public comment, even so-called 'digital natives' (Prensky 2001) continue to use a wide range of communicative practices: 'for the entire population of those ages 12–17, phone conversations and face-to-face meetings are the most frequently chosen ways to communicate with friends outside of school' (Lenhart et al. 2007: iii).

What is of interest from a social practice perspective is to consider what kinds of writing are being produced and used where, by whom and for what purposes and what we seem to find – and this may be an obvious point – is that people use whatever resources are available to them in their specific contexts and make use of these for areas of life that are significant to them. I briefly consider one recent example of popular, political activity in the following section.

USING OLD AND NEW WRITING TECHNOLOGIES: AN EXAMPLE OF POPULAR POLITICAL ACTIVITY

On 15 May 2011 peaceful protests began to sweep across Spain bringing together people of all ages and backgrounds to demonstrate dissatisfaction with political leaders and a political system that seemed to be doing nothing to engage with the increasing numbers of people who felt disenfranchised. Calling themselves <<los indignados>> inspired in part by the French writer Hessel (2010)[5] people occupied major Spanish cities, notably Madrid and Barcelona but also many more. It is calculated that the initial protests involved some 130,000 people, but that around two million people participated in some way in the following months by actively taking part in the demonstrations, living on or visiting the squares. As with other similar movements, much has been made in the media of the use of mobile phones and social networking sites particularly around activities such as arranging times to meet or demonstrate.[6] The question I want to focus on here is: What semiotic resources and – in particular given our focus here – *writing* did people use to engage in activities relating to these demonstrations?

There are several points that are worth mentioning in our focus on the nature of everyday writing. Firstly, alongside the use of mobile technologies, a key semiotic practice involving those in the squares was the regular use and updating of information written by hand on large sheets of paper posted around the squares: these posters listed organisational tasks, such as rotas for tidying up parts of the square, but also agendas for the *asambleas*, semi-structured public meetings called at regular intervals to discuss and debate specific issues, from practical decisions about how to organise 'living on the square' such as child care, meals, cleaning, to debates about specific proposals and political strategy. The large written sheets were central to the *asambleas* as were note-taking on hard copy paper and face-to-face interaction.

On being asked about the range of communication methods she had observed being used as part of the 15-M movement, a twenty-five-year-old student commented as follows: 'Facebook has been the source of information that I've most used in relation to the 15-M movement, both for getting information and to express my opinion. I've used my mobile phone to share photos and videos taken during the demonstrations and *asambleas*' (Translated from the Spanish original).

However, she also stated: '*Asambleas* have been the nucleus of the 15-M movement – and in these everybody who's wanted to has had the opportunity to express themselves freely, using megaphones or microphones, offering ideas or critiques. But also posters and banners have been the best way of reaching those not directly involved, of communicating with people not actively seeking information' (Translated from the Spanish original).[7]

A second key point to note is that participation involved different types of writing, using a range of technologies in immediate and more distant geographical contexts. Handwritten, hand-painted banners were not only in the squares but in places far from these. The image in Figure 4.7 shows a banner hanging from a balcony in small village in northern Spain with its recognisable slogan (verbal, 'I

Figure 4.7   Handmade banner

Figure 4.8   YouTube upload, number of viewings and examples of comments

am also (with) 15 May', and colour – red on white) indicating verbally and visually support for the movement.

This use of 'old' technology echoing at some geographical (and cultural) distance from the protests in urban areas was paralleled by a considerable amount of echoing and participation, via online and mobile technologies, both geographically close and at a greater distance. Following the first few hours of the occupation of the main square in Madrid, 'Spanish revolution' was a 'trending topic' on Twitter. Other hashtags being used were #15M, #acampadaensol, #yescamp (see Velasco 2011).

Likewise on Facebook, videos were being uploaded and there was considerable activity in commenting on these as illustrated in Figure 4.8, which shows the popularity of such sites (14,115 hits) and gives some indication of the range of comments and the geolinguistic contexts of viewers/participants.

- Peace From Tunisia We Support you !! Yeah Democracy Change The System !

marwenHamrawi 1 week ago

- Desde Barcelona, BRAVO LOS HERMANOS DE MADRID!!!! RESISTENCIA!!!! NO A LA VIOLENCIA!!!!!

Ojara985 1 week ago

- big respect to the spanish activists! greetings from germany & viva la revolution!

NokturnalTimes 1 week ago

- Hi, my name is michael from Germany, we have the same problems here too, it s not as worse like in spain but we are working on a solution. Inform about Silvio Gesell and tell it to the people in spain. Silvio Gesell had developt a way out of all economic crises!!! The world belongs all people!!!

The above account briefly illustrates the range of writing using old and new technologies to get this particular activity going and to sustain it beyond immediate localities of the squares using a range of modes, materialities, technologies and languages. The account also underscores the relevance of questions already raised about some core analytical categories in literacy/writing research mentioned above: most obviously 'event' and 'participation'. The initial (publically named) 'event' here, 15-M, was constituted by countless interconnected tiny literacy events and, in fact, the activity in which people engaged obviously predated this particular date and has continued long since. With regard to 'participants' many people shared information and opinion on YouTube, Tuenti, Facebook and banners; some were actively involved on the squares, some participated through their comments at a distance, some visited (both squares and relevant virtual sites) and some did a combination of all these at different moments in time. There are thus many types of production and participation. The writing can be usefully conceptualised in terms of a chain of texts and activity, linked by the shared interests of users mediated and marked by specific semiotic and rhetorical practices. The function of these different kinds of writing at different 'links' in the chain is an empirical question: from the comments by one person (above) we can begin to understand how the different modes and technologies of writing were used, and to what effect. But this is clearly an area that needs further investigation (see Chapter 5 for further discussion of text chains and trajectories and Chapter 6 for heteroglossia in digital spaces).

WRITING AS DIFFERENTIALLY EVALUATED RESOURCE: THE CASE OF FORMAL SCHOOLING

Throughout this chapter, I have emphasised the significant amount of different kinds of writing activity in which people are engaged. At this point it is important to make two obvious, yet important points. The first is that writing is not one thing, but involves many different kinds of materials, technologies and practices including various kinds of relations around texts; writing, like all communication practices, is not an 'open' or neutral bank of resources, available to all, but is made available and learned (or not) through the specific contexts we inhabit and used in different ways for different purposes. Secondly, and relatedly, different kinds of writing are differentially evaluated in and across domains. Writing, again as with all communication practices, is embedded in evaluation practices, often tied in with powerful social institutions that regulate (amongst other things) the norms and conventions governing such practices. And the institution in relation to which differential evaluations of writing nested within literacy more generally has been most fully discussed has been that of formal schooling. Formal schooling, understood here in the sense of formal education across institutions and age ranges has clearly played – and continues to play – a key role, as a site for the teaching and learning of writing, but also in influencing practices and attitudes towards writing.[8] For whilst writing and reading play a role in many peoples' daily lives, regardless of their schooling experience, formal educational contexts are where most people most obviously spend time doing activities labelled explicitly as writing and, as importantly, where they develop a sense of what counts as doing writing and literacy. Consider the following response to a researcher's question about a man's (il)literacy, as part of a larger project on everyday literacy practices in Pakistan (Nabi, forthcoming as reported in Street 2010: 207).

> Researcher: You can write very well, why did you say you are *Jahil* (illiterate)?
> Zia, plumber: I do not have any certificate or paper to show that I am literate, which means I am illiterate.

Schooling plays a central role in codifying socially what counts as writing. It is a key evaluation institution, most obviously in literally codifying who counts as being literate, through exams, certification and so on, and in codifying what counts as acceptable writing, through specific pedagogic practices around writing, such as primers on spelling, grammar and punctuation and curriculum guidelines on key aspects of writing, as well as ideologies around 'good writing' and 'standard' language and literacy practices. Schooling typically involves the valuing of a particular kind of writing, the most obvious dimension to which is its predominantly verbal nature; as discussed in Chapter 2, much has been claimed on the basis of the specific verbal nature of writing for both individual cognitive and wider societal development, so it is not surprising, therefore, that schooling places particular emphasis on this verbal dimension. However, this has meant that historically the non-verbal has tended to be squeezed out of (what count as) potentially valuable resources for meaning making.

The suppression or marginalisation of the potential of such resources has been discussed in relation to current and historical practices. An example of the former is work by Ormerod and Ivanič (2002) who, in their research in UK primary schools, showed how the range of multimodal and multimaterial resources used by children get progressively reduced in production activities in formal schooling; children, left to their own devices used a wide range of resources for text production, including feathers, eggshell, wax, photos, images and a range of pens, papers and colours. A key point noted by the researchers was that the multimodal and multimaterial resources used were progressively reduced over time, with a marked shift from the use (and valuing) of the range considered acceptable by the age of ten. As an example of the historical tracking of the marginalisation of the non-verbal, Baca and Villanueva (2010; see also Baca 2008) chart the multimodal practices of Mesoamerica and argue that Western negative evaluations of such practices were/are based on a fundamental bias towards the verbal dimension of inscription (for examples of such practices, see http://www.ancientscripts.com/aztec.html and see also discussions in Chapter 2).

That (Western) schooling currently values not only particular kinds of semiotic practices, but particular kinds of verbal practices, notably 'essayist literacy' (which I return to in Chapter 6) has been documented in a range of studies including those focusing on the 'home' and 'school' practices of children (Flewitt 2011; Heath 1983; Gregory and Williams 2003; Gutierrez et al. 1999; Michaels 1981; Moss 2001) and of adults (for example, Ivanič et al. 2009; Kell 2010; Richardson 2003). Heath's foundational ethnographic study (1983), mentioned above, explored the 'ways of taking' and making meaning by adults and children in different communities and included an analysis of the extent to which these mapped onto the practices valued in formal schooling. A key example she gives of synergy across these domains is of the practice of bedtime stories in 'mainstream' (white middle-class) homes and the way in which adults orient children to such stories, particularly a focus on *what-explanations*, such as 'asking what the topic is, establishing it as predictable and recognising it in new situational contexts by classifying and categorising it [. . .] with other phenomena' (Heath 1983: 78). In contrast, she found that Roadville adults and children (the black working-class community) actively engaged with literacy but in ways that diverged from mainstream schooling practices. Figure 4.9 is an extract from Heath's account of Roadville practices:

Figure 4.9   What 'Roadville' parents do (Heath 1983: 187)

Roadville parents provide their children with books; they read to them and ask questions about the books' contents. They choose books which emphasize nursery rhymes, alphabet learning, animals, and simplified Bible stories, and they require their children to repeat from these books and to answer formulaic questions about the contents. Roadville adults also ask questions about oral stories which have a point relevant to some marked behaviour of a child. They use proverbs and summary statements to remind their children of stories and to call on them for simple comparisons of the stories' content to their own situations.

Her work challenges the view that any difficulties children face in engaging in school literacy practices are because of any simple oral/literacy culture divide – i.e. that some children are from predominantly oral cultural backgrounds and others from literate cultural backgrounds – and emphasises instead the existence of different orientations to literacy, texts, participation and knowledge making.

Key differences between community-based home literacy practices and school-based literacy practices, noted by Heath, have been emphasised in many studies. Examples of such differences include the following:

- the materials available/accessible for reading and writing
- the technologies available and used
- the kinds of interactions and relationships around written materials and texts
- the kinds of physical/bodily connections with literacy practices, for example, specific practices occurring at different times of the day (related to sleeping for example) or movement alongside different rhetorical practices such as 'steppin' ('spelling words or saying rhymes to dance routines which feature hard body movements', Richardson 2003: 88)
- the values placed on different kinds of practices around written materials, for example the valuing of narrative or song
- the range of languages and/or language mixing related to different reading and writing practices
- orientations towards the truth value (or not) of the written word

Of course researchers' interests do not stop at documenting difference: as with a long tradition in sociolinguistics (Hymes [1973] 1996), such studies raise issues of equality and access and of how sociolinguistic knowledge can be used to redress inequalities. Thus noting difference or more specifically *discontinuity* between home and school practices – including the recognition that some are valued positively and others less so in the domain of formal schooling – is of considerable concern, particularly in the context of communities where educational failure looms large (as is the case with children from particular populations i.e. Hispanic failure in US school system http://eclkc.ohs.acf.hhs.gov/hslc/Head%20Start%20Program/Director/LaVanguardia.htm (accessed 3 Sept. 2011)). One key conclusion reached and which in turn has provided the imperative for further study is the importance of enabling continuity between specific practices in the home and those of the school (here we are focusing on writing and literacy but other key areas of linguistic concern focus on discontinuities in relation to multilingualism, multidialects). This involves the use of notions such as 'funds of knowledge' (Moll et al. 1992) and 'semiotic affordances' (as used for example in English 2011 and Kress 2010), which shift the emphasis away from deficit approaches (what people don't know) towards what people do know and a concern with how existing funds of knowledge can be added to conventional school-based practices so as to ensure that a wide range of resources can be productively used for learning.[9] I return to this question of continuity between home (or 'informal') and school semiotic practices, with particular reference to the use of digital technologies, in Chapter 6.

A NOTE ON THE CHALLENGES OF DESCRIPTION

The question of literacy

With regard to the meta-language being used to describe the fact of multiple and differently evaluated literacy practices, a range of terms has grown up, often using an (implied) binary; for example vernacular/dominant, visible/ invisible (see Box 4.4). The use of such terms is an attempt to avoid the negative/positive evaluation so common in everyday discourse about language, writing and literacy – and to respond to the descriptive imperative of sociolinguistics – but they illustrate well the difficulty of avoiding evaluation, and of avoiding such evaluation through a binary lens. Some terms signal an explicit interest in power in relation to literacy practices (e.g. 'dominant', 'elite'), some signal an explicit hierarchy of value (for example, 'low'), some signal social (mis)recognition of particular practices (for example, 'hidden', 'grassroots').

The question of language

If an important contribution by NLS has been to identify the plurality of literacy(ies), 'language' occupies a problematic position, in that it tends to be used straightforwardly as either a universalistic category (i.e. human language) or as a particularistic phenomenon, as languages, such as 'English', 'French', 'Arabic' etc. Examples of the latter treatment are the ways in which particular literacies are mapped in a uniform way against particular languages: for example, Scribner and Cole (1981) and Street (1984) mapped specific literacy practices against specific languages. The question of the ways in which languages – understood as discrete entities – map onto specific literacy practices is, of course, an empirical one and has been explored to some extent in work on 'contrastive rhetoric' (for summary and critical discussion, see Chapter 3).[10] In contrast, in some literacy focused work, language gets backgrounded altogether, as if the key semiotic stuff of literacy – language (however conceptualised) – were not relevant to the specific literacy practice being discussed.[11]

However, the question of 'language' has been problematised in some work and there is debate around not only the sociolinguistic question of what counts as a language (as compared, for example, with a dialect) but the meaningfulness of using the term 'language' to capture the way in which people use the linguistic resources available to them, a focus brought into relief most obviously in contexts of 'super-diversity' (Vertovec 2007).[12] Thus some literacy focused research has foregrounded practices where resources from multiple languages are brought to bear in an apparently single literacy event, for example in the use of a number of languages (as well as particular orientations to literacy practices surrounding the production of a particular text) as in, for example, Juffermans's (2010) account of the writing of a letter in a village in the Gambia, or as evident in the range of linguistic resources in particular texts, for example notebooks using combinations of French

---

Box 4.4 Signalling differentiation in literacy and writing practices

Commonplace literacy: Used to describe the reading and writing activities of 'ordinary men and women' engaged in prior to and alongside formal schooling (Cook-Gumperz, 2006: 27, after Laqueur 1976).

Lay literacy: Environmental literacy or lay literacy 'is the term used to designate that form of unspecialised competence involved in generally dealing with a literate environment. Such **literacy** need never be taught. It is a type of **literacy** that is acquired through participating in a literate environment in which written signs, labels, trademarks, headlines, sports scores, and the like are ubiquitous'. Glossed as a 'general, if low, level of literacy', Olson in Encyclopaedia Britannica Online http://www.britannica.com/ (accessed 10 June 2010).

Vernacular literacies: 1. 'Vernacular literacy practices are essentially ones which are not regulated by the formal rules and procedures of dominant social institutions and which have their origins in everyday social life' (Barton 2010: 110; see also Barton and Hamilton 1998); 2. Used by Fishman (2010) in his discussion of European vernacular literacies to refer to literacies in modern European languages. These stand in contrast with 'classicals of literacy' (primarily religious literacies), which are Hebrew, Greek, Latin, Arabic, Slavonic, Anglo-Saxon.

Dominant literacy practices: Dominant literacies are those associated with formal organisations, such as those of education, law, religion and the workplace (Barton and Hamilton 1998: 110).

Hidden literacies: Reading and writing practices carried out in everyday activity and not recognised as such by policy makers, educators and participants themselves (Nabi (forthcoming), reported in Street 2010).

Grassroots literacy: A wide variety of 'non-elite' forms of writing – 'writing performed by people who are not fully inserted into elite economies of information, language and literacy' (Blommaert 2008: 7).

---

and Bambara in rural Mali (Mbodj-Pouye and van den Avenne 2007), public notices in a European city using features of several Chinese scripts (Blommaert and Rampton 2011), comments on YouTube as discussed earlier in this chapter, or, as in Chapter 3, 'meshing' in academic writing. Such work illustrates the limitations of the boundaries of mono-language/linguistic frameworks and foregrounds language as a complex semiotic resource; to capture this shift in understanding, the notion of 'languaging' in contrast with 'language' is increasingly being taken up (Box 4.5).

Box 4.5 Language and languaging

Language: As an overarching, universal category, for example language is the key means of human communication

Language(s): As identifiable multiple units which are tied to specific geo-spaces or domains, e.g. French is the official national language of France, French may be used at school and Arabic in the home domain

Language(s): Viewed as ideological constructs rather than neatly, observable distinct entities

Languaging: As a way of emphasising how people do/use language resources which may include a number of resources typically defined as distinct languages as well as mixes and meshes of features from these (Mignolo 1996; Møller and Jørgensen 2009)

CONCLUSION

The key argument in this chapter is that writing – once construed as the act of inscription using available resources and technologies – is clearly an everyday practice. Considerable ethnographically oriented research has been carried out which illustrates and accounts for the range of writing in which people engage. Writing is nested in a whole range of daily activities, across diverse domains – work, home, school, political activity, personal interests. Exactly what writing people do, why and how, has been explored in relation to individuals and communities across many diverse geographical, cultural and linguistic contexts. As activities, resources and social relations around activities change so too do the nature and purposes of writing and there is a need continually to explore all dimensions.

A range of methodological and theoretical tools for making visible and documenting everyday writing, has been discussed. These tools include empirically oriented notions such as events, participants, artefacts and more theoretically oriented notions, such as Street's ideological and autonomous notions of literacy and the widespread (if somewhat varied) use of *practice*; this last is a key notion in social sciences, notably in the work of Bourdieu (e.g. 1977), to connect individual action and agency with larger social structures and processes. Together these empirical and theoretical notions enable literacy and writing researchers to take the notion of function beyond an initial, or even primary concern with text, to focus on what people are doing, where, why and with what consequences. This does not mean that *writing as texts* is ignored but that a concern with writing as a socially defined and oriented activity, or *social functions*, are layered onto a concern to explore *textual functions*. This was touched on in Chapter 3 and is an issue I pick up again in the following chapters.

This chapter has emphasised the sheer amount of writing that is going on – an issue I will further illustrate in Chapter 6 – the most obvious reason for this being an increase in semiotic production more generally using digital and online technologies. However, given that much writing in daily activity is invisible (in the sense of not counting as writing from the perspective of users, analysts and key social institutions, such as schooling) it is hard to compare the amount of writing going on globally using both 'old' and 'new' technologies. But two points seem clear: where online and digital technologies are available to users, they certainly seem to be leading to greater production activity overall, including the production of writing; digital and online resources are being used alongside more traditional technologies, although exactly how requires considerably more research. The brief account of semiotic practice around one recent political activity indicates that people are using all available resources, rather than – as is often implied – dumping the old for the new. Of course – and an important NLS premise which may help us avoid any easy technological determinism – identifying exactly how technologies of writing are being used is an empirical task, and one to which the ethnographic approaches discussed in this chapter can usefully contribute.

Whilst a huge range of writing is taking place across all domains of social life, a key argument made in this chapter is that writing – in terms of its materialities and practices and in terms of the ways in which it is evaluated – is not an open resource. I pointed in particular to the role of formal schooling in establishing a particular evaluative regime which pervades common sense notions about what writing is and should be. I continue with this focus on writing as both a differentially available and differentially evaluated resource in the following chapters.

NOTES

1. These are contested terms but I'm using a distinction here between 'centre' and 'periphery', or 'semi-periphery' from World Systems theory. See Wallerstein 1991. Other terms in use are 'developed' and 'developing' country or 'Third' and 'First' world, or north and south.
2. Of course it's not my intention here to mask unequal access to literacy and this is an issue I return to in Chapters 5 and 6. Working to ensure access to the resources for literacy continues to be a global imperative. 'In 2008, 796 million adults worldwide (15 years and older) reported not being able to read and write and two-thirds of them (64%) were women [. . .] More than half of those unable to read and write – 412 million – lived in Southern Asia. A further 176 million adults were in sub-Saharan Africa. Together, these two regions accounted for three-quarters (74%) of adults unable to read and write worldwide.' http://www.uis.unesco.org/FactSheets/Documents/Fact_Sheet_2010_Lit_EN.pdf (accessed 3 Feb. 2012).
3. For introductory overview of ethnographic methodology and tools, see Blommaert and Jie 2010.
4. I am grateful to Janet Maybin for discussions about the value and limitations of different definitions.
5. Hessel argues that the popular response to the current global economic (and political) crisis should be one of active and public indignation organised around specific issues and concerns (Indignez – vous, Indignaos, de Stéphane Hessel, en formato PDF

y en castellano via http://www.attacmadrid.org/wp/wp-content/uploads/Indignaos.pdf 10 Apr via Tweet Button [http://twitter.com/#!/jbravo/statuses/57179124409696256 (accessed 31 Aug. 2011)].

6. The use of new technologies to spread information and/or call for political action – e.g. in Greece, Spain, Egypt – has been widely discussed (often criticised) in the media. Of course there is also public debate about why regimes attempt to close down these means of communication. For examples of public debate and links to other related articles see http://www.newint.org/books/reference/world-development/case-studies/social-networking-in-the-arab-spring/ (accessed 19 Nov. 2011).

7. This is part of a small ongoing project setting out to explore the semiotic practices of those who have engaged in some way in Spain's 15-M demonstrations.

8. The relationship between schooling, literacy and language and the specific case of 'writing', is a rich area of research and too large an area to do justice to here.

9. Examples of continuity are sometimes identified in existing teaching practices, for example Gregory and Williams 2003, as either being actively worked at by teachers, for example Gutierrez et al. 1999 or as evidenced in children's own agency, Maybin 2006.

10. The relationship between the semiotic affordances of specific languages for specific kinds of literacy practices is a much larger issue and not dealt with in this book. It connects, of course, with foundational debates about the relationship between language(s) and meaning and linguistic relativity, probably the most familiar of which is work by Sapir and Whorf and critically explored by Hymes, in terms of 'first' and 'second' linguistic relativity, as discussed by Blommaert 2005: 70.

11. This is particularly the case with Anglophone based research in (assumed) monolingual settings where 'English' is not made visible, yet conclusions are reached about 'literacy' more generally. I think this is in large part due to the politics of academic research and knowledge making more generally, rather than specifically to language/literacy/writing research (see discussion in Lillis and Curry 2010).

12. Whilst 'super-diversity' is most obviously visible (and lived) in particular contexts, such as multiethnic and multilingual urban areas with large migrant populations, it is also a defining feature of a globalised world in which there is considerable movement of people and transnational/transmedia communication and production.

Chapter 5

Resources, networks and trajectories

INTRODUCTION

This chapter focuses on the resources used for writing and some of the ways in which these are tied into specific communities, practices and values. A key aim of this chapter is to focus in particular on the *dynamic* rather than the (often) assumed fixed nature of writing in three main ways: in terms of the specific textual make-up or *texture* of any writing product, in that any text is built on and out of a range of existing resources; in terms of the processes surrounding the production of writing, in that writing often involves many people across space and time; in terms of its mobile potential, for the material nature of writing means that it can be portable or mobile – travelling along with the people who produce it or alone – although as it moves the meanings attached to it and the ways in which it is evaluated may shift and vary in complex ways. At the same time as emphasising this dynamic nature of writing, the chapter emphasises in particular the ways in which writing resources, networks and trajectories often enact and orient to 'centring institutions' (Blommaert 2005) which have strongly normative orientations. I turn to the issue of less regulated spaces in Chapter 6.

This chapter:

- explores the resources needed for writing and the ways in which these are tied into existing communities, practices and values
- explores the ways in which writing is produced in complex networks of activity
- considers the importance of focusing on the dynamic nature of writing in terms of chains and trajectories across time and space
- outlines some of the analytical tools useful for exploring trajectories of writing and illustrates three examples of trajectories of 'verbal heavy' texts oriented to centring institutions.

RESOURCES FOR WRITING: USE AND RE-USE

Any specific instance of writing, like all communication, is built on and out of existing semiotic resources, key aspects of which have been discussed in previous chapters. The array of resources for writing is not, of course, free floating but tied into what in broad terms can be referred to as 'conventions', and in studies of language and writing these conventions are often construed in terms of genres, discourses and practices (see Chapters 3 and 4). Such resources and conventions are the often unstated, yet powerful, rules surrounding what can be written (by whom and where) which can themselves, at a more abstract level, be understood as nesting within 'discursive' regimes (Fairclough 1992) or 'literacy' regimes (Blommaert 2008): 'Literacy is organised in literacy regimes in structures of distribution, access, value and use that are closely tied to the general make-up of society' (Blommaert 2008: 6). And here I'll make three obvious points:

1. When we write, we don't just write, but we write *something* in ways which we have come to learn as, in broad terms, recognisable as writing, and more specifically 'acceptable' or 'appropriate' to specific uses;
2. The resources we draw on for writing depend to a large extent on how we have come to learn about the particular ways of using such resources, and these vary depending on where we live in the world, our social, cultural, economic and linguistic backgrounds which are mediated by our families, our neighbourhoods, our (sense of) nation states;
3. As with any act of communication, resources used in specific instances of writing (and indeed judgements about what should be used) pre-exist, for the most part, such instances. So all writing, to use Pope's phrase, involves rewriting (2003). Such rewriting may be an obvious dimension to the production of some texts, and far less so with others.

Allan Bell tracked the different sources and resources used in the writing of one newspaper article, set out in Figure 5.1. The identification of such (re)sources, of course, leads into further questions about exactly how and why which particular (re)sources are used in the construction of news, whose interests are served and the consequences of such use.[1]

The idea of reuse or rewriting in news production may be something we are all familiar with at a general level, but it is important to acknowledge such reuse as a pervasive dimension to all writing. A number of analytical categories have been developed to capture how the making of any text always involves the use and reuse of existing resources, key categories being 'intertextuality' (Kristeva 1986) which captures the notion that all communication is inherently intertextual, made up of wordings, meanings, tones and conventions from other texts/uses, and 'recontextualisation' (see Blommaert 2005; Linell 1998) which refers to the practices of writers reusing existing resources, such as words, meanings, discourses and genres. Brief definitions of these and related analytical categories are outlined in Box 5.1.

Of course, the fact that written texts are made up of existing bits of resources does not mean that texts are simple reproductions; recontextualisation occurs in less obvious ways, for example by indirect reference or allusion to other texts, or even by challenging expectations about forms of texts. Wales gives an example of the latter with reference to the words of Shakespeare's 'My mistress' eyes are nothing like the sun' (Sonnet 130) of which Wales states 'the I persona is reacting

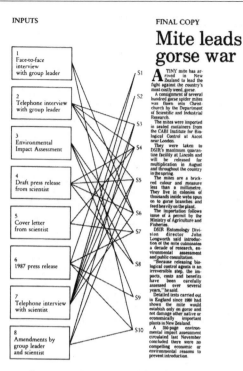

Figure 5.1   The use of sources in news articles (Bell 1991: 63)

against the conventional sonnet conceits in a kind of interactive dialogue, conceits which his contemporaries also must have known about' (Wales 2001: 221). Recontextualisation here then involves the writer challenging (some) expectations about rhetorical features of a recognisable form of writing, and illustrates the importance of the involvement of both writer(s) and reader(s) for this recontextualisation process to work (including knowledge about, for example, how sonnets conventionally work): the writer draws on and plays with existing conventions in ways which (some) readers recognise.

Bazerman (2003: 86–8) usefully lists some of the different ways in which texts draw on other texts, usually for specific purposes.

1. The text may draw on prior texts as a **source of meanings to be used at face value**, for example in a US Supreme Court decision, passages from the US constitution may be cited and taken as authoritative givens.

2. The text may draw on **explicit social dramas** of prior texts engaged in discussion, for example when a newspaper story quotes opposing views of senators, teachers' unions, community activist groups and reports from think tanks concerning a current controversy over school funding, they portray an intertextual social drama.

3. The text may also explicitly use other statements as **background, support**

Box 5.1 Analytical categories used to indicate that writing is always from existing resources

Contextualisation: Used to make the general point that language use is always connected to and made meaningful in contexts. Thus writing, what it is and does, is always bound up with specific contexts of production, distribution and evaluation; at the same time, the production of a text necessarily involves the production of a context specific to that text (see Blommaert 2005).

Entextualisation: Used to refer to the processes whereby any instance of language comes into being, in the case of writing, the ways in which writing gets produced and under what circumstances (Baumann and Briggs 1990; Silverstein and Urban 1996; Blommaert 2005).

Recontextualisation: Used to refer to the way in which texts – in this case writing – always involve the use and reuse of existing bits of language/texts, often with the effect of reframing the meanings of these (Blommaert 2005; Linell 1998). Used in a similar way to intertextuality.

Rewriting: Used to indicate that writing (and reading) are always forms of rewriting (Pope 2003).

Intertextuality: Used to refer to the ways in which all language is connected to existing and prior language use in 'a chain of speech communication' (Kristeva 1986; Bakhtin 1981).

Manifest intertextuality: Used to refer to language/texts which are explicitly present in other texts, for example the use of direct speech from one text and reported in another (Fairclough 1992).

Constitutive intertextuality or interdiscursivity: Used to refer to the way in which texts may echo other texts and discourses in less explicit ways, for example a text echoing a 'commonsense discourse' about immigration (Fairclough 1992).

---

and contrast, for example when a student cites figures from an encyclopaedia or uses quotations from a work of literature to support an analysis.

4. The text may rely on **beliefs, issues, ideas and statements generally circulated** and likely to be familiar to readers, for example US constitutional guarantees of freedom of speech may lie behind a newspaper editorial on a controversial opinion expressed by a community leader, without any specific mention of the Constitution.

5. The text may use certain implicitly **recognizable kinds of language, phrasing and genres** and thus evoke particular social worlds where such language

and language forms are used, for example an academic book uses language recognisably associated with the university, research and textbooks.

(Note: from Bazerman 2003: 86–8, summary closely following the original text; bolding as in original)

Exactly how specific resources are used and reused is a question that has to be explored empirically and whilst this has been a key focus in some traditions of writing studies, notably in media and literary studies, it has more recently become a focus in studies of everyday writing. There is, for example, a growing interest in how texts are made and remade in and for specific institutional purposes, as illustrated in the diagram in Figure 5.2 by Pontille on the making of a 'bioinformatics data base'. The diagram foregrounds, in broad terms, the way in which texts get taken up and incorporated into other texts over time, according to specific institutional trajectories and chronologies. I discuss examples of specific text trajectories later in this chapter.

The particular ways in which writing comes into being therefore always involves socially situated processes of '(en)textualisation', relating to resources, contexts of use and users and interests or goals. In sociolinguistics, the specific ways in which resources are tied into histories of use and users is often explored through the lens of 'community' or 'network' and is an issue I now turn to.

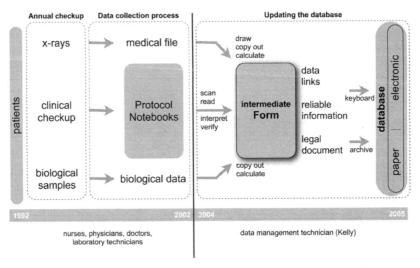

Figure 5.2   The making of a bioinformatics database (Pontille 2010: 62)

COMMUNITIES, NETWORKS AND THE CLUSTERING OF RESOURCES

Communities – speech, discourse and practice

Community is a pervasive if problematic notion in sociolinguistic research signalling as it does the powerful link between individual users of language and the groups of people – or communities – with whom one interacts and re-enacts aspects of language use. Here I am concerned with community particularly regarding access to and use of resources for writing, and the three notions of community that are widely used in sociolinguistics are of relevance here: *speech, discourse* and *practice* community. 'Speech community' is a key notion in sociolinguistics used to refer, in broad terms, to the language(s) or variety of language(s) shared by a group of people. Whilst 'speech' signals a focus on spoken language, and much research has indeed focused on spoken language use in sociolinguistics, the notion is often used to extend beyond spoken language to refer to the range and types of communicative practices shared by people, including explicitly, in some instances, writing as well as speech (for example Firth 1968; see also community and literacy practices in Chapter 4). Within this framing, language is often construed as a particular national or official language, for example Spanish, and community may be used to signal more immediate contacts (family, local community, single nation) or in a more dispersed way, for example to refer to the 'Spanish speaking community(ies)' around the world. Speech community is also used to signal not only knowledge of a shared language, but a shared knowledge of rules or conventions governing language use (Hymes 1974); or indeed a shared set of norms, even where the linguistic forms differ (Labov 1972). This may involve, for example, in a multilingual context, knowing when and where it is socially appropriate to use a specific language or to switch from one language to another or to mix languages and registers. This emphasis on knowledge of conventions indicates that 'community' is a more complex phenomenon than might at first appear, most obviously in that tensions may arise within what may be construed, at some level, as the same 'speech community'. For instance, I may share a language, English, with 1.5 billion people worldwide, but I may also find that the rules governing our uses of English in any specific context vary considerably. This latter point signals that 'speech community' is a useful notion for connecting individual language use with that of others, but that it is a notion to be used critically as well as referentially, to avoid assumptions about the workings of any 'language' in any presumed 'community'.

In contrast with speech community, which emphasises language use in general terms, *discourse community* is used to emphasise the particular uses of language associated with particular interests or functions of groups of people and often to refer to written rather than spoken language. For example, sociolinguists, a specific religious community or a group of online gamers engage in the use of specific written text types or genres according to their interests: sociolinguists' texts may include academic articles, textbooks, grant proposals, discussion lists; key written texts of an institutionalised religious community may involve weekly newsletters, calendars of events and orders of service; online gamers may use hard copy and digital manuals, fan websites and blogs. Swales (1990: 24ff.), whose work on genre and community with regard to academic writing in particular has been highly influential, sets out three reasons why a notion of discourse community is needed in contradistinction to speech community.

1. 'Speech' will not do as an exclusive modifier of communities that are often heavily engaged in writing, not just because of the medium but because of what it suggests about the nature of the activity; literacy takes away locality and parochiality, with members (of the discourse community) more likely to communicate with others in distant places and to respond to writings from the past.

2. There is a need to distinguish between a sociolinguistic grouping and a socior-hetorical one. In the former the primary determinants of linguistic behaviour are social (for example socialisation and solidarity). In a sociorhetorical community, the primary determinants are functional, that is, to sustain and maintain the goals of the specific community.

3. In terms of the fabric of society, speech communities are 'centripetal' (they tend to absorb people into that fabric) whereas discourse communities are 'centrifugal' (they tend to separate people into occupational or speciality-interest groups). A speech community typically inherits its members by birth, accident or adoption; a discourse community recruits its members by persuasion, training or relevant qualification.

(from Swales 1990: 23–4, summary closely following the original text)

The distinctions Swales makes are useful for a variety of reasons, not least in arguing for the need to highlight the specific and often unacknowledged ways in which written texts mediate people's organised goals and needs (see Chapter 6 for further discussion of notions of centrifugal and centripetal). But the specific details of the distinctions he makes are problematic to the extent that they also echo the dichotomy between speech and writing, already challenged in preceding chapters. These include the assumption that literacy is necessarily less context specific (taking away locality), that there are clear distinctions between modes in relation to functions and purposes, and that a specific mode is necessarily more closely associated with sociolinguistic dimensions (what people do because of birth, family, immediate community etc.) rather than with sociorhetorical dimensions (choosing to do something as part of, or in order to be part of, a particular community). Of course, all of these distinctions may be true in specific instances, but we should be wary of such generalisations and rather seek to explore what each instance of writing is and does empirically. I will offer a particular take on Swales's useful point about centrifugal/centripetal dimensions below, and in more detail in Chapter 6.

A third notion, *community of practice*, connects strongly with discourse community in that it emphasises the way in which people come together around specific purposes. Whilst both emphasise activity, discourse community tends to be used to foreground texts, whereas community of practice, as the qualifier *practice* suggests, emphasises the activities or practices in which people engage, although of course in studies of communication both aspects are often emphasised. Eckert and McConnell-Ginet (1992: 490) define a community of practice as 'an aggregate of people who come together around the mutual engagement in some common endeavour'. A key contribution of work which foregrounds practice, drawing predominantly on the work of Wenger (1998), is that there is a need to focus on what people do/are doing, and as part of this focus then to explore how all kinds of shared 'stuff' (including writing) are involved. A key example of shared stuff, drawing on Wenger's 1998 study of the practices of claims processors in the offices of a US insurance company, are written texts of all kinds – forms, notes, letters, emails – which are routinely used to get work done. Wenger refers to these as 'reifications', which we can also refer to as 'entextualisations', to signal the processes surrounding textual production. Community of practice powerfully connects specific bits of writing with the specific organisational and institutional contexts in which writing circulates.

All three notions of community are widely used in sociolinguistics and they are as useful as they are problematic (a strong criticism of all three is the idealisation and homogeneity that they imply; see Rampton 1998). For the purposes of the discussion on writing here, they can be useful if we draw on (some) aspects of all three when considering resources for writing and the practices in which they are embedded. Thus the notion of speech community, which is often dismissed in writing research because of its apparent emphasis on the mode of *spoken* language, can be useful precisely because it makes 'languages/ing' visible as part of the cluster of resources that a writer has (or has had) access to and draws on in any specific instance of writing (for resources and identity Chapter 6); *discourse* community is useful for signalling that people engage in a range of activities and purposes that are mediated by discourses which have established themselves over time as intrinsic to those activities; and communities of *practice* is useful for reminding us that people do writing as part of other activities and that familiarity with particular types of writing usually comes about through regular engagement in these.

Identifying clusters of resources

It's worth pausing to consider actual instances of writing at this point. Consider the three examples of writing below. Figure 5.3 is the writing of a twelve-year-old British Pakistani girl in the UK about how she feels her schooling is going. She was asked to write this by a teacher who was concerned about her being unhappy and withdrawn in the classroom. Figure 5.4 is an extract of a draft of an academic paper written by a Spanish scholar. Figure 5.5 is an extract from a young woman's social networking site: a screen shot of a news feed page. It's useful to look again at Figure 2.3 (Chapter 2) which are posts that appear in her news feed pages and which I will also comment on here. In thinking about the resources for each instance of writing, consider the following questions: What cluster of resources are being drawn on in

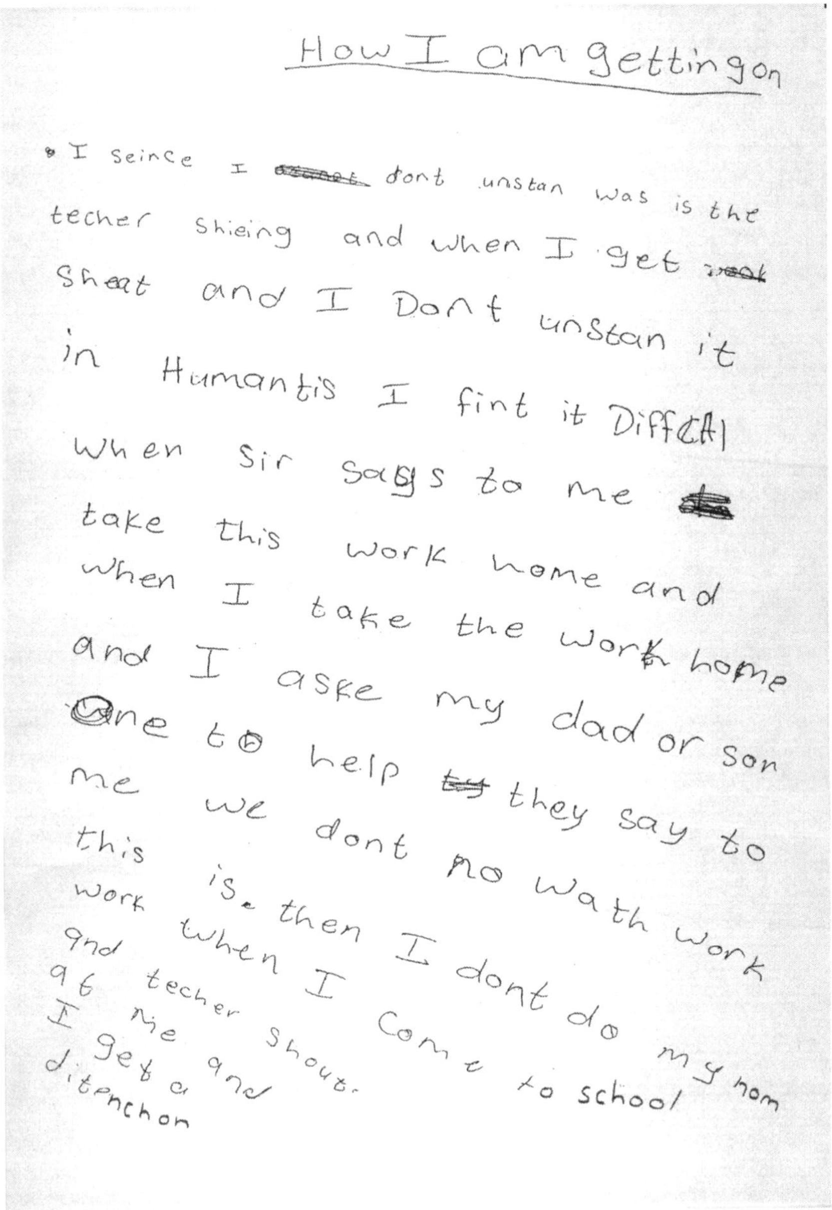

How I am getting on

I seince I ~~want~~ dont unstan was is the techer shieing and when I get ~~week~~ sheet and I Dont unstan it in Humantis I fint it Diffcfl when Sir says to me ~~take~~ take this work home and when I take the work home and I aske my dad or son One to help ~~to~~ they say to me we dont no wath work this is. then I dont do my hom work when I come to school and techer shout. me and I get a ditenchon

Figure 5.3   Extract from school-based writing (Lillis 1996)[2]

each case? To what extent are the three notions of 'community' useful in helping us to connect these resources to particular groups and histories of use?

Figure 5.4   Extract from draft of an academic paper (Lillis and Curry 2010: 77)

> [1] Results of this research *provienen del analisis de un* questionnaire, that it *indaga* about the next points: labour *trayectoria*, initial and continuous formation, *condiciones de trabajo y vision de la* profesion. [2] It will be analyse the relationship *que* existed *entre estos rasgos de los docentes y su concepcion de identidad.*

In each example we get a strong sense of the cluster of resources that are being drawn on. Most obviously we can identify *materials, tools* and *technologies*: thus pen and paper in Figure 5.3, word processor in Figure 5.4, a personal computer and specific web environment in Figure 5.5. We can also see the *languages, varieties of language* and *languaging work*: in Figure 5.3 we see a variety of English being used, together with specific orthographic and layout features – 'irregular' use of capitalisation and use of page space (these are features sometimes identified as 'grassroots literacy', see Chapter 4); and in Figure 5.4 we see the use of Spanish and English, both of which are being drawn on in drafting ideas. In Figure 2.3 we again see the use of English and Spanish, including commentary on the use of Spanish, as well as still and moving images, sound, colour, range of fonts.

In considering how and why writers are using such resources, *speech community* – once pluralised as *communities* to acknowledge that people may be moving through many – is useful in that the linguistic stuff of writing is bound up with

Figure 5.5   Extracts from one person's social networking site: a news feed update page (see also Figure 2.3)

people's broader language use, not just their literacy practices; *discourse commu-nity* is also useful, for articulating not only who/what writers are engaged in but the particular discourse practices that have come to be associated with particular communities. Thus, for example, in Figure 5.3 the writer is clearly drawing on and orienting to genres and practices associated with UK schooling, notably a particular notion of formality (writing in full sentences), monolingualism (English only should be used in this context), particular writing genres (description and narrative); in Figure 5.4 the extract shows the writer's use of currently dominant academic discourse practices, most obviously working towards English as the target language, crafting a separate section for Results, a key feature of academic articles. In Figure 5.5 and 2.3 the writer is clearly engaging in chat with friends (sharing details about immediate or recent events) as well as sharing political news (YouTube upload showing demonstrations in Spain; see Chapter 4 for fuller dis-cussion). Extracts from all three examples indicate that the writers' involvement is oriented towards something beyond the specific text and that they are engaged in particular practices connected to particular purposes and contexts which notions of 'community' can be helpful to define and name (most obviously, school, academia, friendship groups etc.).

As already discussed, there are limitations with the notion of 'community' in relation to writing and production activity more generally. A key limitation worth signalling here is with regard to the notion of 'membership' which is a dominant trope across discussion of any notion of community and which is problematic theo-retically and empirically. What does it mean to refer to members of a community? How – and from whose perspective – can someone be defined as a member? A related critique is the often implied rigidity of both 'community membership' and the communicative norms presumed to be governing community practices. This has been taken up particularly with regard to digitally mediated practices, often infused with popular culture (as content and forms), such as those illustrated in Figures 5.5 and 2.3 and for which Gee (2004) offers the notion of 'affinity group' or 'affinity spaces', which signals a looser set of relationships and norms and is perhaps a useful notion when considering writing and production in less strongly regulated spaces (this is an issue I return to in Chapter 6).

All three examples point to the importance of 'uptake' in considering what a written text does, or more accurately, gets to do, depending on how texts are taken up – that is read, understood, acted on, and the extent to which they can be considered successful. Example 5.3 can be considered successful in that the writer communicates some of the difficulties she is facing about doing school work and the lack of resources to support school work at home; Example 5.4 can be consid-ered successful in terms of generating key ideas as a draft towards the production of an article in English; Examples 5.5 and 2.3 can be considered successful in that the writer is adding contributions, has 'friends' with whom she is interacting and exchanging information, ideas, views etc. But they might all also be considered unsuccessful if they were, for instance, being assessed as 'finished' pieces of writing (at school or as submitted to an academic journal) or, with regard to 5.4 and 5.5

(and 2.3) in terms of individual authorship (a prevailing criterion in evaluating writing). I return to the question of 'uptake' across chains or histories of texts below (see also Chapter 7 for a discussion of the frames used to research and analyse writing).

Networks and brokers

Whilst community has proved useful in situating individual language use within a history of others' use (past and present), *network* and *social network* have proved useful in sociolinguistics for empirically tracking relations around language use and the way in which specific connections or *ties* between people influence specific language usages (see for example Milroy 1987). In research on writing (and literacy more generally) the notion of network is often used to move 'beyond a focus on individuals and individual encounters, towards one which shows how literacy links across people and localities' (Barton and Hamilton 1998: 16). A focus on networks points to the ways in which different resources – people and materials – are called upon in the writing of any texts. When used as an analytical tool it can also be useful for tracking the production of texts, that is, precisely how and when moments of entextualisation and recontextualisation occur. For example, in our work on academic writing for publication (Lillis and Curry 2010; Curry and Lillis 2010) 'community' proved useful for conceptualising the localities where academics were writing from, and thinking in broad terms about who scholars were writing for; whereas 'network', and analytical tools nested within this concept (see Box 5.2) were useful for tracking relations around language and texts and the impact of these on specific texts or 'text histories' (see Figure 5.6). We used some key tools from network studies to characterise the type of networks in which scholars lived and worked – focusing on their local and transnational networks of activity – to track how scholars gained access to the specific kinds of resources necessary for writing for English medium publication and the specific entextualisation processes this involved. Some key examples of resources made available by networked activity included access to academic publications, access to scholars with a knowledge of (academic/specialist/general) English, access to scholars in similar fields. The ways in which ties to specific people in networks function both as a resource for writing and as a way of bringing texts into being is illustrated in the diagram in Figure 5.6.

Figure 5.6 illustrates a moment in a network's activity and history as it relates to the production of several interrelated academic texts. The larger two circles represent two research projects in which Fidel, FG, is involved, with the smaller white circles indicating a network of local scholars and those in black a network of scholars from a different national context. The overlapping circle indicates the three 'local' scholars who are involved in both research projects. The main point to note here is that the production of particular academic texts is nested within this research activity and that the strong ties indicated between FG and T1 signal their pivotal role in text production (for full discussion see Lillis and Curry 2010).

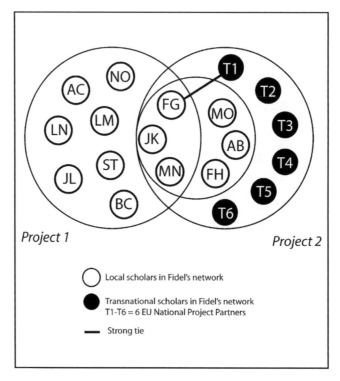

Figure 5.6   Example of a scholar's network around academic text production in two research projects (Lillis and Curry 2010: 79)

Box 5.2 Tools to describe and track networks of activity around writing

Networks: Specific links or connections between people as they go about their everyday writing

Roles: People adopt different roles in relation to writing in different contexts, for example, women often take on personal writing tasks such as greeting card writing

Resources: The material, semiotic and human resources that people draw on in order to get writing done

Brokers: People who support writing in some way, facilitate access to resources and/or who gate-keep access to resources

Ties: Links and relationships between people and/or resources which are used for writing

Pivots: Key people and resources in any specific writing activity

THE PORTABILITY AND MOBILITY OF WRITING

As discussed in Chapter 4, work in New Literacy Studies pays particular attention to writing (and literacy) in its social context, with considerable emphasis on
understanding writing as a local and immediate practice. However, whilst staying
close to the local (people, places, specific moments etc.), it is also important not to
stay bounded by the local in exploring what writing is and does: a key affordance
of writing is its *portability* (it can be carried by/along with people) and *mobility* (it
can travel alone). Latour refers to writing as an example of a 'stable mobile' to signal
how texts can mediate activity both close and far from the site of a text's production
(Latour 1987). This is a point emphasised by Brandt and Clinton (2002) who argue
that the significance of this mobile potential of writing is often misunderstood in
NLS:

> We are not suggesting that the technology of literacy carries its own imperatives
> no matter where it goes. But we want to grant the technologies of literacy certain
> kinds of undeniable capacities – particularly, a capacity to travel, a capacity to
> stay intact, and a capacity to be visible and animate outside the interactions of
> immediate literacy events. These capacities stem from the legibility and durability
> of literacy: its material forms, its technological apparatus, its objectivity, that is,
> its (some)thing-ness.
>
> (Brandt and Clinton 2002: 9)

Of course texts have always travelled, most obviously as documents, letters and
cards through a range of courier and postal systems (briefly discussed in Chapter 4).
A key question here is, what exactly stays intact as texts travel? For whilst texts may
remain intact as artefacts (in their material nature), their meanings and significance
may shift. Furthermore, in the context of globalisation, mobility is a key dimension
to (re)entextualisation processes involving complex and contested meanings and
practices. In illustrating these (re)entextualisation practices, I use the term 'text trajectories' as an overarching category in this chapter, but I also show how some other
specific notions are being used (see Box 5.3).

Centring institutions, text trajectories and the question of uptake

If the writtenness of texts enables them to become mobile, this does not mean that
they are free floating, existing outside of histories and contexts of use, or ideologies
of production and evaluation. The trajectories of many texts are in fact strongly pre-
scripted, powerfully anchored to what Blommaert (2005, after Silverstein 1998)
refers to as 'centring institutions'. We have already briefly considered examples of
such centring institutions; most obviously formal schooling (above and in Chapter
4) and the academy (above with regard to writing for publication; see also Lillis
2012). Centring institutions are institutions at all levels of society, nationally and
transnationally, which regulate activities and to which people orient in constructing
their/our imaginary of what counts as 'appropriate'. The nation state is an obvious

---

Box 5.3 Analytical categories seeking to reflect the mobility of writing-as-text

Literacy-in-action: Used in contrast to 'literacy event' by Brandt and Clinton 2002 to draw attention to: the mobility of literacy artefacts (print, instruments, paper, other technologies) across time and space, irrespective of the producers and users of these artefacts; the importance of engaging in explorations of literacy as a mobile phenomenon, rather than something only anchored to one place and time.

Text trajectories: Used to signal a focus on how texts come into being through a process of entextualisation and recontextualisation. In tracing text trajectories it is possible not only to track what changes, but who is involved, why, under what conditions and with what consequences (Silverstein and Urban 1996; Blommaert 2005).

Text Histories: Used to refer to a methodology for empirically tracking the drafting and redrafting of written texts across time and for exploring the impact of literacy 'brokers' on specific changes in the text (Lillis and Curry 2010).

Genre chains: Used by Fairclough (2003: 31) to refer to clusters of text types that are regularly linked together, involving systematic transformations from genre to genre (for example [with regard to the media] official documents, associated press releases or press conferences, reports in the press or on television).

Text chains (la chaine d'écriture): Used by Fraenkel (2001) to refer to the way texts are linked in organisational contexts to form an integral part of the sequencing of institutional practices.

Genre set: Used by Devitt (2004) to signal the way in which texts are connected by their social purpose although they may have very different formal and material features. An example of a set given by Devitt is a marriage proposal that is 'tied to wedding invitations, cards of congratulations, guest books, marriage vows, thank you notes' (Devitt 2004: 55).[3]

Genre suite: Used by Berkenkotter and Hanganu-Bresch (2011) to refer to clusters of texts that together constitute a particular meaning or argument and call for a particular uptake/action.

---

centring institution, regulating as it does all manner of social, political and economic activity, including schooling. A key point about centring institutions – real or as part of a particular imaginary – is that they necessarily work towards normativity:

> This centering almost always involves either perceptions or real processes of homogenisation and uniformisation: orienting towards such a centre involves

the (real or perceived) reduction of difference and the creation of recognisably 'normative' meaning.

(Blommaert 2005: 75)

We saw traces of such normativity in writers' orientations in Examples Figures 5.3 and 5.4, most obviously in the emphasis on monolingualism, standard languages and English as the language of science. Consider the irony in the 'normative' comment in Figure 5.5 where one writer questions the mixing of Spanish and English 'why pones below si you are español?'; the writer is clearly being ironic in such 'gatekeeping' comments, in that after the admonishment about mixing, he continues to mix the languages in his own writing (see Chapter 6 for heteroglossia in digital contexts).

In order to get at how normativity works in the production of texts, we need to look not at individual texts or single moments of entextualisation processes, but chains of texts, including their uptake. As already mentioned, the way in which texts come into being is influenced by explicit and implicit regulatory regimes and how individuals orient to these. These include ideologies around what counts as writing (both in terms of production and evaluation) and what counts as 'reading'/uptake. Furthermore, specific uptake may be shaped not only by 'reading', as attention to the verbal aspects of a text, but also by 'looking', that is attention to the visual dimensions or look of a text, and both looking/reading shape (mis)readings (for looking, see Chapter 2; for useful discussions of uptake, see Blommaert 2005: 70–8; Freadman 2002; Bawarshi 2010). By focusing on the ways in which texts connect with other texts, using notions such as text trajectories, text histories and genre suites, our attention is directed towards the written text, but also to when and where writing takes place, who is involved, under what conditions, with what resources and with what uptake. I now consider in detail three examples of text trajectories, focusing on the particular ways in which these are pre-scripted, that is, oriented to specific centring institutions.

Seeking asylum (Blommaert 2005)

Drawing on an interview and text-based study with some fifty applicants seeking asylum in Belgium, Blommaert describes the complex administrative procedures surrounding application for asylum. A key part of the procedures is the applicant's narrative in which the applicant seeks to explain and justify why he is seeking asylum. These 'home narratives' (Blommaert 2005) involve intricate descriptions of the specific political context from which the speaker has travelled, and the personal involvement in and knowledge of this context. An extract from such a spoken narrative is provided below:

Figure 5.7   Extract from a home narrative (Blommaert 2005: 58–9)[4]

Fragment (1)
oui/l'autre président [. . .] (xxxxxx)/ on l'a empoisonné/ c'est le président Mobutu/ qui a mis le poison retardé/ il est parti au russe/ l'URSS/ pour traîter/

il a retourné/ il est mort/ mais on a abandonné son corps hein/ oui/ {{*Question: c'était un président de MPLA*?}} c'était le même mouvement MPLA/ dans le temps / année septante-cinq/ quand il est mort on dit/ comme on =il est marxisme/ on a pris on a choisi =on= on a fait faux testament/ cette testament c'était au temps du russe qui a fait ça/ comme toi tu =le= le président il est mort/ il a décidé Eduardo qui va me remplacer/ sans vote/ parce que il est toujours du même parti/ Eduardo il est d'origine angolais/ mais il est des Cap Verdiens/ parce que ce sont des anciens prisonniers/ et Portugais il a mis à l'île hein.

Translation

yes/the other president [. . .] (xxxxxx)/they have poisoned him/ it's president Mobutu/ who put the delayed poison/ he has left to Russian/ the USSR/ to treat/ he gave back/ he died/ but they have left his corpse, right/ yes/ {{*Question: it was a president of the MPLA*?}}/ it was the same movement MPLA/ in those days/ year seventy-five/ when he died they say/ like they=he is Marxism/ they took they chose=they=they have made false testament/ those testament it was in the time of Russian that has made it/ since you you=the=the president is dead/ he decided Eduardo who is going to replace me/ without vote/ because he is always of the same party/ Eduardo he is of Angolan origin/ but he is of the Cape Verdians/ because they are former prisoners/ and Portuguese has put on the island, right.

The spoken narrative involves the use of what Blommaert describes as a 'broken' variety of French, acquired probably during the man's stay in the Congo and is, he says, 'like the English and Dutch of many others, a product of refugee life and it mirrors the marginality in which they find themselves wherever they go' (Blommaert 2005: 60). Such spoken narratives by asylum seekers are often listened to and interpreted by an official(s) from a very different linguistic life-world who has the task of re-entextualising such spoken narratives (or quotations from these) into written texts, such as case reports, notes and letters some of which are exchanged between administrators and lawyers, and all of which feed into the summary verdict on the asylum case. The application of the man whose narrative was briefly illustrated in Figure 5.7 was rejected and an extract from the letter of rejection is in Figure 5.8.

Figure 5.8   Extract from official letter of asylum rejection (Original Dutch translated into English by Blommaert [2005: 63])

The concerned was interrogated on November 23, 1993 at the Commissariat-General [for Refugees and Stateless Persons], in the presence of [name], his attorney.

He claimed to be a 'political informant' of the MPLA. On October 18, 1992 however, he passed on information to UNITA. At the UNITA office, however, he met with Major [name], who works for the MPLA [. . .]

It has to be noted that the concerned remains very vague at certain points. Thus he is unable to provide details about the precise content of his job as 'political informant'. Furthermore the account of his escape lacks credibility. Thus it is unlikely that the concerned could steal military clothes and weapons without being noticed and that he could subsequently climb over the prison wall [. . .]

the itinerary of the concerned is impossible to verify due to a lack of travel documents (the concerned sent back the passports).

The statements of the concerned contain contradictions when compared to his wife's account. Thus he declares that the passports which they received from the priest [name] were already completely in order at the time they left Angola. His wife claims that they still had to apply for a visa in Zaire.

Blommaert discusses this case in detail. Here I indicate some key points arising from this case and how they illustrate important issues about text trajectories and their consequences: decisions about the veracity of a person's case are made on the basis of a spoken narrative, the complex semiotic resources of which are not acknowledged – for example that the specific linguistic variety used may not be the applicant's preferred variety or indeed that the applicant may not have a preferred variety or a standard variety of any language; such resources get re-entextualised as a standard variety of one language, French or Dutch, making invisible the semiotic resources used by the speaker and thus obscuring the 'story' – that is the life – that the applicant is actually telling (and here then is an example of the normative, centripetal dimensions of a specific institution at work); given common ideological orientations to language – that people have one language rather than another, and that language can be identified as a specific boundaried resource (see Chapter 4) – the uptake of officials is likely to present problems for any applicant attempting to produce a 'credible' account, that is one that can be recognised as valid by the administrators; the written text, that is the summary case, is not produced in one go but over a period of time and involves a number of people re-contextualising earlier words and evaluative stances towards such words; and the final report represents itself as outside of the process of text production as if the report were the 'story of the applicant'. Yet, as Blommaert argues, the story of the applicant is in fact 'the whole text trajectory' (Blommaert 2005: 63). This includes the specific cluster of resources used by the applicant in the oral narrative, the resources used by the officials in re-entextualising this narrative into written documents and ideologies around what counts as language(s) and the relationship between use of language(s) and truth. A final point to note here relating to the discussion about 'communities' in this chapter is that this trajectory illustrates why the notion of 'speech' communities – both as descriptors and ideologies – is useful when seeking to understand writing.

Writing for academic publication (Lillis and Curry 2010)

In a study setting out to explore the practices and experiences of scholars writing for publication, we followed the trajectories of some 250 texts (Lillis and Curry 2010) from early drafting to submission to academic journals. Given the context in which scholars were working, non-Anglophone semi-peripheral (Sousa-Santos 1994), the texts were literally being moved from one geopolitical site to another; for example from a group of scholars in a Hungarian research centre to a centre-based Anglophone journal.[5] In reporting on this research, we have discussed how a number of people, brokers, other than authors are involved in the production of such texts (Lillis and Curry 2010). Here I want to focus on the impact of the gatekeeper, in one specific text trajectory. This particular text can be said to have 'travelled well' – from one specific place and group of scholars to another place –in that the intended uptake is secured and a text is published. However, it's important to explore the changing nature of the text in its trajectory, the conditions under which it gets to be published and the questions it raises about practices of knowledge circulation globally.

This Text History concerns a paper produced by a close-knit group of experienced researchers from Central Europe who had researched and co-authored for some eight years. After submission to an Anglophone-centre journal, they received a response from the editor who, following reviews, declared his interest in the paper, but proposed the involvement of an additional scholar, a statistician, whose involvement the editor subsequently organised. The authors agreed and eventually the text was published in the journal. However, in the trajectory towards publication a significant change is made in the overall argument, as illustrated in the extracts in Figure 5.9. In the version submitted to the journal, emphasis is on signalling the difference between the findings of the study reported and a key previous study. In the published version the claim to difference is replaced with claims to confirmation; that is, the study in the paper is reported as confirming the findings of the previous study.

The changes towards confirmation begin to occur in the drafts when the statistician is involved, indicating that he played a significant part in developing such a shift. It is also clear that the editor favoured or indeed encouraged such a shift, stating in one correspondence that he valued the 'confirmatory aspect' of the study. The main author appreciated the involvement of both literacy brokers, acknowledged the shift in argument and stated that it would be easier to publish 'if we focus on the similarities rather than the differences'. However at the same time the author expressed mixed feelings. In considering the shift from contrast to confirmation, the author foregrounded the position of her national context as a peripheral location for academic production: 'Saying something from [Central Europe] which is new is not good, not allowed. Of course it's absolutely their perspective to see [Central Europe] as, I don't know, a tribe trying to do something scientific' (Lillis and Curry 2010: 107).

As with the asylum application, the most consequential text in the text trajectory – that is the text that is finally published – is not produced in one go, and involves

Figure 5.9   Extracts from submitted and published versions of an academic text
(Lillis and Curry 2010: 106)

Extracts from submitted text	Extracts from published text
Another difference from the Z et al. study is that in our procedure . . . (I)* *The difference between* the strongest factor of Z (author) *and ours* . . . (I) *In our case* this is accompanied by – while in Z *(author) study* . . . (D)	The results (see Table 1) *are consistent* with those of Z et al. in that . . . (R and D) These results *appear to be supported* in a different linguistic and cultural setting . . . (R and D)
In our case the X factor explanatory value (among other factors) *was greater than in the case of Z et al.* (D)	The X also *correlated significantly* with . . . (R and D)

I, R, D refer to different content sections of the text: I = Introduction, D = Discussion, R = Results

a number of people's views about and interventions into the text's production. It also illustrates the role that a range of resources plays in text production: as with the asylum case, language is a key issue in that the scholars are writing in English and for an Anglophone journal. Whilst highly competent in English, the authors of this and other articles regularly receive comments on their 'English' or 'style' although, as with the asylum application, in which orientations to language are not made visible, these are often presented as if they played no significant role in the evaluation and (mis)recognition of the text. It is the clustering of textual features and specific responses to this cluster that mediates (positive or negative) uptake and value. In terms of positive uptake, in this instance it seems that even though the scholars were using the global 'language of science' they could only be granted a certain voice. As a text from the periphery, its value lies in its potential to confirm – from the margins – something that has been done in the centre. Therefore, if our interest is in understanding what this writing is and does, it needs to be understood in terms of the whole trajectory, not only what it becomes in its most public form (published) but in how it comes into being.

Medical certification processes in nineteenth-century England (Berkenkotter and Hanganu-Bresch 2011)

Whilst the above text trajectories are from contemporary contexts and practices, analysis of historical text trajectories are important not only because of what they tell us about past institutional practices but also for what they can show us about the historical bases of contemporary practices. Berkenkotter and Hanganu-Bresch (2011) track the medical certification process in nineteenth-century England, a process with profound social and personal consequences, that of the 'confinement of individuals judged to be "of unsound mind"' (Berkenkotter and Hanganu-Bresch: 2011: 220). As part of their study they collected and analysed a range of texts, including medical certificates, an extract from one of which is included in Figure 5.10.

Figure 5.10   Extract from medical certificate (Berkenkotter and Hanganu-
            Bresch 2011: 238)

I, the undersigned John James being a Bachelor of the University of London and Fellow of the Royal College of Physicians, and being in actual practice as a surgeon, Personally examined Walter James Marshall, at [gives Marshall's address] and find him to be a person of unsound mind and a proper Person to be taken charge of and detained under Care and Treatment. I have formed this opinion upon the following grounds; viz.:

1. Facts indicating insanity observed by myself: On introduction to him today, he did not desire another medical man after Dr. Seaton, then began to read aloud the Book of Common Prayer, an epistle and some collects; then said he was very clever and would go into Parliament, that he endured afflictions and insult unjustly inflicted because it was acceptable with God; his manner was excited, & ideas rambling from point to point; these observations do not seem [. . .] but his friends [writing becomes illegible here].
2. Other facts (if any) indicating Insanity communicated to me by others: Mr. J. Myers, Mr. Ernest Myers, Mr. Douglass, tell me that he is normally a quiet, retir[ing] man, gentle and polite, lately he has become violent in language, enters into pecuniary transactions with great rashness viz. Amongst others (are) and a first interview with a [word illegible] previously unknown to him, Mr. Marshall, suddenly agreed to give him five thousand pounds at 4 percent because the corn chandler whom he alleged [to be] a gentleman, and would at once go into Parliament with him.

Signed Name, John M. James. M.B. London, FRCS, 11 Thurlor Square
Dated this third Day of May, 1876. (AR 6328/16) [. . .]

Berkenkotter and Hanganu-Bresch argue that the 'medical certificate' should not be analysed in isolation but as one element in a text trajectory, or to use their term, as a 'genre suite' consisting of four documents – the order, the two medical certificates (an extract from which is in Figure 5.10) and the notice of admission itself. For whilst they each exist as separate documents, their meaning is constituted by their mutual existence, uptake and enactment; 'Each of these documents must be filled out and signed if the "Notice" is to succeed as a "performative"' (after Austin 1962, Berkenkotter and Hanganu-Bresch 2011), that is, as being taken up, and thus literally the documents performing an action. In this instance the final uptake is that of admitting a patient into an asylum.

The use of 'genre suite' here is interesting for the questions it raises about the extent and ways in which genre can be construed as a textual or a practice/action phenomenon, an issue raised in Chapter 3. Two interesting points can be made using this particular case as an example. Firstly, we see that what are often presented as distinct textual genres often locatable in distinct texts, narrative and argument, are in fact found in one text. As can be seen from the extract in Figure 5.10 elements of narrative – the recounting of events, description of people, time, places – are centrally embedded in the certificate; these include 'on introduction to him today', 'he did not desire another medical man after Dr. Seaton', 'then began to read aloud the Book of Common Prayer'. But the purpose of the narrative elements is to serve as evidence for the overall argument that the doctor is making: that Marshall is of unsound mind and therefore that the Commissioners should agree to have him confined to an asylum. Secondly, Berkenkotter and Hanganu-Bresch argue that this one text needs to be viewed in terms of the whole chain of texts, genre suite, illustrated in Figure 5.11 which can be viewed as an 'illocutionary act of complex argumentation' (van Eemeren and Grootendorst 1984, cited in Berkenkotter and Hanganu-Bresch 2011). They use 'genre suite' to signal how the texts combine to constitute a specific rhetorically co-ordinated action with material consequences. This particular genre suite is heavily pre-scripted, that is, production followed by uptake of one text drives the uptake of another (and can only be revoked if challenged through another process, as occurred in the case of Marshall in this instance, see Berkenkotter and Hanganu-Bresch 2011). The previous two text trajectories are likewise heavily pre-scripted, nested as they are within specific sets of institutional imperatives and gatekeeping practices which orient producers and evaluators (albeit sometimes differently) in quite rigid ways.

CONCLUSION

Writing involves using existing and available resources – in terms of language(s), materials, technologies. The resources that are used for specific instances of writing are not free floating but are powerfully bound up with the histories of their use. A key way of capturing this situatedness is to talk in terms of the communities we inhabit, come into contact with, or even ignore: drawing on the notion of community in specific relation to *speech*, *discourse* and *practice* may be relevant when seeking to understand the nature of such resources, how they get used, where and why.

A key dimension to writing is its materiality and thus its portability or mobility. However, texts or bits of texts travel across time and space rather than, as we often imagine, writing being extextualised at one point and remaining 'intact'; in fact what any instance of writing means and does and how it is valued, shifts. And here it's important to return to the notion of function when exploring what (aspects) of writing get (mis)recognised and by whom. As discussed in Chapter 3, there is often what I have described as a fruitful convergence between form and function; an emphasis on function serves to tie form – of any semiotic resource – to social purpose and use. However, there are problems with the way in which the

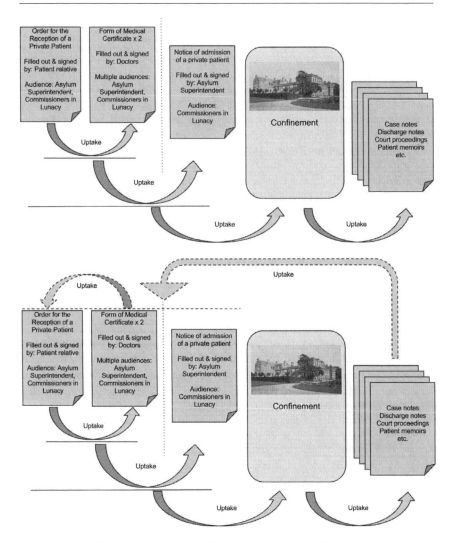

Figure 5.11　The chain of 'uptakes' following the request ('Order') to confine a patient in an asylum (Berkenkotter and Hanganu-Bresch 2011)

widespread use of 'function' as a common sense category seems to flatten out any complications and contestation around what texts do. Key causes of this problem are the empirical tendency to read off functions from textual forms alone, at a specific moment in time and, within applied and sociolinguistics, the theoretical tendency to frame function within a strongly normative evolutionary discourse – that forms simply (und unproblematically) evolve to fulfil communicative functions (discussed in Chapter 1, see also Note 1). The notions of text trajectory, text history and genre suite discussed in this chapter go some way towards responding to this challenge, by empirically grounding what texts do – and how in fact they come to be (entextualised). Following trajectories may be one way of avoiding slipping into any straightforward claims about function (although there are always dangers).

Methodologically the chapter has picked up on a key notion in writing research, discussed in Chapter 3, that of genre. The notions of text trajectories, genre suite and genre chains offer a more dynamic representation of the workings of written texts in social context because they shift the emphasis away from questions about specific texts and questions about their type (for example, is it an example of this or that genre) towards the idea that certain texts routinely cluster together, not because of their formal or textual features but because of the ways these texts are produced, received and – importantly – acted upon. Here then a stronger link is made between the notion of genre as 'text' and genre as action. When the notion of 'chains of genre' is used alongside the notion of 'uptake' – for example, literally how texts or bits of text are taken up and acted upon – we can see how genre can be a useful empirical notion that can enable the tracking of specific texts and their specific outcomes.

A key focus in this chapter has been on text trajectories in 'centring institutions'; here we can see how function – what texts do – are tied into these institutional agendas and pre-scriptions. In Chapter 6, I continue to explore writing in centring institutions in terms of regulation but I also explore how agency is enacted in these as well as less regulated semiotic spaces.

NOTES

1. At the time of writing, the question of the politics and ethics surrounding the use of (re) sources in the media is a subject of major inquiry in the UK. See http://www.leveson inquiry.org.uk/ (accessed 24 Nov. 2011).
2. In science I don't understand what is the/ teacher saying and when I get/ shouted and I don't understand it/ in Humanities I find it difficult/ when sir says to me/ take this work home and/ when I take the work home/ and I ask my dad or some/ one to help they say to/ me we don't know what work/ this is. then I don't do my hom/ work when I come to school/ and teacher shout/ at me and/ I get a detention.
3. This is the example used by Devitt but clearly sets vary historically and geoculturally.
4. See Blommaert 2005: 240 for details of transcription conventions used and discussion of the difficulties of transcribing and translating such speech.
5. These are contested terms but I'm using a distinction here between 'centre' and 'periph-ery', or 'semi-periphery' from World Systems theory. See Wallerstein 1991. Other terms in use are 'developed' and 'developing' country or 'Third' and 'First' world, or north and south.

Chapter 6

Identity, inscription and voice

INTRODUCTION

This chapter focuses on identity in studies of writing and explores how identity is theorised and explored. In this chapter the notion of writing as material inscription (discussed in Chapter 2) is layered onto the notion of writing as the making, or inscription, of the self.

The aims of this chapter are:

- to explore why identity is an important focus in writing research
- to consider some of the different ways in which writing involves the doing of 'identity work'
- to explore ways in which existing semiotic resources for writing are inscribed with particular (resources for) identities and how these are taken up for identity work
- to consider the ways and extent to which writing practices are regulated in different social semiotic spaces and how agency is enacted

WHY FOCUS ON IDENTITY?

Research seeking to explore the relationship between language and identity is part of a broader recognition in the social sciences that issues of identity are of considerable concern, bound up with 'some of the most troubling phenomena of our times: communal violence, xenophobia and exclusion and discrimination on the basis of gender, ethnicity, sexuality, disability and religion' ('Identities and Social Action' research, in Rampton 2010: 234). Once we move away from the idea of language being an autonomous system (see Chapter 4) the potential significance of identity in and for language use – the relationship between who we are, how and why we use language, how we evaluate ours and others' uses of language – comes to the fore. In general terms, we can think of identity as having anything to do with the ways in which a person or group ascribe to themselves, or are ascribed by others, particular categories of social being, with common markers of identity being gender, sexuality, race, ethnicity, social class, nationality and linguistic profile.[1] Each category is not hermetically sealed or separate from other categories, for example, categorising someone as a woman may at the same time (even if unstated) involve categorising her also as working class, Norwegian, bilingual.

In some traditions of sociolinguistic research, identity markers are construed as social variables to be mapped against specific linguistic variables or clusters of these, for example, quantitative variationist studies mapping the use of 'standard' and 'non' standard linguistic features against gender (see Cameron 2009 for recent discussion of 'sex/gender' as constructs used in studies of language). But of course *identity* – what it is and means in any specific context is not fixed – and identity *markers* – the categories that we use to mark identity – are not straightforward. Thus in line with much work in the social sciences, most socially oriented approaches to language, including writing, construe identity not so much as a specific social category layered onto a specific feature of language use, but as active and dynamic, using terms such as 'identity work' or 'identification' to indicate the complex and processual nature of the relationship between identity in language use and communication.

Identity is also an important dimension to discussions of agency – the human capacity to act (Giddens 1979) – signalling that the kinds of actions and decisions people make at specific moments are bound up in complex ways with who they/ we are, or who they/we are imagined or imagine our/themselves to be, with some studies indicating that such 'imaginings' are often framed in terms of what is valued by key 'centring institutions', as illustrated in the text trajectories in Chapter 5 (for imagining community/ies see also Norton 2000). In exploring how issues of identity, language and agency are interwoven, other notions are also used to tease out and articulate this complexity, such as *interest, voice, subjectivity* and *desire*. Each signals a particular emphasis drawing on particular academic or ideological traditions (for brief overview, see Box 6.1). In this chapter I use 'identity work' in a general way to encompass the range of traditions signalling the active nature of being, doing and construing identity.

With regard to writing, 'identity work' has come to the fore, I would suggest, for two principal reasons. Firstly – and often because of the particular status it is ascribed socially and historically – writing is a highly consequential social activity. On the basis of writing, as texts and practices, people gain or are denied access to a whole range of important social resources (obvious examples are education, work, welfare and citizenship, as illustrated in Chapter 5). How we gain access to the essential or primary resources that enable us to access further resources or capital (material and semiotic) relates to who and where we are in the world – a combination of geographical location, social positioning, linguistic and cultural experiences – and how our writing is evaluated is not only in terms of what we write but who we are considered to be, or the identity(ies) that are ascribed to our writing. Secondly, influenced by poststructuralist theories of discourse (see for example Weedon 1987), the notion of writing as a material act of inscription has extended beyond the purely material to foreground its symbolic significance in the making of the self. Within this framework, inscription is no longer only a description of the material activity of marking or inscribing something on a material substance (discussed in Chapter 2), that is as something external to us, but rather becomes a way of describing how in our everyday actions we are constantly and repeatedly (re)inscribing ourselves and others into particular ways of doing/thinking/being. Attention to the fundamentally bodily or visceral nature of inscription is captured in Bourdieu's notion of *habitus* discussed below (and echoed in Gee's 2007, widely cited use of 'D/ discourse'; see definitions of discourse in Chapter 3, Box 3.2). The notion of inscription therefore usefully connects the material acts of specific inscriptions with the writing or inscribing of our selves (both symbolic and bodily-material) into specific discourse practices. In this chapter I illustrate some examples of inscription practices and also the highly consequential nature of identity work with regard to writing in different contexts.

Box 6.1 Identity – terms and traditions

Identity: Refers to aspects of who a person is, or feels to be as defined by themselves or others. Categories widely used are ethnicity, social class or status, gender, age, sexuality. Used in everyday discourse and across the social sciences.

Identification/identity work: Refers to the processes and practices of identifying the self with others, semiotic resources, language(s), institutions. Used by discourse theorists such as Fairclough (1992), Gee (2007).

Agency: Refers to the capacity, possibility or will to act in any given context (Giddens 1979). Widely used across the social sciences to emphasise individual action/opportunity in contrast to the social structures/uring of individuals' actions and life opportunities (for example relating to the teaching and learning of academic writing: see Horner 2000).

Interest: Used by Kress (2010) to signal the motivation driving an individual's meaning making, including decisions and choices about which semiotic resources are used for which purposes.

Desire: Used to refer to the stated/unstated and conscious/unconscious emotional, physical and intellectual impulses driving communication. It can refer to any form of desire but significant work in relation to sociolinguistics has focused on erotic desire (e.g. Cameron and Kulick 2006). With regard to writing, desire tends to be used to signal a writer's dissatisfaction with dominant conventions and wanting alternative ways of making meaning (for example in relation to academic writing, see Lillis 2011).

Voice: Used in writing research to signal connections between people's sense of identity, the content and form of what they write, and their capacity for what they understand to be key aspects of all three to be recognised or taken up. Voice is sometimes used to signal the person/groups of people (for example the voices of women poets) and sometimes to refer to what is said. It can be used to signal a strong authentic self, or to signal multiplicity of selves. The work of Bakhtin (e.g. 1981, 1986) is highly influential with researchers drawing on notions such as 'heteroglossia' (see below this chapter), 'ventriloquation', 'double voicing' (for examples of voice with regard to academic writing, see Lillis 2001, 2011; Scott 2012).

Stance: Refers to the ways in which writers (re)present themselves, their ideas and perspectives in texts. Considerable work on stance in academic writing has been carried out by Hyland who defines stances in terms of how writers 'communicate their integrity, credibility, involvement, and a relationship to their subject matter and their readers' (Hyland 1999: 101).

Habitus: A notion developed by Bourdieu (1977) to refer to 'the set of dispositions or habits that are learned throughout childhood and beyond and lead people to act and react in different ways [. . .] Language and communication are viewed as key aspects of these dispositions' (Swann et al. 2004: 131) (see discussion in this chapter).

Subject(ivity) subject position(ing): Used in discourse oriented studies where individuals are construed less as free agents and more as acting within (and against) available discourses (e.g. Fairclough 1992, Weedon 1987). Thus individuals can be viewed as being 'subjected' to particular discourses or as taking up particular positions within discourses (with regard to academic writing see this chapter).

WRITING AS IDENTITY WORK

There are a number of ways of thinking about writing as identity work. In this section I discuss identity work in terms of three interrelated dimensions or levels: the social structuring of (opportunities for) writing; the relationship between socially embodied individuals, through the notion of habitus, and writing; the socially available resources for writing and the ways in which such resources are inscribed with particular identities.

The social structuring of opportunities for writing

Writing practices are socially patterned and structured, thus involving issues of identity in many ways. Identity is most obviously connected to the social structuring of writing practices through the regulation of who gets to write and under what conditions. Historically writing has often been a tightly restricted resource, with certain (large) groups of people being excluded from its use, both with regard to specific writing practices and purposes (such as the scribing of religious texts) and with regard to writing more generally. A key example of the latter was the prohibition of the teaching of writing to the enslaved populations of America, as illustrated in the 1740 Carolina Negro Act:

> Be it therefore Enacted by the Authority aforesaid, That all and every Person and Persons whatsoever, who shall hereafter teach or cause any Slave to be taught to write, or shall use or employ any slave as a Scribe in any Manner of Writing what-soever, hereafter taught to write; every such Person or Persons shall, for every such offense, forfeit the Sum of One Hundred Pounds current Money.
>
> (quoted in Rasmussen 2010: 202)

Rights to write are bound up with political rights, ranging from the right to engage in the act of inscription itself to the right to write in particular ways, most obviously, to write in particular languages. The development of literacy, as a central goal of education, is currently viewed as a fundamental human right and consist-ently campaigned for by international bodies such as UNESCO.[2] But people's opportunities for writing are restricted and regulated in a number of indirect and direct ways, the most obvious restrictions arising from the lack of opportunities to take part in writing (whether in informal contexts or formal schooling) including limited access to the necessary material resources for writing (for example of literacy and development debates, see Street 2001). Another key way in which writing is restricted is through limiting who can write in particular authorised ways, evident in gate–keeping practices relating to professional and official bodies whereby only those authorised to write get to do so, for example in medicine and law. How people gain access to and engage with these authorised writing practices has been explored in a number of ways, but the link with identity is made on two counts: firstly, in terms of which social groups gain access to these professions (using categories such as gender, social class, ethnicity), and secondly, and more closely linked to writing, in terms of the tensions and challenges people face in taking on new or additional layers of iden-tity, for example, the authority or expert stance of lawyers, doctors or social workers (for discussion, see Abner and Kierstead 2011, Ivanič 1998, Lillis 2001, Rai 2004).

A key focus in ongoing explorations of how writing and identity are socially structured is that of gender. Barton and Hamilton (1998; see also Chapter 4) talk of the gendered patterning of literacy practices in the home, drawing on their ethno-graphic study of literacy practices in a town in the north–west of England. Whilst pointing out that there are individual counter-examples to the ones they describe, they found that men often engaged in reading and writing related to 'official' exter-nally oriented activities, such as responding to and paying bills, while women often engaged in 'personal' activities or activities requiring more personal interaction, such as writing Christmas cards, or letters to their children's school or complaint letters. Likewise, more women than men were involved in literacy activities with children, such as reading, helping with homework or buying books. These findings echo other work on the gendering of literacy practices in urban settings; Rockhill (1994), for example, exploring the literacy practices of Spanish speaking adults in a working–class community in Los Angeles, found that women did most of the lit-eracy work of the household (see also Chapter 4 for gender and weblogs).

This domestic gendering of writing (and literacy more generally) involves complex ideologies around opportunity, responsibility and aspiration. On the one hand, the key role played by women in literacy activities in the home can be viewed in a positive light, in that women are active participants in theirs and their family's general literacy practices and educational development. Indeed, the importance of women in developing literacy/education has often been stressed in international campaigns: consider versions of the widely used proverb-based slogan, 'If you educate a man you educate an individual, but if you educate a woman you educate a family/you educate a nation.'[3] However, some studies have also emphasised the negative nature of these ideologies around gender and literacy; most obviously that the home and children are construed as the sole or main responsibility of women and the doing of particular kinds of literacy work – domestic, caring – as being part of being a 'good mother'. Some studies show how women's desire and aspirations to literacies associated with other kinds of (non-domestic) identities, for example, professional, academic, are thwarted by educational programmes which offer routes towards the very same domestic literacy practices that women are in fact already expert in, and want to move beyond (see for example Horsman 1990 on the experiences of rural women in Canada) or by being offered 'schooled' literacy learning which bears no resemblance to the complex tasks and activities in which women are already engaged (as in, for example, Kell's 2010 account of a woman community leader in a South African shanty town).[4] There is a danger that such programmes can tie women into a particular type of literacy identity and close down opportunities for other more prestigious types associated with higher status literacy work, for example, currently, particular digital literacy activities, such as software design and programming (for discussion of 'gender digital divide' see Castaño 2008). I continue this focus on gendering throughout this chapter both as an important dimension to identity work in writing practices, and also as an illustration of how identity gets bound up with or inscribed into specific conventionalised resources for writing.

The key point here is that the social structuring of writing is not something that sits outside of us as individuals but is powerfully bound up with who we are, come to feel to be and also, importantly, how we are 'recognised' or misrecognised by others. To get at this embodiment of writing, Bourdieu's notion of *habitus* is useful, and widely used.

Habitus and writing practices

Bourdieu's notion of 'habitus' refers to the ways in which our individual ways of being, acting, knowing and feeling are powerfully shaped by the specific material, cultural and semiotic worlds we inhabit. Habitus refers to an 'internalised style of knowing and relating to the world that is grounded in the body itself' (Bourdieu 1977; see also Box 6.1). Habitus is an attempt to capture the way in which culture imprints itself on our bodies as much as our minds, and in this bodily experience of culture, some dimensions of which are more powerfully *sedimented* than others – that is deeply layered into the way we engage in the world (for discussion of sedimentation, see Rowsell and Pahl 2007). Whilst habitus does not deny the possibility of agency, it emphasises the way in which agency is mediated and shaped by the social contexts we inhabit – and which, in turn, inhabit us. With specific regard to writing, we are surrounded by particular social patternings and structuring of writing practices, as discussed above, and the particular ways we come to experience these vary depending on our specific social backgrounds, particularly early socialisation in the home and immediate communities of contact. Lived experiences lead to the development of 'dispositions' towards writing – that is, understandings and perceptions about what writing is, who does it and why and what we feel about it, which helps to explain why learning to write in specific ways may present particular difficulties for people who experience discontinuities between familiar and new writing practices. The existence of such dispositions often becomes evident once we engage in a new practice, for example, academic writing which, as illustrated across this chapter, may stand in contrast to – or socially distant from – many students' previous language and literacy experiences.

Engaging in new or less familiar practices may not be easily learned or taught if existing resources – and identities – are (implicitly or explicitly) denied or rejected. If we take the case of formal schooling (discussed briefly in Chapter 4) there is considerable difference between the levels of continuity and discontinuity of practices between home (work, political activity etc.) and formal schooling. Nomdo (2006) uses the notion in his study of a fellowship scheme aimed at enhancing the academic experiences and trajectories of 'promising "black" undergraduates' (Nomdo 2006: 182). The ways in which they experience the scheme, including their writing, is closely bound up with their sense of who they are, with students foregrounding social class in particular. Thus for Lyanda from an 'upwardly mobile' urban background, there is considerable continuity between the discourses of academia and her previous lived home and community experience, which contrasts with the lived experience of Sipho from a working-class township community. Talking of her experience in academia, Sipho states:

> The economic factor is very alienating, that's the worst part of all. I still experience a tension between those who grew up in the townships and those who grew up in the suburbs, meaning between working class and middle class black students [. . .] I'm still in the township, not like I was, for me the township is not *was*, it *is*.

She indicates how such feelings play out in her writing:

> When you write you are not expected to come from your home. I remember most comments I got for my essays was like 'why do you always have to be political about things'.

(Nomdo 2006: 192, 199)

Certain kinds of identities are expected to be set aside in certain (usually institutionalised) writing spaces which accounts for, in part, why the doing of writing in particular ways in particular contexts can be an emotionally fraught activity, and why writing cannot be construed solely (or primarily) as a transactional, cognitive or rationalist activity.

However, whilst continuity (of practices, resources and identities) is important, it is obviously not always positive and indeed can be highly constraining, as illustrated earlier in this chapter with regard to women's literacy aspirations. Ivanič et al. (2009: 66) point to the ways in which some students at college feel constrained by peer pressure to read in particular ways, rather than adopting new ways of reading or opportunities for reading that the formal institution has on offer. And, indeed, engaging with and experiencing some forms of discontinuity is what education and learning – wherever it takes place – is presumed to be about. But here is where the notion of agency and ownership seems to be important. In thinking about habitus and dis/continuity, it's important to recognise that whilst the dispositions developed in early daily lived experience may be powerful, they are not rigid or ossified, particularly where opportunities for new semiotic and meaning making encounters occur. A range of notions is used to capture moments where we recognise that we may want or need to modify or transform our existing resources and practices. For example, in her study of 'mature students'' writing in higher education, Ivanič draws on Candlin's notion of 'crucial moments in discourse' (Candlin 1989, discussed in Ivanič 1998: 5) to signal specific instances of disjuncture between students' existing habits of writing (and meaning) and the demands and conventions required by the university.[5] Whilst such moments may be highly problematic (as I discuss further below), they may also lead to the creative use of existing and new resources, captured in the notion of 'improvisation'. For example, Holland and Cain use 'improvisations', to refer to 'the sort of impromptu actions that occur when our past, brought to the present as habitus, meets with a particular combination of circumstances and conditions for which we have no set response' (Holland et al. 1998: 17, discussed in Pahl and Rowsell 2010: 9). Drawing on this notion Pahl and Rowsell give the example of a Turkish child at school making a map using his mother's prayer beads, which they describe as 'an improvisation on the practice of prayer and on mapmaking' (Pahl and Rowsell 2010: 9). Whether the use of new resources or old resources in new ways is successful depends of course not just on the user/producer but on uptake. This is an issue I have raised in Chapter 5 and I return to below.

Resources for writing inscribed with particular identities

There is a close relationship between writing *practices* and the *resources* used for such practices, and identity work is nested in both. Broadly speaking, by engaging in a particular writing practice we are maintaining and sustaining (the value of) a particular semiotic resource; and by drawing on and using a particular resource we are maintaining a particular type of social practice. The point here is not that any semiotic resource is intrinsically marked with a specific identity(ies) but rather that such resources carry with them particular histories of use, including histories of evaluation of such use. Bakhtin's widely quoted comment on the nature of actual language usage, or to use Bakhtin's term 'utterance', is helpful here, particularly if we conceptualise the 'utterance' as referring to the use of any type of semiotic resource (and not limit it to referring only to the verbal meaning). Of the utterance Bakhtin states:

> It is entangled, shot through with shared thoughts, points of view, alien value judgements and accents. The word, directed toward its object, enters a dialogically agitated and tension-filled environment of alien words, value judgements and accents, weaves in and out of complex interrelationships, merges with some, recoils from others, intersects with yet a third group: and all this may crucially shape discourse, may leave a trace in all its semantic layers, may complicate its expression and influence its entire stylistic profile.
>
> (Bakhtin 1981: 276)

We can consider examples of the ways in which specific utterances at all levels of language use are 'shot through with shared thoughts, points of view, alien value judgments and accents' and are necessarily bound up with aspects of identity work. For example, at the level of orthography or material inscription, writing marks identity in a number of ways, not least nationality, ethnicity, gender, political affiliation. Thus the decision not to use in Czech the diacritics used in Polish was because of the desire to mark a cultural–political boundary with Poland, rather than because of the usefulness or otherwise of the diacritics per se (Sebba 2001; see also Johnson 2005 for debates around spelling reform Germany in the mid-1990s; see also Chapter 2). Likewise, the establishment of a particular script (over another) can be a powerful signifier of group membership, identifying the users as belonging to or differing from other groups (Sebba 2009: 42) and change at different historical moments; for example, the use of Latin rather than Cyrillic script for representing non-Russian languages of the former Soviet Union (see Mesthrie et al. 2009: 377 ff.). In a similar way, inscription practices at the level of handwriting have historically been ascribed a range of particular uses and identities, including, for example, gendered and class identities (see Graddol 2007). The short poem below is an interesting eighteenth–century commentary on a 'lady's writing' and how handwriting is linked to what are considered to be appropriate physical and mental attributes;

Figure 6.1   On a Lady's Writing (*Poems* 1773 Anna Lætita Aikin/ Barbauld).
Available at http://www.rc.umd.edu/editions/contemps/barbauld/
poems1773/introduction.html (accessed 10 Sept. 2011)

HER even lines her steady temper show;
Neat as her dress, and polish'd as her brow;
Strong as her judgment, easy as her air;
Correct though free, and regular though fair;
And the same graces o'er her pen preside
That form her manners and her footsteps guide

Of course the function and purpose of such apparently small and insignificant markings (the use or not of a particular diacritic or a particular cluster of letter shapes) with such potentially big and specific indexicalities cannot be taken as given or simply read off from inscriptions and markings themselves, but are rather questions to be explored. This is illustrated in Cushman's work on a syllabary developed for Cherokee: Cushman challenges the assumption that the syllabary designed by Sequoyah reflected his lack of knowledge of English and, using documentary evidence to indicate that he knew English, argues that he explicitly chose to develop an alternative system. Thus, rather than the syllabary reflecting a limited knowledge of English orthography it was an explicit attempt to capture Cherokee meanings and to index a particular political and cultural identity (see Cushman 2010).

At this point, it seems useful to pause and consider the different orientations or pulls on the ways in which writing as a semiotic resource and practice gets inscribed with identity(ies), taking account in particular of orientations to centring institutions (discussed in Chapter 5). And here, using the notions of centripetal (centralising or unifying forces) and centrifugal (diversifying) after Bakhtin 1981, I'll consider three.

1. **Centripetal pulls towards centring institutions with obvious normative gatekeeping interests and ideologies.** An example of a centring institution is the nation state, and public institutions under the auspices of the nation state, such as formal schooling. Here there are categorical positions on what kinds of inscription practices are acceptable or important (in Western sites, these are usually verbal, usually alphabetic, monolingual, in the standard variety of a language) and often clear ideological positions on which specific features of writing reflect and enact socially valued aspects of identity.

2. **Centrifugal pulls that stay within the ideological semiotic space of centring institutions.** These are pulls that seem to loosen many presumed straightforward relationships between specific details of inscription practices (at the level of micro or macro features) and identities but which nevertheless are made within the same ideological semiotic space as those valued by centring institutions. Thus dominant semiotic values remain intact. These are strongly evident in commercial practices (advertising, shop labelling) where playing with (rather than conforming with) conventions around semiotic modes is viewed as appropriate. Most obviously, advertising has long since worked with colour and image alongside the verbal, using all available resources (and identities) to engage people's interest in and to play with notions of correctness/incorrectness rather than correctness per se being a key value or ideology (see Cook 2001).

3. **Centrifugal pulls that work to destabilise the dominant ideological semiotic space.** Examples include challenges to the norms and values of centring institutions. These might be at the micro level of semiotic signs, as in the use of <k> rather than <c> (and <ni> for <ň>, <tx> for <ch>) to challenge the hegemony of Castilian dominance in Spain (Sebba 2007; see Chapter 2) or

more macro level challenges to acceptable material sites of inscription, such as graffiti on public buildings. They may also include challenges to the notion that in order to be employed 'appropriately' languages need to be used in discrete, semiotic spaces, through practices such as code-meshing (discussed in Chapter 3) as well as challenges to the verbal-heavy emphasis that are found in both contemporary digital and 'hard copy' writing, but particularly in the former. The extent to which centring practices are being destabilised is one to be explored but that these are growing in terms of sheer number and attracting considerable engagement is evident, particularly in what Gee calls 'passionate affinity-based learning' contexts (Gee, http://www.jamespaulgee.com/ (accessed 28 Oct. 2011)), a notion I return to below.

The ideological nature of the use of any signs is far from straightforward, and attempting to reach conclusions about the ideological workings of signs on the basis of signs alone can take us only so far. With the increase globally in production and in the number of producers, the reasons for any specific inscriptions may be multiple and various. Thus, for example, whilst the use of <k> rather than <c> may signal a political statement challenging the hegemony of Castilian, it may also reflect the dominant influence of English globally, or a playing with 'Englishness', or indeed a combination of all three (there has been little study of mixing in multilingual written texts, but see Sebba et al. 2012).

An example of a centripetal resource: essayist literacy

Just as resources for writing at the levels of orthography and script design are bound up with identity work, so too are the resources of genres and discourses. An example of this is 'essayist literacy' (after Scollon and Scollon 1981), a literacy practice which is pervasive across institutions of higher education, increasingly globally through the ever rising symbolic status of English.[6] Scollon and Scollon describe essayist literacy as rooted in the European Enlightenment tradition of clarity and transparency whereby – as long as the correct language is used – it is assumed that language can encode meaning straightforwardly into any text:

> The ideal of essayist literacy that all meaning resides in the text is of course impossible to achieve. As an ideal, however, it expresses a view of the world as rational and of an identity between rational knowledge and linguistic expression (Foucault 1973). The ultimate knowability of the world is matched by the assumption of its complete expressability in text. One only has to observe clearly, think clearly, and clear expression will follow automatically.
>
> (Scollon and Scollon 1981: 49)

Scollon and Scollon (1981) foregrounded the relationship between essayist literacy as a particular semiotic resource and issues of identity by contrasting the ways of knowing, presenting and being that essayist literacy demands with alternative traditions, notably, in their research, the Athabascan communities in Alaska. They point to, for example, the importance of knowledge display in essayist literacy, regardless of who the writer is addressing and illustrate how such display is only considered appropriate in Athabascan practices when the person doing the displaying is in a position of dominance/higher status over the audience. They argue that where the relationship is unknown, Athabascans prefer silence. A particularly strong critique of the dominance and imposition of essayist literacy which foregrounds identity has emerged from feminist researchers who argue that the conventions enacted in essayist literacy inscribe not only ways of meaning making but particular ways of doing identity work (Campbell 1992; Frey 1990; hooks 1988; Nye 1990).[7] The nature of essayist literacy has been analysed therefore in terms not only of its generic conventions but also in terms of the kind of opportunities for meaning, intellectual work and self-hood it offers, or affords (see Figure 6.2).

Figure 6.2   Essayist literacy: resources for identity work (Lillis 2011: 412)

Privileges one specific. . .	
kind of textual unity	→ one key theme/argument (as dialectic)
kind of relationship between reader and writer	→ 'anonymous', 'neutral', 'disembodied'
kind of identity/ subjectivity	→ rational, neutral, male?, middle class, Anglophone centre . . .
kind of aesthetic value	→ rational, logical, verbal
form of language	→ 'standard', formal, monolingual
language (globally)	→ English
kind of text	→ linear, transparent
mode	→ verbal, written
kind of learning/writing trajectory	→ from novice to expert

Often the only way identity in conventionalised resources becomes visible is when people experience a jarring between who they feel they are/want to be and the ways in which they feel positioned by the required use of particular semiotic resources, discussed in terms of 'dispositions' above; for example when a student feels that writing in standard English using academic conventions signals a particular social class identity (middle class) which is at odds with her sense of self as working class. Of course, the link between available semiotic resources, their uses and their affordances and constraints for identity work is far from straightforward, and shifts and varies according, not least, to specific domains, contexts and moments in an individual's life trajectory. Using semiotic resources, particularly those which are more or less rigidly regulated and gatekeepered, often involves a complex mix of negotiation, resistance and accommodation (for discussion of these notions in relation to student writing, see Chase 1988).

REGULATION AND AGENCY

Strongly regulated writing spaces

Regulation of writing is most obviously evident in institutional contexts, where, for a wide range of reasons there is a strong imperative to govern, constrain and evaluate what writing goes on. Regulation is evident in the many bureaucratic and procedural recording practices demanded by institutions, which are increasingly mediated by digital technologies, and driving work–based practices. We considered examples of such pre-scripted practices in the text trajectories in Chapter 5 (see also Figure 5.2).

Perhaps the most extreme context of institutional regulation of writing (apart from actual prohibition) is prison, where, depending on the historical, geographical context and reason for imprisonment, rules vary about the materials you can use, when you can write, what you can write. But even where there are such totalising frames for regulation, agency is often evident in many ways; political prisoners, for example, may work to secure materials, spaces and opportunities for writing and often succeed in production and dissemination (for example, Irish hunger strikers in the early 1980s (Beresford 1987) and the Iranaian journalist, Akbar Ganji in http://freeganji.blogspot.com/2005/07/second-letter-to-free-people-of-world.html (accessed 10 Sept. 2011)). Furthermore, as Wilson's prison ethnographies show, writing (and literacy more generally) is used to transform the highly regulated space in prisons. She shows how prisoners use writing to recontextualise their space to create identities for living that challenge that of prisoner/imprisoned and enables prisoners to work at identities that stand in contrast to their identification as 'prisoners': a friend (through the writing of letters); a father (through the making of cards); an artist (by decorating texts); a poet (by writing poetry). Wilson (2003, 2010) illustrates the agency of prisoners with regard to their use of literacy artefacts and the construction of 'non prison spaces' that she describes (after Bhaba 1994) as a 'third space' – a space created by people that transcends the immediate material space they inhabit. She describes, for example, how a pillow gets 'relocated as a site of graffiti' and in so doing the prisoner makes a link with the 'outside world' where graffiti usually occurs (see Chapter 2, Figure 2.2). In carrying out such writing, prisoners are enacting agency in strongly regulated contexts; the author of the graffiti-pillow actually named himself ('John Lomax') and thus risked punishment for damaging institutional property. More fundamentally, the creation of such third spaces helps prisoners hold onto the very existence or possibility of self.

Other institutions regulate writing in less direct ways. But once the issue of identity is allowed (or encouraged) to be discussed in the context of writing, people signal how writing is bound up with identity work in all sorts of ways. This can be illustrated if we return to focus on essayist literacy and draw on my research with 'non-traditional' students; identity was a significant dimension to their experience of writing in higher education. For example, the reflections of Sara, a successful student from a Pakistani-British background indicate the kind of identity work involved for her:

See, when I say I think of myself as English (when she writes academic essays) what I mean is that I'm trying to imagine how an English person would be writing, thinking in that sense-trying to programme myself, to make myself think as if I'm an English person writing this out. It just helps me sort of concentrate a bit more, you know, leave my Urdu aside – if they're (tutors) asking specifically for my experiences and what I feel, then that's fine. But if not, then you have to think, you have to put yourself away from that, you know, basically write what they want you to write.

(Lillis 2001: 88)

The relationship between particular semiotic resources, the identity of writers and the identities of their (imagined) addressees is also evident in student writers' comments on wordings they use (see Lillis 2001, 2003 for use of Bakhtin's notion of addressivity in student writing). Consider the comments of another student-writer Reba, in Figure 6.3, in the same research, when asked about particular wordings in her text.

Figure 6.3   Extract from Reba's text and her comments on the text
             (Lillis 2001: 84)

Extract from Reba's texts	**Extract from Reba's comments on her text**
The media reflects what society thinks as a whole, or just reflects the hierarchy ideas. Women are portrayed in the media as being **total airheads**.	R: (laughs) *Can you not use that? [total airheads]* T: *Well, what do you think?* R: *No you can't.* T: *Why not?* R: *Because it's slang.* T: *It was good to see it in a way, but in terms of an academic essay, it probably wouldn't be looked on too well.* R: *I know.* T: *So, can you think of another word, or words instead of that?* R: *Er, in a derogatory way. But I don't like using these words cause it sounds . . .* T: *It sounds what?* R: *It sounds as if it's been copied off somewhere . . . It doesn't sound like my work.*

Reba clearly knows the phrasings that would be considered appropriate in this context but does not use them because she does not identify them as 'hers' (see below for issue of ownership). To use a discourse approach to this instance, we could say that she is resisting the way in which dominant academic discourse seems to position her. And consider another student's strong feelings about the conventions she is expected to adhere to, commenting on the need for more formal wordings:

It makes me sick . . . I don't think it's important at all (laughs). But you have to do it? It's like I'm imprisoned, honest to God (laughs). That's how I feel. And that's why a lot of people are not interested . . . I am not. What am I saying? I know what I'm saying, but it's like, what for? Everybody knows what 'I'm not' means. It's like trying to segregate, you know, you've got like a boundary that sets, you know, you apart from other people. Why?

(Lillis 2001: 85)

In all the above extracts the student writers signal the importance of regulation not only with regard to their production of texts but with regard to 'uptake', that is how their writing (and indeed they) will be read. Taking account of uptake is clearly important; in the case of students, negative uptake may lead to failure of a course.

But even where there are what we can refer to as strongly normative regimes of regulation (governing what writers must do in order for there to be uptake according to particular evaluative regimes), there may also be active agency. Thus, for example, student writers may choose to mask identities which they consider will be misrecognised, so there may be agency in complying with, as well as resisting, dominant conventions, as seemed to be the case with Sara, above. People may also choose to recontextualise aspects of highly regulated practices for their own purposes, other than those initially intended. This is illustrated in Maybin's work on young people's practices at school, where a range of 'unofficial' writings, that is writings driven by children's interests – such as notes passed in class, copying down and sharing the words of popular songs (among girls), graffiti and lists for made-up clubs – are shaped and built out of 'official' school–based practices. Maybin argues that 'literacy in classrooms involves a hybrid mix of official, semi-official and unofficial readings and writings, each associated with different patterns of relationship, identity and formalised and unformalised knowledge' (Maybin 2006: 183) and talks of the need to avoid conceptualising social spaces and the literacy practices associated and practised within these as monolithic (i.e. either official or unofficial) spaces.

Whilst there is agency evident in the active recontextualisation of highly regulated practices, there are also ongoing attempts to open up highly regulated semiotic spaces to a wider range of meaning making and, thus, more diverse opportunities for identity work. Focusing on writing in higher education, for example, English argues that there is a need to rethink genre as a creative resource. Particular genres orient people not only towards the production of particular texts but towards particular discursive identity(ies) and, English argues, once 'genre' is reconceptualised as a resource, student writers can be invited to explore and play with a range of ways of meaning making and of doing identity work in the academy. English states: 'Genre studies have tended to focus on what genres look like (structural properties) or what they are used for (functional approaches) whereas in my study I have tried to focus on what genres let us do' (English 2011: 200).

Using an analytic framework designed to reframe genre as a resource (see Figure 6.4), English illustrates a pedagogically oriented activity which she refers to as 're-genring'. She, as teacher, invited students to consider the affordances and constraints of conventional essayist genres by regenring the essays.

The framework she uses in foregrounding different orientations – contextual, discursive, thematic and semiotic – is aimed at enabling writers to consider the affordances and constraints of different genres and to make decisions about which kinds of genres – or elements – they wish to use.[8] In the case of the example illustrated in Figure 6.4, this specific regenring enabled the writer to claim greater authority over what he was doing and to shift the way he oriented to potential readers: 'There wasn't so much of a paranoia about it [the second version]. While I was writing this one there wasn't the thought of having someone telling me that I was wrong' (English 2010: 116).

Weakly regulated writing spaces

As already indicated, distinctions are often made in literacy studies – between the 'official and unofficial', 'dominant and vernacular', 'public and personal', with the second in each pair of binaries often assumed to involve greater possibilities for agency than the former. It is clear that there are distinctions between the levels of regulation in different contexts for writing; we have briefly seen how centring institutions constrain and in many cases explicitly govern what people can do with writing, both in terms of production and uptake. I've also indicated, however, that agency doesn't disappear in institutionalised semiotic spaces – people can also be identified as being agentive seeking ways to accommodate to regulatory space, recreating and recontextualisng resources to create different spaces – but it is also the case that options for choice are more tightly constrained, through practices and ideologies around gatekeeping.

In contrast, there are communicative spaces where there is less direct regulation and gatekeeping about which semiotic resources can be used, when and why and by whom. The most obvious spaces being discussed currently are those linked with digital and mobile technologies, such as texting on mobile phones, social networking and gaming which are highly imbued with popular culture and part of an explosion of production activity by people across the age range and in many parts of the world. Gee, drawing in particular on his research on video gaming in relation to learning, refers to these as 'affinity spaces' and 'affinity groups' (Gee 2004).

> Passionate affinity-based learning occurs when people organize themselves in the real world and/or via the Internet (or a virtual world) to learn something connected to a shared endeavor, interest, or passion. The people have an affinity (attraction) to the shared endeavor, interest, or passion first and foremost and then to other people because of their shared affinity
> (Gee at http://www.jamespaulgee.com/ (accessed 28 Oct. 2011))

Of course regulation doesn't disappear and exactly who gets to participate and under what conditions is an ongoing focus of research. But some research on what is happening in such spaces does indicate that they may certainly be less restrictive

Figure 6.4   Analytic framework for analysing genre as a resource (English 2010: 109, 111)

The Social		
	Essay	**Children's Information 'article'**
Contextual Orientation		
Design	Responding *to* client's design	Designing *for* client
Production	Essayist (student essay)	Expository (for young readers)
Distribution	For institutional assessment *Normative* practice, reproduction of . . . Evaluation against normative implicit disciplinary (and institutionalized) criteria and/or values	For institutional assessment *Alternative* practice, experiment, reconfiguration of . . . Interpretive effect – for assessment/evaluation against non-normative disciplinary criteria and/or values
Discursive Orientation		
Purpose	Display knowledge of client's design Work with disciplinary material Display learning	Experiment with learning/ writing Tell (teach) about disciplinary material 'Infotainment'
Process	Acquire Reflect Synthesize Report Create	Reflect Synthesize Recontextualize Create Inform
Identity	Novice *as though* expert	Expert *as if* children's book writer
Role	Performer	Informer
Agency	Mediated Disguised/unidentifiable Intertextual	Unmediated Visible Interpersonal

Figure 6.4 (contd)

The Material		
	Essay	**Children's Information 'article**
Thematic Orientation		
Organization	Essay management (introduction, 'body' conclusion i.e. sequence of information/ideas) Discussion, descriptions, explanations, examples	Organization (introduction, 'body' and conclusion) Discussion, descriptions, explanations, examples
Topics	Disciplinary topics linguistic terms of reference Swahili loan words, history of borrowing, etc.	Disciplinary topics 'everyday' terms of reference Colonial history as background English and Swahili as languages that each borrow words
Semiotic Orientation		
Modes	**Writing**	**Writing**
Textual Materials	Impersonal forms (e.g. 'it' fronted, passives, nominalizations) Density of expression/clause density Embedded/indirect questions Disciplinary terminology Formal (writing-like) expression (e.g. full forms, subordination) Implicitness (assumed knowledge) 12 point Palatino	Personal forms (e.g. subject fronted, addressivity) Looseness of expression/ clause intricacy Direct (rhetorical) questions 'Everyday' terms Colloquial (speaking-like) expression (e.g. contracted forms, co-ordinators in first position – so, and) Explicitness (assumed 'ignorance') 14 point Palatino

about the kinds of resources that people can get to use – in terms of both production and uptake. In his study of computer mediated discourse (CMD), Androutsopoulos (2011) layers the notion of semiotic and modal variety onto Bakhtin's notion of heteroglossia – the use and invocation of multiple social voices and languages. Androutsopoulos argues that 'heteroglossia' helps illuminate and articulate what is going on in CMD Web 2 environments, that is interactive digital environments such as social networking sites. In order to illustrate what he means by heteroglossia in CMD, it's useful to consider an example – a comment on a YouTube video involving a Bavarian styled global pop song – alongside an extract from the analysis made by Androutsopoulos.

Figure 6.5   YouTube comment and analysis (Androutsopoulos 2011: 8)

Extract

xXxCroatiaStylexXx (2 months ago)

des is doch echt so geil zefix oida^^
so sama hoit mia bayern :D^^

Analysis
The comment gives praise to the video (the first line reads: 'this is really great, mate') and asserts a collective local identity (second line: 'that's how we are, we Bavarians'). Both sentences are in Bavarian dialect, as evidenced in the orthographic representation of dialect features and the use of dialect lexis (such as the interjection *zefix*).---

What strikes me here is less the comment's alignment to the language style of the commented video than the contrast between the comment proper and the screen name. While the former uses dialect to praise the video and claim (jocularly, perhaps) local identity, the latter is cast in English and signifies at the propositional level a different identity (namely, Croatian). I interpret this as heteroglossic: two different languages explicitly indexing two different identities, moulded together into one post yet at the same time differentiated in terms of its functional components. Here, as elsewhere, the elements participating in a heteroglossic contrast belong to different parts of a genre, and previous research suggests that the difference between a post proper and accompanying emblematic elements, such as names and mottos, is consequential to style and language choices.

Androutsopoulos argues that computer mediated discourses are 'sites of tension and contrast between linguistic resources, social identities and ideologies' (Androutsopoulos 2011: 283) but importantly, we might note for the discussion here on the regulation of writing, they are sites where these tensions and contrasts are often made visible rather than suppressed. Obvious contrasts can be made between the range of resources used here – and the corresponding range of opportunities for identity work (and play) – as compared with the constraints experienced by Sara writing an essay (discussed above) which included the suppression of language/identities in orienting to the monolingual/monocultural assumptions and expectations of the institution. Another key difference of course is that the site described by Androutsopolous is a site of 'convergence' (Jenkins 2006 and discussed in Williams 2009: 6; see also Chapter 7), that is where multiple semiotic resources are used and the boundaries between the different participant roles in production activity are blurred, for example, on YouTube you can be both a producer and a receiver/listener/consumer whereas with a student essay you are (usually) either a writer or a reader.

The notion of style or 'styling' is of relevance to both instances here and an example of where sociolinguistic thinking developed in the study of spoken interaction (for example the work of Rampton 1995) might be usefully applied to the study of written texts. For whereas, in studies of writing, 'style' tends to be treated as a dimension of the written text, what we see clearly here is that it is also a dimension to performing identity and agency: Sara consciously styled herself as 'English', in contrast to the writer of the YouTube comment who seemed to be styling himself as both Bavarian and Croatian.[9]

The CMD example above is a highly multimodal digital semiotic space (the data extract above shows only a verbal, single colour comment but of course in YouTube this comment was alongside others, in different fonts and colours, images and video). There are other digital spaces that are similar in their verbal emphasis to many of the writing practices valued in formal education, but are not regulated according to the same regimes of production and evaluation. FanFiction (http://www.FanFiction.net/) is an example of a digital space, which although multimodal, tends to be verbal heavy. It is a site where people can write and upload stories about characters from books, films and music that they are interested in – current popular examples are Harry Potter, Twilight, Naruto – and is an interesting phenomenon in any discussion of young people's writing and literacy practices. Building on existing fan fiction practices it was founded by a computer software designer in the late 1990s and it has had incredible success in attracting contributions: as of October 2011 there were 3,744,842 stories uploaded and accessible to the public on the site (http://ffnresearch.blogspot.com/2010/07/FanFictionnet-story-totals.html (accessed 10 Oct. 2011)). There is huge productivity on such sites, standing in contrast to young people's documented limited production activity in formal schooling. In fact, educational researchers are increasingly interested in exploring not only what these sites afford young people in their own terms but how they contrast with formal schooling and what might be learned from these for formal teaching and learning. Black, for example, was intrigued by the involvement of 'English language learners' (ELLs is her term for users of English as an additional language) in FanFiction sites and the different opportunities that such sites seemed to offer. Using online participant observation, she explored how ELLs engaged with the site – what they wrote, how they marked their identities and the responses they received. Below is an extract from a fanfiction discussed by Black. It is an example of a particular FanFiction category, where the fictions are based on the Japanese animation or anime series Card Captor Sakura (for details see Black 2005: 120). In this fiction, written by a fourteen-year-old Mandarin Chinese speaker, the characters and plot are reworked to some extent using the plot of a US film, *You've Got Mail*.

Figure 6.6   Extract from fanfiction (Black 2005: 125)

Note: The excerpt depicts the characters Sakura and Syaoran from Card Captor. Fanfiction abbreviations: A/N = author's note; S+S = Sakura and Syaoran, a preferred couple pairing; E+T = Eriol and Tomoyo, a preferred couple pairing.

Access and affiliation

Love Letters
A/N: Konnichiwa minna-san! This is my new story
^_^. Please excuse my grammar and spelling mis-
takes. Because English is my second language. Also,
I'm still trying to improve my writing skills . . . so this
story might be really sucks . . .—;;
Summary: Sakura and Syaoran met in a chat room.
They have been e-mailing each other for almost 1.5
years, then fall in love. But in real life, Sakura and
Syaoran are roommates that hated each other's gut!
What happens when they find out each other's secret?
S+S E+T
Chapter 1
An auburn haired girl was sitting on the soft sand,
with her lab-top opening on her lap. The fresh wind
blew against her silky hair gently, as she sighed dream-
ily. The girl yawned; her emerald green eyes were fixed
on her computer screen. She read though the e-mail
and smiled brightly. It was a letter from a very special
friend of hers; his nickname is 'Little Wolf'. She
opened a new window to type out her reply for this email.

(Tanaka Nanako, 2002)

Black draws on such data gathered as part of her participant observation in the site, and alongside a range of other data including interviews, to make points about what this particular practice affords writers who are learners of English, which include the following: writers feel able to self identify as second language learners who, whilst expressing concern about possible errors (as indicated in the extract above, the format enables her to insert notes) are not inhibited from participating; writers are able to state explicitly what they would like comment on (form and/ or content) thus taking some control over the kind of engagement they want from readers; the functionalities of the site enable readers/reviewers to post their responses to the specific comments requested by the author. Furthermore of specific relevance to the focus in this chapter on identity, Black and others argue (Black 2005, 2006, 2009; Lam 2000) that 'electronic environments' enable ELLs to take on and play with identities not easily accessed in formal contexts of learning. These include taking on the voice and authority of an English language user as well as playing with identities through characters in their fictions. Black states:

> Fan authors often construct hybridised identities that are enacted through their texts. It is not uncommon for authors to insert themselves into their fictions as characters that possess a mixture of idealized and authentic personality traits.
>
> (Black 2005: 122)

Whilst we might consider that some of these practices are to be found in the formal curriculum, for example in English or creative writing, we might also note that creative writing is often not a curriculum space on offer in second language classrooms. Furthermore, I think a key point here with regard to identity and agency relates to the writer's control over what are in fact quite complex writing sites and the sense of safety against being judged negatively. I return to the issue of control in relationship to ownership below. In terms of the affordances of sites such as FanFiction and their value to users – in this case to users of English as a second language – Black argues that they offer opportunities for doing writing in ways not available in formal schooling, not least because of the different rules governing uptake, that is what readers do:

> Readers also focused a great deal on the content rather than the conventions of her stories. In this way, FanFiction.net provided a safe space where Nanako as a learner could experiment and practice with different genres and forms of writing in English.
>
> (Black 2006: 101)

Such sites offer semiotic opportunities for some users who may not find similar opportunities elsewhere. However, it is also important to note the following. Firstly, as with any resource, such sites are not necessarily accessible to all – by far the greatest number of contributors to FanFiction are from the US (female and in their teens). Secondly, these digital sites are not solely agency or user driven; the templates and functionalities come ready made, driving in part particular kinds of communication and interaction (see Androutsopolous 2011 for layout of Myspace). Thirdly, commercial interests are highly visible: Tesco and O2 were advertising on the FanFiction.net site at time of writing (accessed 11 Oct. 2011).

The huge appeal nevertheless of such sites lies to a great extent in the opportunities they offer for engaging in popular culture and the excitement and pleasure such engagement affords (e.g. Buckingham 2007). And this interest in a particular type of content, popular culture, also shapes the form, that is, how users want to build meanings and the relationships around writing, and who they want to engage with and be engaged by. Marsh et al. (2005) report on the ways in which adults support children's engagement with popular culture via digital media and the importance of such activity in fostering enjoyment and play at the same time as building children's self-esteem. Williams (2009) describes the effort young people put into practices such as FanFiction and YouTube and the considerable pleasure people enjoy in creative endeavours, including a strong awareness of the ways in which these are ongoing processes; for example, Ashley who had been writing fanfiction 'for my own pure enjoyment' for five years, was keen to draw on readers' feedback to develop her writing; Peter who had just finished making his first video and had posted it on YouTube saw it as 'just a start. Now that I've done that, the next one will be better' (William 2009: 181).

Agency here, then, lies in opportunities for participating in practices where users feel they have some personal enjoyment, investment and control. In the last section of this chapter I want to focus briefly on the question of ownership of writing – both in terms of the material means and in terms of control over writing – as a key dimension to identity work in and for writing.

Ownership and becoming: the material resources for identity work in writing

If creating a space for choice and control over writing, including what counts as writing and how it may be read, emerges as an important attraction to writing in (some) digital spaces, it is important to note that this interest in the use of writing in less regulated writing spaces has a long history. Most obviously, it is evident in the existence of diaries and journals, which Johnson (2011) tracks as an activity in some form as old as the emergence of writing, and which continue to be produced currently, both in more recent digital versions, for example some types of blogs (see also Chapter 3), as well as in the ubiquitous hard copy notebook. The nature and function of these writings have been much studied and debated, for example over whether they are personal or public, oriented to the writer or oriented to the reader(s), as sites of individual reflection and introspection or as sites for recording externally observable facts and events (see Mallon 1984 on types of diaries; for overview of wider range of diaries and notebooks, see Mbodj-Pouye 2010). On the debate around the private/public dimension of such writings in digital form, Miller and Shepherd (2004) state, 'like the diary, the blog is a phenomenon that illustrates the debate without resolving it': specific texts vary enormously, and may be analysed or understood along any combination of the aforementioned dimensions. What seems to be important across all of these modes and technologies of writing, however, is the extent to which they afford writers some sense of control over a semiotic space for meaning making. And part of this control relates to ownership of, or access to, the necessary material means. This does not mean, for example, that the notebook is necessarily an individual product, written in, by and for an individual person; in fact research on notebooks indicates that many people may be involved in their production, using a range of scripts and languages and they are often illustrative of the kind of heteroglossic activity identified above in CMD contexts (see examples in Mbodj-Pouye and van den Avenne 2007). Some form of material ownership/access to material resources is important for opening up opportunities for some kinds of identity and self work in writing. In his study of notebooks in rural Mali, Mbodj-Pouye states: 'Keeping a personal notebook appears to be a way of setting aside some personal information and thoughts, which is a way of objectifying the existence of a domain of one's own' (Mbodj-Pouye 2010: 141).

This ownership or strong connection to a notebook links with the importance of literacy artefacts more generally and how they are imbued with a sense of belonging, connected to habitus (see for example Juffermans 2010 for analysis of notebooks as 'valuable objects' in the Gambia). Getting to own such an object seems to function like a critical moment or 'improvisation', a notion discussed earlier in this chapter.

Paper notebooks have long since been a way of doing all sorts of writing, from recording observations and information about the world (as in Darwin's diaries) to creating personal spaces and inscribing voices and identities that may not have had space elsewhere. And the hard copy notebook seems to continue to be ubiquitous, being used alongside digital media (typically in resource rich Western contexts), or as sole (or major) medium for writing (often in resource poor global south contexts) for a wide range of functions, including aspects of what we might think of as diary keeping, such as chronological accounts and reflections, as well as all manner of work and domestic recording, such as keeping details of bills, names and addresses (see dedication at the beginning of this book where extracts from a millwright's diary include measurements, the names of horses backed in races and names of people).

CONCLUSION

This chapter has focused on the relationship between writing and identity and the range of conceptual tools used to articulate this relationship. The importance of writing as identity work has been discussed in terms of the social structuring of opportunities for writing, including the right to write and access to material resources, the significance of habitus and the way in which existing resources are inscribed with identity positions. Writing may be used as a specific activity to carve out a space for identity work in terms of voice or existence of a self but is more often nested within other activities and bound up with identity work relating to such activities. Dimensions to identity that have become marked as socially significant (for material and or ideological reasons), for example gender, are layered onto other dimensions of identity according to specific domains of social activity (for example work – writing as part of the identity work of a lawyer, a teacher etc.).

The chapter has foregrounded the ways in which existing resources for writing carry with them long histories of use and are therefore often inscribed with particular identities; as such they provide ways of doing identity in particular ways associated with those histories of use. Discontinuity or jarring between writing identities is most often visible in contexts where people are required to write towards a centring institution imaginary, in terms of practices, norms and values, but which is at odds in some ways with their sense of who they are or want to be. Regulation of meaning making in writing, and thus of identities, is strongly evident in practices oriented towards centring institutions although people also clearly make decisions about how to engage with such regulation.

The question of agency has been discussed in relation to dimensions of ownership and control. Whilst regulation exists in all communicative contexts – communication and language use necessarily involve acceptance of some conventions – there are spaces where regulation is weaker and where writers play or challenge dominant practices; these may include using a range of modes alongside the verbal, mixing languages in what are conventionally considered to be singular/monolingual spaces, crossing content boundaries by mixing for example a strong interest in popular culture with politics, science and personal reflection. Much emphasis in current language research is on the way in which particular technologies are opening up opportunities for innovative communicative practices: for example, Moje and Luke (2009) note that in current work on the use of new technologies in literacy studies, there is a tendency 'to celebrate the agent as inventor of literate practice' (Moje and Luke 2009: 416). Whilst it seems to be the case that online and digital technologies do indeed afford a range of practices which challenge many boundaries and binaries, what's particularly significant is that attention to such practices opens up debate about what people do or can potentially do with a much wider range semiotic resources (including but not exclusively digital resources) than has been conventionally imagined or recognised. This may lead to a rethinking of writing – what it is, what it does and what it could do – in terms of production and uptake in both more strongly and more weakly regulated semiotic spaces.

NOTES

1. This last includes geolinguistic categories of languages and dialects, as well as indicators relating to assumed level of competence in a language or sequence of learning, for example, first or second language user.
2. For example of the discussion of the explicit suppression of language rights, see Skutnabb Kangas 2000. For an interesting selection of posters from around the world advertising the importance of supporting literacy development, see UNESCO http://www.unesco.org/education/uie/publications/European%20Literacy%20Posters.html (accessed 4 Sept. 2011).
3. See for example, http://womennewsnetwork.net/2007/08/28/%E2%80%9Ceducate-a-woman-you-educate-a-nation%E2%80%9D-%E2%80%93-south-africa-aims-to-improve-its-education-for-girls/ (accessed 6 Oct. 2011).
4. For an interesting overview of a range of positions on the relationship between gender and specific sites of literacy, see special issue 'Women and Literacy: Moving to Power and Participation', *Women's Studies Quarterly*, 2004: 1–2.
5. Forthcoming work by Thesen and Cooper (eds) offers a nuanced and detailed account of the meanings of risk in particular for writers 'on the periphery'.
6. It's important to distinguish between essayist literacy and the essay(ist) tradition. See Spellmeyer 1989 for interesting discussion of the importance of the essay as a 'transgressive' form.
7. Strong critiques have also been made of the dominance of this rhetorical practice in the context of the global dominance of English, see for recent example Bennett 2011.

8. English's encouragement/pedagogical invitation to 're-genre' is similar to Pope's position on 'rewriting' (Pope 2003), perhaps the main difference being the particular academic disciplines they are seeking to engage – Pope with English and literary studies and English with applied linguistics and writing pedagogy. English focuses on *genre* in particular and argues for the need to rethink genre as a resource for meaning making rather than as a rigid category to be achieved or reproduced.

9. Whilst in this instance Androutsopoulos's analysis is based on the text/screen, he emphasises the importance of avoiding making text/screen based assumptions about what people are doing and why and the need for ethnographic data (Androutsopoulos 2011).

Chapter 7

Theorising writing-reading-texts: domains and frames

INTRODUCTION

This chapter draws together discussions from previous chapters to foreground some of the key ways in which writers and writing are conceptualised. It summarises some of the approaches most evident in this book, notably writing as a social (discursive) practice and as social semiotic, sets these alongside two contrasting approaches to writing which continue to be highly influential (if often implicit) in any discussion of writing – the *poetic-aesthetic* and *transactional-rationalist* – and also discusses an approach highly relevant in the contemporary context, that of 'participatory culture' (Jenkins 2006). A key goal of this chapter is to outline the range of approaches available for exploring writing as a phenomenon whilst at the same time to caution against conflating the domain of activity we are observing, i.e. the particular type of writing, with the domain – or frame – through which such observation is being made.

This chapter:

- considers different approaches to theorising writers and writing and the academic domains from which these have arisen
- considers the ways in which language is conceptualised within these different approaches, and how relations between writer-text-reader are configured
- considers some of the problems arising from the (common) conflation between the domains of writing activity being observed and the academic frames through which observation is made
- illustrates the importance of bringing to bear a range of approaches to exploring what's involved in writing, by focusing on two of my own research interests, student writing and everyday 'work' based writing.

CONCEPTUALISING WHAT WRITERS DO: DIFFERENT APPROACHES TO WRITERS-READERS-TEXTS

In the academic study of writing, there are several highly influential approaches which are discipline specific; for example, writing is a key area of interest in literary studies, New Literacy Studies, composition and rhetoric and each disciplinary field has developed particular conceptual and analytical tools for exploring writing. In this book, I have foregrounded aspects from those academic domains which connect most obviously with the key principles of sociolinguistics, outlined in Chapter 1: these are the importance of the 'social', the centrality of the empirical study of naturally occurring language and the basic premise that everyday language is worthy of study.

Of course mapping the range of ways in which writing and relations around writing – most obviously between writers-readers-texts, or as discussed across this book, between production and uptake – have been understood across different academic domains is a complex task. Furthermore, any such mapping necessarily oversimplifies the work and ideas of specific researchers and theorists, and how ideas have shifted historically and across different cultural and geographical contexts; and certainly underplays the leakages across approaches. However, for those of us seeking to research and explore everyday writing in contemporary society it is important to tease out what kinds of approaches are available to us and the underlying assumptions about 'writing', language and literacy that are nested within specific approaches. Once we have a sharper sense of what's involved in the different approaches that are currently used to make sense of and theorise writing, we can consider how and why we might draw on these for researching and understanding specific instances of writing and for considering what other approaches we might need to develop or draw on from other disciplinary areas.

In the following sections I offer brief overviews of what seem to me to be eight key approaches to writing, aspects of most of which have been illustrated in preceding chapters: these are also summarised in Table 7.1. I begin with two contrasting approaches to writing that continue to be highly influential in studies and ideologies of writing in general – which I refer to as the 'poetic-aesthetic' and the 'transactional-rationalist' – and traces of which are often found in other approaches, as well as in common sense discourses around writing. I then move on to a summary of the social approaches most evident in this book – social semiotic, socio-discursive and social practice – and also include reference to socio-cognitive approaches, which were briefly discussed in Chapter 3 in relation to the notion of 'genre'. I conclude this section by briefly outlining a 'participatory culture' approach (Jenkins 2006) which is of importance in the current context of increasing productive activity, before considering some of the challenges we face in using any approach and, in particular, the danger of conflating the domains of writing activity being observed with the academic frames through which observation is made.

Poetic-aesthetic

Writer and *author* along with the many positive connotations attached to these terms are most commonly associated with culturally prestigious writing, notably literary writing, and are most obviously evident in what I am calling here a 'poetic-aesthetic' approach to writing. This approach to writing is most commonly found in the academic domains of literary studies and stylistics (see Chapter 3).[1]

This approach is strongly influenced by Romantic notions of authoring which emphasise the individual writer and the creativity or artistry in which she engages; notions such as inspiration, genius (discussed in Pope 2004), 'duende' (a notion used by Lorca 1933), the 'divine' (Shelley 1821) are called on to explain (in part) the creative process. Whilst there is considerable debate about authoring and the author's varying positions in relation to the text and its meanings, with a range of notions developed to explore these, such as real v. implied author, narrator, authorial voice, persona(e), the 'author-writer' is always construed as significant. In researching and analysing writing within this approach, therefore, considerable attention is paid to who the author is, for example, was the text written by Shakespeare (see Bate 1998). At the same time, considerable debate exists around where and with whom the meanings of any texts resides: the *writer* as creator/originator; the *text* whereby meanings are crafted and encoded; the *reader* who interprets both and in so doing, can be described as creating the text. The key point for our discussion here is that once an instance of writing is assumed to belong to a socially prestigious category (for example, literary), there is considerable interest in explicating and analysing all three aspects.

Language within this framework is construed as what we can usefully think of as an 'open resource', that is, as a complex resource but one which is potentially available to all to use (usually thought of as one language, such as English, Spanish and so on). The key interest is in exactly how it is used, and discussions around whether it is used to best artistic effect are often assumed to depend on the individual's capacity or genius (for example of recent debate see Cook 2011). As the heading to this section suggests, particular attention is paid to what is often referred to as the aesthetic or 'poetic function' of language, after Jakobson (1960) who identified six functions of language, the poetic function involving a 'focus on the message for its own sake' (Jakobson 1960: 356), by foregrounding language in different ways, as discussed in Chapter 3. Whilst Jakobson was careful about not conflating the poetic function with particular kinds of language or writing, the poetic-aesthetic dimension has most often been related to literary writings and used in evaluating the worth of such writings. However, there is an increasing interest in the poetic-aesthetic dimension to everyday spoken language, often under the category of 'creativity' (e.g. Swann et al. 2011) and I have drawn attention across the book to some ways in which this dimension is being explored with regard to everyday writing; for example the aesthetic dimension to people's responses to different traditions of Chinese characters in public signs (Chapter 2), the creativity and play evident in a souvenir label (Chapter 3), the use of metaphor in personal letters (Chapter 6), the 'styling' evident in computer mediated discourse such as a YouTube commentary (Chapter 6).

Transactional-rationalist

A transactional-rationalist transmission approach to writing is, I would argue, the default, or common sense approach to all writing that is not attributed a specific 'literary' or 'creative' function. Indeed, this is the dominant approach to communication more generally, much influenced by conduit (Reddy 1979) models of communication and language, as in work by de Saussure (1916) and Shannon and Weaver (1949; see also Figure 7.4). Communication within this approach is represented as a speaker/writer encoding a message that is transmitted to and picked up by a listener/receiver; language is viewed as a conduit, to convey thoughts, ideas from one person to another (sender-receiver). In the case of writing, the writer encodes meaning into a text and the reader decodes the meaning from the text.

The function of writing (and communication more generally) within this framework is conceptualised as primarily transactional, that is as getting something (else) done, with the primary goal of the writer assumed to be that of conveying information and ideas to a reader. The language used in such a text is assumed to be transparent and in the service of rationality: that is, the words used reflect ideas, information and clear thinking, with the assumption being that if the writer has done her job properly, the reader should be able to abstract or decode the textual meanings intended by the writer. Within this frame, there is an assumption that language does not (and should not be allowed to) get in the way of clear meaning, expression and argument. In contrast to the poetic-aesthetic approach, which construes a complex relationship between writer-text-reader, the reader here is viewed as a passive consumer of the words with meanings laid bare by the writer.

Within this approach, which has a powerful history in Western academia (see discussion in Turner 2011), the identities and histories of specific individual writers and readers – unlike in literary texts – are not given particular importance. The writer is understood to be the producer of the words and information but is not construed as being particularly artful with language, or indeed as having any interest in such aspects. Most obviously such texts are not expected to demonstrate artfulness or beauty but rather to be (usually verbally) 'clear'. That some writing has a transactional goal, as understood from the perspectives of users, is evident: for example, conveying information would seem to be the goal in some Wikipedia (Chapter 4) entries, and is clearly a goal in the increasing use of texting to remind people about hospital appointments (see for example Downer et al. 2006). However, as much discussion and analysis in this book shows, there are many more dimensions to writing than the purely transactional; a key point to note here is that the pervasive ideology of language and writing as only or primarily transactional rationalist is problematic because it obscures the many other dimensions involved.

Process-expressionist

A process approach to writers and writing reflects aspects of both the poetic-aesthetic and the transactional-rationalist: with regard to the former it tends to focus on individual production and expression, whilst with regard to the latter it often foregrounds the transactional aspect – encapsulated in the emphasis on goals and audience. A key difference, however, is that a process approach emphasises in many ways the textual *work* involved in writing, by pointing to the many stages of producing a text – planning, drafting, redrafting, rewriting, editing – and because such stages can be made visible and explored, emphasis on process is widely considered to be useful in the teaching of writing. An emphasis on process challenges the idea that a writer (doing whatever kind of writing) simply produces a written text in one go (through 'inspiration' for example) and rather suggests that most written texts involve considerable time, redrafting and reworking. The reader in this approach is often backgrounded, as the emphasis is on the work the writer does to produce the text. Language is likewise backgrounded and, where mentioned, tends to be treated as a transparent and open resource. The assumption is that it is the iterative processes involved in writing that will eventually enable the writer to say/write what she wants to say or 'express', hence expressionist/m is often used alongside 'process' to signal this approach. Process approaches have been emphasised in some educational contexts as a way of teaching writing (for example, US Composition Studies) and are also embedded in some socio-cognitive approaches which pay significant attention to writers' understandings about what's involved in learning how to write.[2] In this book, my attention to process has been nested in the focus on situated text production practices (emphasising en/recontextualisation processes), examples of which include academic text production and medical certification, as discussed in detail in Chapter 5.

Socio-cognitive

Socio-cognitive approaches tend to emphasise writing as a mental or cognitive activity that takes place in social context. Within these approaches two principal traditions can be noted: one that prioritises the individual writer's internal representations of the writing process and purposes; and a second that emphasises the importance of writing as a socially situated activity mediated by available tools (such as language, technologies). I will focus here on the latter tradition as being most directly relevant to the discussion in this book, particularly in the way it engages with the notion of genre.[3]

Drawing on activity theory (for example, Leont'ev 1981) writing is construed as an activity, involving subjects (people) who have particular goals and mediated by the use of specific tools, such as language(s), technologies, materials. The emphasis on tools foreshadows in many ways the more recent interest in modes and materialities in applied and sociolinguistics, discussed in Chapter 2, as well as the considerable interest in *actor network theory* (ANT) in studies of digital communication. ANT, like activity theory, emphasises the networks of activity in which tools mediate human action but explicitly treats non-human and human 'actors' as equally important in any analysis (Latour 1987; for useful study and discussion see Prior 1998). Within an *activity theory* approach to writing, the writer is construed as someone engaged in activity, of which writing may be a part or the sole goal, and whose writing is powerfully mediated (shaped, influenced) by available tools. In this approach considerable emphasis is placed on: the networks in which the writer moves/writes and indeed writing as a networked activity; and the tools that mediate such activity. It is the 'activity system' that is of central interest to the researcher and how writing fits into this system, and indeed helps generate the system. Less attention is accorded, therefore, to a dyadic relationship around writing – that is as between a writer and a reader – as is often emphasised in many approaches to writing (see Box 7.1).

This approach shares with a transactional approach an interest in how writing is used to get things done, but its analytic framework is significantly different in that, rather than focusing on the texts alone, or on how ideas are communicated via a text by A to B, it focuses on the texts as part of an activity system, involving a range of people with shared/different purposes (objects or goals) using a range of tools. Emphasis is on understanding what written texts *do* in particular activity systems and how texts build on, connect with, differ from other texts within the same system or related systems. As discussed in Chapter 4, 'genre' is used to refer to typified activity (rather than typified texts) serving as a key mediational tool for instantiating organisational practices and interests. This is illustrated in Figure 7.4 where three interrelated activity systems are identified (in three triangles) relating to writing in cell biology, and the relationship between them marked through the larger circles. Thus AS 1 and 2 share the same goal – an understanding of cells – although the texts that they produce differ, relating to the specific nature of each AS, whether a university course or scientific researchers. Connections between AS 2 and 3 are evident – students and teachers in AS 2 are bound up with the practices of AS 3 the university, yet they also have their separate specific goals and target texts.

Social semiotic

A social semiotic approach to writing is one of the approaches outlined in this book, illustrated most obviously in Chapter 2 where a key focus is on exploring the material and multimodal nature of the resources that are available for writing – of which verbal language is just (albeit an important) one – and examples of which are illustrated across the chapters. In semiotic and some multimodal approaches, much attention is given currently to articulating the specific nature of these resources and to developing a 'language of description' or terminology for describing these resources, rather than exploring the specific uses and users of such resources. However some researchers also pay attention to the latter, as briefly illustrated in Chapters 2 and 6. Kress has outlined a model of the semiotic process, involving two key stages and emphasising the notion of 'interest':

> Stage 1 – is dominated by the *interest* of the initial maker of the *sign-complex*, the *rhetor*, with his or her intent of disseminating the *sign-complex* as a *message* and for the *message* to be taken as a *prompt*;
>
> Stage 2 – the *interest* and *attention* of an *interpreter* is in focus: it leads to *selection* of what is criterial for the *interpreter* in the initial message and to the *framing* of the selected aspects of the initial *message* as a *prompt*, which is subsequently *interpreted*.
>
> (Kress 2010: 36–7)

The active role of the reader signalled in Stage 2 here connects with the interpretive power accorded to the reader in some literary approaches to writer-reader-text relations (not surprisingly given the influence across both literary studies and semiotics of the work of Barthes 1977). The role of the reader in selecting and therefore creating her text rather than decoding or receiving meanings of the text as laid out by the writer (as in a transactional-rationalist approach) is emphasised: this approach is picked up currently in relation to some digitally mediated practices, as when for example a reader moves around web pages and thus becomes a designer of his own reading. This choice in design trajectory is akin to all kinds of semiotic practices, for example, in the ways in which visitors can choose their routes through art galleries and museums, engaging with some material and ignoring others (see Kress 2010: 39). However, whether with older or newer technologies, it's important not to exaggerate or generalise about the levels of choice or design trajectories: most obviously the pre-existing design of spaces – both virtual and physical – constrain writing, reading and uptake practices and trajectories.

Kress makes a distinction between *rhetor* and *designer* in production processes: 'the *rhetor* has a political purpose: to bring about alignment between her or his message [. . .] and the position of the audience [. . .] the *designer* has a semiotic purpose: to *shape* the message, using the available representational resources [. . .]' (Kress 2010: 49).[4] Of course the rhetor and designer may be the same person in any instance of writing; they may also be different people, or groups of people. Examples abound in the production of public media, such as news stories, advertisements, public signs. Likewise, there may be many interpreters, readers/audiences of texts who pick up on different aspects of the text (see Cook 2001: Chapter 9 for discussion of multiple senders and receivers, as well as hearers/observers, in relation to advertisements). A social semiotic approach which foregrounds practice, therefore – along with approaches which focus on activity and practice – often tends to shift attention away from individuals or dyads in production and interpretation processes (here writers/readers), signalling that production has often involved/may often involve many people and the text may be directed towards and picked up by many readers/ings (see Box 7.1).

Socio-discursive

A socio-discursive approach to writing tends to background the specific writer(s)/producers and to foreground text-as-discourse. This approach is strongly reflected in critical discourse analytic (CDA) approaches which emphasise the contextual dimension, with a distinction often being made between the context of situation and context of culture (Malinowski 1923, 1935; broadly speaking, these are used to distinguish between the more immediate, observable context (for example, what is going on in a particular classroom) and the less easily observable, but highly significant beliefs and ideologies helping to shape that particular observable context (for example beliefs and ideologies of schooling). Here, discourse is understood as 'ways of representing, understanding and being in the world' (Swann et al. 2004: 83), but the analytical

---

Box 7.1 Writing, design and production – beyond dyadic framings

The production of early books

The creation of a book involved many people. Several copyists might work on the same book, each responsible for different pages. An assistant might read the original aloud, working from the other side of the desk. When the scribe had finished, the manuscript would be passed to the 'rubricator', who added any headings and initials in red colour. Finally, an artist – the illumina-tor – would create the elaborate miniature paintings which adorn the finer manuscripts.

(Graddol 2007: 168)

The production of current news

The news is seldom a solo performance. News media offer the classic case of language produced by multiple parties. Journalists, editors, printers, news-readers, sound technicians and camera operators are just some of the people who can directly influence the form of news discourse.

(Bell 2007: 94. See also example in Chapter 5)

The production of academic articles

A wide range of brokers are involved in English-medium text production, including friends, editors, reviewers, academic peers, and translators. All of these brokers mediate text production in a number of ways, with potentially significant consequences for how texts will be received and evaluated as they travel from one part of the academic globe to another.

(Lillis and Curry 2010: 87. See also Chapter 5)

The production and circulation of media content

Participatory culture is intended to contrast with older notions of media spec-tatorship. In this emerging media system, what might traditionally be under-stood as media producers and consumers are transformed into participants who are expected to interact with each other according to a new set of rules which none of us fully understands.

(http://www.henryjenkins.org/2006/06/welcome_to_
convergence_culture.html (accessed 10 Jan. 2012))

---

emphasis tends to be on approaching discourse through texts, whether spoken or written. The writer and the reader within this framework are construed as being 'positioned' by discourse(s) in some way, with discourse(s) making available particular 'subject positions' to be taken up. Thus particular types of discourse set up particu-lar subject positions in specific texts: one obvious example is bureaucratic discourse which frames both the nature of texts (for example forms or templates) and relations around those texts (tick boxing, closed responses); another example is educational discourse which involves a range of discursive practices with regard to writing (written exams, dissertations and so on) which set up particular ways for both the writer and reader to engage (see Chapter 6). Furthermore, as one diagrammatic representation of this approach illustrates (see Figure 7.4e), analysis and interpretation is not so much concerned with explicating specific writer-text-reader relations as with how these reflect and instantiate larger processes of social production and interpretation.

Language within this framework is not construed as an open resource, that is a resource on which anybody can draw (as in a Romantic notion of authoring), but as particular socially and historically situated discourses, which make available both specific ways of meaning and specific ways of being. Furthermore, some of these ways of meaning are more easily available to some social groups than others and thus discourse is always bound up with issues of power and access. The individual – writer and reader – figures in the extent to which she takes up or resists these available meanings. A socio-discursive approach to writing is most clearly illustrated in this book in Chapter 4 with examples of critical discourse analysis (CDA). But a discourse approach can be traced in all social approaches to writing in the recognition that semiotic resources for meaning making and production are social products and effects, with social consequences. A clear example of this is the tracking of the asylum seeking documents in Chapter 5, where analytically a discourse orientation to language is combined with ethnographic attention to specific instances and workings of text production and uptake.

Social practice

A social practice approach to writing has been foregrounded in this book, often used as an overarching framework for social semiotic and socio-discursive approaches. This is most clearly set out in Chapter 4 but is illustrated across the book.

Within this framework, both the writer and the writing are construed as historically and socially situated. The writer is construed as engaging in a social practice by both drawing on socially available ways of writing and enacting particular ways of writing. Practice, as discussed in Chapter 4, offers a way of linking language with what individuals, as socially situated actors, do, at the levels of context of situation and culture – discussed above – in three specific ways. Firstly, an emphasis on practice signals that specific instances of language use – spoken and written texts – do not exist in isolation but are bound up with what people do – practices – in the material, social world. Secondly, ways of doing things with texts become part of everyday, implicit life routines both of the individual, habitus in Bourdieu's (1991) terms, and of social institutions. Specific instances of language use involve drawing on available and, in institutional contexts, legitimised representational resources (Kress 1996: 18). Here, language might best be understood as practice-resource (see Lillis 2001: see also Chapter 6) which keys into a third level of practice, that of social structure and stratification; for by engaging in an existing practice we are maintaining a particular type of representational resource; by drawing on a particular type of representational resource, we are maintaining a particular type of socially structured and stratified (semiotic) practice.

What tends to distinguish this approach from others, precisely because of an interest in shifting attention away from texts towards practices, is an ethnographic methodology in order to pay attention to describing and understanding what writers do, why and in which contexts. As discussed particularly in Chapter 4, this approach has given rise to a language of description which extends the focus outwards beyond texts towards networks, roles, communities and trajectories, and works with the tension between emic/etic accounts and perspectives to generate insights into what writing means and does (see Chapter 4). The importance of the social identity of both writers and readers has been foregrounded in much recent research, which connects in some ways with the careful attention given in literary studies to the author: most obviously, a key working assumption is that what gets written is bound up with who is doing the writing – and who the writer is, wants to be (and doesn't want to be) – and who she seeks to address in her texts (see Chapter 6). However, other key aspects of the poetic-aesthetic approach tend to be backgrounded in all social approaches to writing – aspects such as pleasure, beauty and desire; this reflects perhaps more a rejection of the particular ways in which these dimensions have tended to be valued in socially prestigious texts, rather than a rejection of the existence of these dimensions to writing per se (see Janks 2010 for importance of desire in critical approaches to language and literacy). And attention to pleasure and play is evident in social practice approaches to particular domains of writing activity, for example children's writing (the writing of and for children) and most obviously on the agenda currently in studies of young people's digital and online writing practices (for instance, Marsh et al. 2005), as well as digitally mediated production activity in general, illustrated particularly in Chapter 6. Attention to pleasure in production has long since been a focus in media studies and is evident in the final approach I discuss in this section on 'participatory culture'.

Participatory culture

A final approach I want to signal briefly here is that of writing as 'participatory culture' (Jenkins 2006) to signal work which is exploring the significance of popular culture in shaping people's semiotic production and participation practices. This is not an approach that would commonly be included in sociolinguistic or applied language studies because of its key interest in content as much as form and function (see discussion in Chapter 3). In this work (for example, Jenkins 2006; Williams 2009) the starting point is neither language nor semiotics (nor writing) but rather popular culture and its considerable power to motivate people to engage in a whole range of practices which include: reading, writing, making and watching videos and podcasts, making and mixing modes and media and content. Jenkins (2006) uses the notion 'convergence culture' to refer to

> the flow of content across multiple media platforms, the cooperation between
> multiple media industries, and the migratory behaviour of media audiences who

Table 7.1   Overview of key academic domains and frames for theorising writing

	Poetic-aesthetic	Transactional-rationalist	Process-expressionist	Socio-cognitive
Emphasis on writer as . . .	Individual composer, genius, crafter of artistic form	Encoder of information and meanings	Individual working at producing text through various stages	One or more people engaged in producing text towards a social goal/action
Emphasis on nature of language/text as . . .	Open (verbal) resource to be forged in artistic creation Attention to language/form for its own sake	Open (verbal) resource, transparent reflection of ideas	Open (verbal) resource, transparent reflection of ideas Emphasis on work of writer	Tool which, along with other tools, such as pens, pcs, texts, mediates and affords activity in specific ways
Key values and attention given to . . .	Originality, beauty, artfulness, pleasure, inspiration	Clarity, rationality, truth	Activity, goals, tasks	Tools, cognition, learning
Communication as. . .	Author as originator, of meanings and personae in texts and owner of these Reader's position contested; either to tease out author intended meanings and/or to construct meanings	Writer as encoder of meanings and reader as decoder of same meanings	Emphasis on writer Reader backgrounded, framed as 'target' of text	Writer and reader as part of same activity mediated by tools
Academic domain from which approach generated *Domain of observation*	Literary Studies Creative writing Media Studies Stylistics	Linguistics Communication Studies	Writing pedagogy Composition	Social psychology Education Sociology of knowledge Activity theory Actor network theory
Academic domain where frame most commonly applied *Domain being observed*	Literary studies, creative writing	Most writing outside of designated creative/literary writing	The teaching of writing/studies of the teaching of writing	Studies of writing as part of everyday routines, for example work contexts, often involves notions of novice/experts

would go almost anywhere in search of the kinds of entertainment experiences they wanted – convergence culture is getting defined top-down by decisions being made in corporate boardrooms and bottom-up by decisions made in teenagers' bedrooms.

> (http://www.henryjenkins.org/2006/06/welcome_to_
> convergence_culture.html (accessed 10 Jan. 2012))

Here values such as participating, networking, having fun and enjoyment are to the fore. We have seen some examples across the book, most obviously in Chapter 6, where enjoyment of popular culture was clearly a driving force in people's engagement with sites such as FanFiction.net and YouTube. Williams (2009: 185) talks of the 'force of emotion' in popular culture and how this drives forms of participation: this force of emotion clearly connects with the huge amount of productive activity

Social semiotic	Socio-discursive	Social practice	Participatory culture
Producers (one or more people) as: *rhetor* – interest – and *designer* – assembler of resources, verbal visual etc.	Socially situated user or users of available discourses	Socially situated producer of meanings and practices	Participant in popular cultural practices – producer of forms and content
One (important) semiotic resource to be used for meaning making	Socially available discourse(s), some discourses more dominant than others	Practice/resource, that is bound up with writer's history and social context in which writing takes place	One element in cluster of materials (semiotic, cultural, technological) made available by popular culture/al practices for participation and remaking
Semiotic resource(fullness), semiotic potential, design	Social context, power, discourse, access and inequality	Use(fulness) and meaning(fullness) in everyday practice	Pleasure, fun, participation
Writer as rhetor and designer Reader as interpreter of text designed by writer or/and as designer of meanings range of which made available by writer	Writer and reader as subjects of texts – that is as both producing and being produced by text as discourse	Writer as socially situated producer Reader (real/ imagined) as embedded in both production and consumption	Writer/reader distinction collapsed viewed as producers, participants, interactants involved in production and reproduction
Semiotics Linguistics Multimodality	Applied Linguistics Sociolinguistics Critical Discourse Studies	Anthropology Linguistic ethnography Sociolinguistics New Literacy Studies Academic Literacies New Rhetoric	Cultural studies (New) Media Studies
Studies of multimodality/ communication using new technologies	Studies of media, public texts	Studies of everyday writing and reading practices in range of contexts	Studies of popular culture, popular culture (re)production in digital contexts

in which many people are currently engaged which has been mentioned at different points in the book.

RECOGNITION AND EVALUATION OF WRITING: DOMAINS AND FRAMES

Whilst the approaches summarised above are identifiable in research and discussions about writing (in academic, media, informal discussions), they are of course not as discrete or self-contained as the description or Table 7.1 implies. There are some clear overlaps; most obviously from the summary, all the 'socio' marked approaches share a perspective on the writing as social phenomena and, less obviously (from the summary), this attention to the social is nested within some poetic-aesthetic approaches (for examples of literary criticism adopting a social practice account, see Eagleton 1983; Pope 2005). Discussions of writing in this book have drawn on some aspects of all of these approaches, illustrating both how they are being brought to bear in studies of writing currently, and to indicate how some could be used in future studies.

However, it is also the case that there are some notable lacks in overlap in approaches and the key point I want to make here is that by pre-selecting a specific approach, or perhaps as more commonly happens, some aspects of an approach, from which to research a specific instance of writing, a researcher may conflate the domain (or frame) of observation with the domain being observed (see Figure 7.1). Thus, for example, in broad terms the poetic-aesthetic frame, from the academic domain of literary studies, tends to be applied to writing designated as literary or creative and such writing is therefore looked at through a poetic-aesthetic lens; the transactional-rationalist frame tends to be applied to writing which is designated as having a primarily transactional purpose, for example routine report writing in many work contexts, an area I return to below. This use of domain specific frames makes perfect sense at one level: in order for writing to be designated as 'literary' 'scientific', 'creative', 'useful' 'clear' it must fulfil the recognition and evaluation criteria that are used to designate it as such.

Figure 7.1   Domains and frames

Domain (general) = A sphere of activity

Domain 1 = Domain being observed. A sphere of writing activity to be observed/analysed. Example, student writing at university.

Domain 2 = Frame of observation. A sphere of activity or approach through/ from which writing is observed/analysed. Example, transactional-rationalist (see Table 7.1).

However, this kind of mirroring activity may lead to acts of misrecognition which is problematic if our goal is to develop a sociolinguistic stance towards writing, that is, a stance that seeks to explore, describe and understand writing in social context. Misrecognition can involve aspects both from what we might think of as academic-disciplinary practices – as in the different approaches listed in Table 7.1 – and institutional or domain specific practices – that is, in terms of the specific domain or institutional functions a particular instance of writing is presumed to have. So, for example, if we only ever look at student writing through an institutional frame – as an essay written by a student in a first year undergraduate psychology course – we may fail to see or recognise what's involved in this specific piece of writing, includ-ing what the writer is doing and why (as illustrated in Chapter 6).

A related problem here is that we may also be conflating two dimensions of evaluation; that is *recognising* and *judging*. This links very strongly with the foun-dational (albeit problematic) principle in sociolinguistics (see Chapter 1): the need for description rather than prescription in the study of language use. This is a tricky area to navigate because recognition necessarily involves evaluation; but what we need to do is to attempt to make visible the kinds of evaluation practices in which we engage. Very different kinds of evaluation criteria tend to be used and invoked as soon as texts (and genres) are designated as belonging to different domains of activity. For example, specific evaluative criteria are used to confirm whether texts are literary or are scientific – by focusing on the generic or rhetorical labels used to categorise the texts. These evaluative criteria, of course, are part of historically established institutional regimes, whereby evaluative criteria are continuously enacted and maintained – for example, in the case of academic publishing, through reviewing and editing practices. Where these criteria are not met, texts tend to be negatively evaluated, or indeed not 'recognised' as being a particular type of text (an example of the latter was illustrated in the asylum case in Chapter 5).

It's easy to see how recognition is bound up with evaluation by considering the evaluation criteria for two types of writing that are widely considered to be distinct – scientific and literary – and juxtaposing these against a more recent and generally weakly regulated writing practice – academic blogging. See Figure 7.2 as an example of an academic blog page, and the criteria listed and queried, in Figure 7.3.

The main point I want to make here is that there is a problem with conflating domain of activity and domain of observation. Such a conflation may be considered appropriate in institutional terms, that is to say, if the goal is to evaluate (judge) the extent to which a particular text has fulfilled specific pre-scripted criteria – as in assessing a student essay, reviewing an academic paper. But it is not appropriate as a research stance, because by using only one (predetermined) lens, we may fail to recognise what we are looking at, including what may be at stake for writers, readers, designers and interpreters. At a fundamental level, therefore, as sociolinguists interested in writing, if we restrict our recognition-evaluative lens to a specific

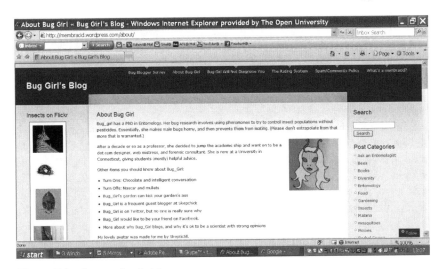

Figure 7.2   An academic blog page

Figure 7.3   Recognition and evaluative criteria when looking at writing in
different domains

Recognition/ evaluation criteria	Domains of activity being observed		
	Scientific writing	**Literary writing**	**Academic blogging**
Type of semiotic resource expected	*Verbal language Diagrammatic*	*Verbal language**	*Verbal language Image Colour Audio Video ???*
Type of material expected	*Paper (articles, books) Mostly black on white Electronic versions of paper copy*	*Paper Mostly black on white Electronic versions of paper copy*	*Digital Image Colour Audio Video*
Rhetorical expectations	*Rationality, transparency*	*Emotive, creative, evocative*	*???*
Semiotic values	*Clarity, transparency*	*Beauty, artfulness, pleasure*	*???*

* Of course there is a long tradition of multimodality in some literary writings,
most obviously children's writing, and this continues in digital contexts. For
useful overview, see Goodman 2006a, b.

domain-designated writing frame, we may limit our perceptions and understandings of what writing is and does in any specific social context.

Challenging the frames we use to explore everyday communication more generally has been brought to the fore in recent work on multimodality and digital
technologies, as discussed and illustrated across this book. The need for blurring
the boundaries becomes particularly obvious when examining writing using a range
of recent technologies, where not only does the binary between spoken/written
language collapse, so too do domain specific frames for exploring and categorising
what's going on in writing. Figure 7.3 illustrates not only that we have no clearly
established 'recognising/evaluating' criteria with which to approach more recent
practices such as academic blogging (see Kirkup 2010 for blogging as an emerging

academic practice), but that in general the ways in which we recognise and evaluate writing are closely intertwined.

In exploring writing, therefore, we need to draw on available approaches and lenses but at the same time to be aware of only seeing, that is recognising, what a specific approach enables us to see. We need to increase our lenses when exploring all kinds of everyday writing. To illustrate this, I will explore what happens when we bring to bear a particular domain of observation not usually used in relation to a specific domain of writing activity, and to illustrate what might be ignored when exploring such writing.

SHIFTING THE FRAME: THE AESTHETICS OF ROUTINE WRITING

The poetic-aesthetic dimension typically associated with literary and creative writing – in terms of the writer's experience of engaging in writing and her attention to the crafting of the text– is not usually applied to routine or institutionally regulated writing. Here I'll briefly illustrate what happens when this dimension is allowed to become visible: in student writing for assessment and writers at work.

Student writing

Student writing in formal institutions is a routine, everyday practice (for those taking part in such institutions), which is highly regulated (albeit in different and sometimes vague ways) and is often researched and analysed in terms of its institutional domain of use. As a phenomenon, it is a good example of the conflation between the domain being observed and the domain of observation. Student writing is often viewed through a transactional-rationalist lens – as 'skills' (often in policy documentation) – but has also been researched using socio-cognitive approaches which often adopt a model of the student writer's trajectory in higher education as being that of novice to expert. Within the (widely used) transactional-rationalist and socio-cognitive approaches to student writing, what we can call 'research recognition' criteria have been highly influenced by 'institutional evaluative' criteria, powerfully shaped by the generic labels used to label student writing; thus, the essay is construed as a particular genre, with particular structural and rhetorical features and students' writings tend to be recognised and evaluated according to those features; for example, a key rhetorical feature of the essay is deemed to be rational argument, thus argument is both looked for and analysed in students' writing. There are important reasons why analysts with a pedagogic imperative want to explore the extent to which students' writing meets institutional criteria (most obviously the pedagogic assessment imperative) but it is problematic if – as we often see – institutional criteria become the only or primary driving force in researching student writing. In researching student writing – like any writing – we need to distinguish between the domain of observation and the domain being observed in order to capture the meanings of such writing.

We have already seen examples of the way in which identity is bound up with student academic writing (Chapter 6), aspects of which are more often associated with creative or poetic-aesthetic dimensions and approaches to writing. The creative pleasure of writing is also evident in some writers' comments: consider the comments by one writer on her use of 'new' words – 'they bring a little tingle to my ear [. . .] Some words sound really really nice and I like them' (in Lillis 2001: 91). And another writer, Sara, comments:

> My mind is like a storm brewing in my head [. . .] I've got so many ideas just wafting around in my head – And then I start having dreams about it (her studying) and, like I told you, I was answering the question in my dream (laughs) it was like I was discussing it with another person, you know – you've still got the adrenaline rush going and you think 'yeah I've got to write this down, I've got to include this as well' [. . .] This studying, you know, it's amazing.
>
> (Lillis 2001: 128)

Here we see traces of experiences often associated with poetic/creative writing, and captured in notions such as 'inspiration'. Such experiences are noted by the writers as also strongly physical (note the 'tingling' the 'adrenaline rush') with the crafting of the text itself ('I've got to get this down'). The poetic-aesthetic dimension has been hinted at in some discussions of writing and identity (Ivanič 1998; Lillis 2001, 2011) where writers' concerns and desires about the crafting of texts and specific bits of text are taken seriously and paid analytical attention. However, the aesthetic dimension of student writing (and academic writing more generally) remains largely unexplored (but see Lillis 2011; Scott 2012 and Thesen and Cooper forthcoming).

Workplace writing

Writing in workplaces is an everyday occurrence. It is clearly a sociolinguistic phenomenon involving people using language in going about their everyday lives. At the same time, work-based writing is often either invisible in discussions about writing or, where discussed at all, is viewed through a largely transactional-rationalist approach with the emphasis on correctness, clarity and writing as encoding information.

Brandt, a US researcher, has been studying what she calls 'workaday writing' and 'workaday writers' for some years, exploring in particular the legal and ideological dimensions to such writing (2005, 2009). By workaday writers she means 'people who make a living in various sectors of the information-services society as salaried employees, freelancers, or entrepreneurs' (Brandt 2009: 173) and her study has involved workers in the areas of law, business, technology, health care, agriculture, insurance, government, library services, manufacturing, banking and financial services, research, communications, publishing, journalism, marketing, the ministry and sales. Examples of the kinds of workaday writing that such workers do include: emails, reports, analyses, columns, press releases, databases, software, blogs, book-length manuals and textbooks.

There are several key points arising from her research which are directly relevant to our discussion here about who writers are, what counts as writing and the ways in which the approaches we use to explore writing influence what we come to recognise and understand. Firstly, workaday writers are often not attributed ownership or authorship in either a (literary) romantic sense or a legal sense. With regard to the latter, their writing, as part of their daily work, is owned and authorised by the employer. Secondly, such work, because it is ordinary, routine or 'humdrum' (Orbach 2002) is assumed not to have any aesthetic or emotional dimensions. Brandt states:

> workaday writing has negligible worth in itself, not only because its creators are considered interchangeable (their personalities being irrelevant to the creation) but also because its value is used up in the course of a particular communication. Once a piece of writing does its immediate job (conveys a message, wins a case, implements a policy, seals a deal, etc.) it has no residual value to worry about or protect. It is considered utterly instrumental.
>
> (Brandt 2009: 178)

However, although the institution may view such writing as transactional-rationalist this does not mean that it should be analysed and understood (solely) through a transactional lens, as can be illustrated in extracts from interviews carried out by Brandt. A writer 'with a string of jobs' with mostly technical and industrial clients preparing brochures, websites and other so-called 'authorless' texts, states as follows:

> I feel like I've grown intellectually and maybe even emotionally.
> If I'm writing about anything that has any value to me personally,
> it can be really gratifying to sink your teeth into a set of ideas, make
> them your own, and then say them in your own words. I have had
> a couple of projects for people who are doing really interesting,
> cool things and just the process of getting to learn what they do
> well enough to become comfortable enough to speak about it, I
> grow and I change as a result of that process.
>
> (Brandt 2009: 180)

His personal pleasure in crafting the texts is evident. Similar comments are made by other workaday writers. For example a police officer states about report writing: 'I get enjoyment in finding the right word. That's the way I interject myself into any particular story, through the words that I use, the way that I structure the sentences that I write' (Brandt 2009: 179). And he signals a poetic-aesthetic dimension to his experiences of engaging in everyday writing practice. Describing how he writes his incident or arrest reports, he states:

> I write my reports as if I were writing a movie. I want you to be able to read my report and visualise everything that happened. I want to envelope the whole human element while I'm writing about the facts.
>
> (Brandt 2009: 179)

Drawing on her extensive study, Brandt summaries her perspective on what workaday writers are telling her:

> In their interviews with me, workaday writers routinely reported having aesthetic, intellectual, ethical and political experiences while writing at work. They also often reported carrying away changes in themselves as a result of having written. I want to call all of this experience the residue of authorship, a value that can neither be separated from their person nor accounted for in any legal or economic sense.
>
> (Brandt 2009: 178)

It's unclear whether Brandt construes this 'residue of authorship' as a core dimension to all writing, or whether she is arguing that this poetic-aesthetic discourse of authoring is so powerful that it pervades our thinking about anything we label as 'writing'. But what is clear is that in order to understand what's involved in this routinised writing, we need to consider aspects that go beyond transactional-rationalist accounts of writing and draw on aspects usually associated with a poetic-aesthetic domain and frame.

Just as pleasure is evident in the accounts of work-based writing production, so too is pain. In our research on routine writing in social work practice (Lillis and Rai 2011, 2012) social workers in addition to talking about the sheer amount of writing they had to do, commented on the creative effort and challenges needed to produce some types of writing within the context of busy and fragmented opportunities for writing:

> I often find it hugely challenging, and a particular area of difficulty for me is life story work, and later life letters, so when I have to give an account to a child of what's happened to them throughout their life, and why decisions have been taken and why their parents weren't able to care for them but in a child friendly focused way. Hugely challenging. And that takes me hours to write, and I start and I delete it and I write and I just think I don't know how to tell this child. This is so painful.
>
> (Lillis and Rai 2012)

Papen and Tusting (2008) also signal the poetic-aesthetic dimension to routine work-related writing. In their discussion they focus on creativity in relation to the texts they have researched in two distinct contexts: the first is voluntary work (unpaid) involving routine text making – the weekly bulletin – in a Catholic Church community in the UK; the second focuses on advertising texts relating to community-based tourism in Namibia. Whilst both foreground the aesthetics of text production, the emphasis in the former – producing the weekly bulletin – is on decisions and choices about content, and designing the bulletin; the latter focus – community-based tourism – signals the creativity involved in resource-poor contexts, and the ways in which people draw on materials and people to generate texts collaboratively. Papen and Tusting (2008) usefully introduce the phrase 'recurrent creativity' to capture something of the creativity involved in routine writing.

One way of challenging our assumptions about writing is to become aware of the range of approaches and assumptions that exist, such as those summarised in the previous section. As part of this work, it can also be useful to consider available diagrammatic representations of writing, some of which are included in the book (e.g. Figures 5.2, 5.6 and 5.11). Consider also the examples in Figure 7.4, with each diagram seeking to represent a particular dimension to writing from a particular perspective. Perhaps the least familiar will be that used by Andrews and Smith (2011: 157) who argue for a reframing of what we mean by 'writing development' towards an emphasis on engagement and control over repertoires and designs. They suggest that Figure 7.4c may be useful as a visual metaphor, challenging as it does linear models of development, signalling spurts, multidirectionality, spiralling.

> In this visual metaphor, the reader can imagine development in motion as a writer draws from existing experiences, forms and practices, expanding their facility with and adaptability to new tools and audiences, resulting in a pattern of development unique to each individual writer.
>
> (Andrews and Smith 2011: 158).

CONCLUSION

There is a range of traditions and approaches for exploring what's involved in writing, which have developed in different academic domains, including literary studies, linguistics, education, psychology and anthropology. Whilst there is fluidity across these fields – with some conceptual tools, theories and methodologies being picked up and recontextualised from one field to another – there are also key differences which are useful to explore when trying to understand the range of approaches available to us. These differences include ideologies around production and uptake, the writer, the reader, the text, language and relations between all of these. My main interest in this chapter has been to attempt to articulate some of these differences but also to raise a concern about the danger of conflating our domain of observation with the object of our observation and thus of limiting our capacity to observe and understand what writing is and does in any specific context. With regard to everyday writing, the simple but important point here is that if we restrict our frame to a particular academic or institutional domain of observation, we may not notice or recognise what is going on.

I have suggested eight influential frames of reference for exploring writing and, whilst acknowledging that such a categorisation oversimplifies the work and ideas of specific researchers, I think it is useful to attempt to articulate the range of approaches and the nested assumptions and ideologies within these, for two reasons. Firstly, when engaging in the study of writing, we need to be aware of the implicit and explicit assumptions nested in different approaches to studying writing. Secondly, and a more general point arising from the discussion in this chapter, we need to engage with the ongoing challenge of engaging in description whilst avoiding (implicit) prescriptions or evaluations about what it is we are looking at when

Figure 7.4   Examples of diagrammatic representations of writing

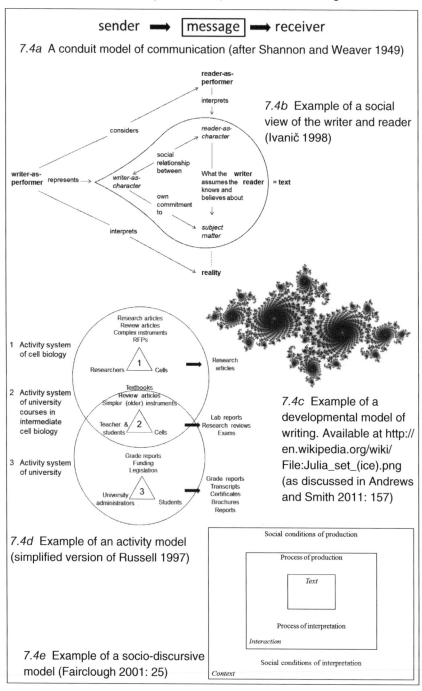

sender ➡ message ➡ receiver

7.4a A conduit model of communication (after Shannon and Weaver 1949)

7.4b Example of a social view of the writer and reader (Ivanič 1998)

7.4c Example of a developmental model of writing. Available at http://en.wikipedia.org/wiki/File:Julia_set_(ice).png (as discussed in Andrews and Smith 2011: 157)

7.4d Example of an activity model (simplified version of Russell 1997)

7.4e Example of a socio-discursive model (Fairclough 2001: 25)

we study writing. If we only engage in a kind of mirroring activity – recognising what our particular frame of reference allows us to recognise – we are effectively already engaged in a form of prescription; thus an academic text which is evocative or emotive may not be described as such, but rather evaluated negatively because it includes dimensions conventionally associated with another domain of activity, such as creative, personal, literary writing. Why should this matter? In terms of a sociolinguistic goal of description it matters because we may be failing to recognise the phenomenon we are seeking to understand. This is of considerable social significance because exactly how texts (and people) get produced, taken up and evaluated is highly consequential for all involved. Processes of production and uptake are highly complex in a globalised world where semiotic practices and values shift and differ and therefore it becomes important to make (mis)recognition practices visible and a focus of debate.

NOTES

1. Approaches to writing and the written text are often distinguished in these domains in a number of ways including their primary focus – literary studies tend to focus on expert readings of texts, for example by critics, whereas stylistics tends to focus on the workings of the text and how these might be taken up by 'ordinary' readers. See discussions in Allington and Swann 2009 and Swann and Allington 2009.
2. See Crowley 1998 in particular for an account of institutional connections between English literature and composition in the US and which may account for the Romantic emphasis in the widely taken up process approach in US Composition Studies; see also Ivanič 1998: 94–7 for overview.
3. The work of Flower and Hayes (1981) and Flower (1994) is foundational in this approach. Within this frame, emphasis is on writers as meaning makers, facing and making decisions about what should and should not be written, why and how. Drawing on Vygotsky, particular attention is paid to exploring and understanding the mental representations the writer has of her self, her task, her readers, with specific interest in how people learn to write and of developing ways of supporting the learning of writing in educational contexts.
4. The distinctions made here correspond in some ways to those in classical rhetoric between *inventio* and *elocutio* discussed in Chapter 4, but a key difference is the emphasis in Kress's work on the socio and historically situated nature of representational resources and how these shape both production and reception/engagement practices. For full discussion of Kress's social semiotic theory of communication, see Kress 2010.

Chapter 8

Conclusions

INTRODUCTION

The aim of this book has been to claim a place for writing as a legitimate focus in sociolinguistics. Writing as a phenomenon does figure in sociolinguistics, but it does so in ways that are bound up with the particular concerns, interests and frames of reference that have historically shaped and continue to shape sociolinguistics as a field; a key aspect of the sociolinguistic imaginary is the positioning of writing as verbal, as fundamentally connected with notions of 'standard' (language and literacy) and as primarily linked to socially prestigious texts. Whilst a concern with writing has been evident for some time in areas at the edges of sociolinguistics, notably in New Literacy Studies, the key position advanced in such work – that writing is an everyday social practice – is often backgrounded in mainstream sociolinguistics. A key goal of this book has been to illustrate some of the ways in which writing is an everyday social practice, to illustrate key analytical tools for description and analysis and to argue that writing – as part of production practices more generally – is on the increase and therefore of considerable interest to anyone interested in semiotic and communication practices in contemporary society.

In this final chapter my aim is to summarise key points made about writing in this book, and to highlight a particular issue of wider empirical, theoretical and analytical concern: that is the identification of *function* and the ways in which such identification is nested within academic, institutional and common sense practices of *evaluation*. Whilst the relationship between function and evaluation has long since been on the agenda in sociolinguistics – most obviously captured in description/prescription debates (see Chapter 1) – I think a discussion of the relationship between function and evaluation in relation to writing helps to foreground the particular challenges we face as researchers and analysts seeking to explore twenty-first-century communication practices. These communication and semiotic practices are characterised by the use of an increasing range and mix of linguistic, material and technological resources, differential access to the use of such resources and control over how these are evaluated, as well as complex patterns of participation and uptake.

A SUMMARY OF KEY POINTS IN THIS BOOK

The key points made about writing in this book are summarised below. I indicate those chapters where the points are most obviously made:

- writing can usefully be seen as an everyday social practice (Chapter 4, across the book)
- a considerable amount and range of writing is taking place across all domains of social life using a wide range of modes, materials and technologies (Chapter 2 and across the book)
- writing involves both strong and weak regulation, depending on the extent and ways in which specific writing is gatekeepered (Chapters 2, 5 and 6)
- a wide range of tools and analytical notions have been developed and are available for researching and analysing writing as a social practice (Chapters 4 and 5)
- there is clearly a strong verbal dimension to many instances of written texts which has usefully led to the development of an array of tools for verbal analysis (Chapter 3)
- the historical emphasis on the verbal dimension to written texts (notably in Western linguistics) is increasingly being challenged, with attention being paid to the multimodal nature of writing, both in terms of its texture (for example its visual as well as verbal nature) and the contexts in which writing appears, that is that writing even of the 'verbal heavy' kind often occurs and sits alongside other modes of communication (Chapters 2 and across the book)
- writing involves both material and symbolic acts of inscription (Chapter 6)
- the material and symbolic resources available for writing are socioculturally and sociohistorically situated (Chapters 4, 5 and 6)
- writing is a dynamic phenomenon in terms of its production and uptake (Chapters 2 and 5)
- focusing on specific instances and patterns of uptake (as well as production) is central to reaching an understanding about what writing means and does (Chapter 5)
- the ways in which writing is understood by researchers – what it is, what it does – is powerfully shaped by the particular theoretical frameworks used and the academic traditions followed (Chapter 7 and illustrated across the book)

THE QUESTION OF FUNCTION

I began this book by pointing to the binary distinction often made between spoken and written language. The obvious question to ask at this point is why this 'great divide' prevails? To a large extent, I think, this binary is sustained not so much because of an ongoing concern to distinguish between spoken and written language (although there are strong traces of this stance within sociolinguistics), but is rather the effect of a powerfully normative and *a priori* stance towards *function*. A normative stance towards function makes the continuing categorical distinctions between spoken and written language – and indeed between any identified modes – possible and warrantable; thus spoken language – or particular types – are assumed to have a particular function, with writing – or particular kinds – assumed to have specific others. A similar stance is often adopted towards different technologies of writing, for example, that writing by hand has a particular purpose, sending messages via mobile phones has another. Function is a key notion in sociolinguistics, usefully anchoring form to use. But as Hymes pointed out some considerable time ago, 'linguists have mostly taken the functions of language for granted, but it is necessary to investigate them' (1996: 45). I would argue that this is particularly the case with regard to writing where so many common sense assumptions abound as to what writing is and should be.

The different ways in which function is investigated with regard to writing have been discussed in this book as follows:

- *in terms of text*: in text-oriented analyses there are at least three particular ways in which the form/function connection is productively used with regard to writing: by layering function onto form; by collapsing the form/function dichotomy; by (temporarily) elevating form over function. These ways of relating form to function in texts are discussed in Chapter 3 with regard to the verbal dimension of writing but they are also equally evident in some multimodal approaches (see Chapter 2).
- *in terms of practice*: researchers vary in the extent to which they seek to contextualise their analysis and understanding of function – with some focusing mainly or primarily on the text and some seeking to draw on users' accounts and perspectives as well as observations. Researchers explicitly working from practice approaches emphasise the need for ethnographic studies of writing, including paying attention to *emic* as much as *etic* accounts in order to identify specific functions (see Chapter 4).

My own view is that if the research goal is to reach contextualised understandings of the functions and purposes of specific instances of writing – what it is and does, what it means to whom, what the consequences are in any specific moment – there are major limitations in working only with texts or text analysis. The function and purpose of small marks with potentially big and specific indexicalities cannot be taken as given or simply read off from inscriptions and markings themselves but are rather questions to be explored and tracked. Whilst not without its challenges and certainly not a straightforward solution, the more context sensitive approach made possible through ethnography – using a range of methods including text analysis, observations, interviews – and working with dynamic rather than static notions of text production and uptake may be one way of avoiding slipping into unhelpfully limited claims about the functions of writing in any specific context.

Furthermore, in paying attention to the relationship between form and function we need also to layer in the range of dimensions discussed and illustrated across this book – such as modality, materiality and technology – in recognition that function will necessarily shift and change in relation to these, but not in ways that we might necessarily presuppose. In general, there is a need to avoid any *a priori* assumptions about the relationship between function and form across modes and materialities, and to avoid positing monoglossic assumptions or conclusions, whether at a micro level, for example, what the function or purpose is of the use of the letter <*k*>, or at a macro level, for example, what the function is of a particular mode or a particular technology (see Chapter 2).

THE QUESTION OF VALUE AND EVALUATION

Identification of function is powerfully bound up with practices of evaluation and there has been a call for some time for sociolinguistic researchers to acknowledge that evaluation is necessarily embedded in their research and analytical practices, even as they/we strive towards description rather than prescription. I have argued that when it comes to the study of writing there tends to be what seems an acceptable slippage towards a normative evaluative stance. Stated simply, research and analysis of writing tends to be powerfully, albeit implicitly, shaped by assumptions about what writing should be, rather than paying attention to what it is. And, as discussed in Chapter 7, these assumptions are bound up with prevailing common sense notions about writing, the particular disciplinary traditions or academic fields on which we draw, as well as ideologically and institutionally bound assumptions about the function of writing in any specific context. This is evident as much in discussions about conventional writing (notably about what are considered to be appropriate writing practices in the context of formal schooling) as in discussions of more recent, digitally mediated writing; thus, with regard to the latter, we find examples both of researchers celebrating the explosion of all forms of writing and production activity (see discussion in Moje and Luke 2009) as well as researchers expressing doom about such – unregulated – activity, for example, Baron's concerns about what she refers to as 'flooding the scriptorium' (Baron 2008).

Cameron has argued that the problem with evaluation is not the fact that it necessarily forms part of what researchers and analysts do, but that it tends to be denied. We need to make visible the evaluation practices nested within writing research, including any research and analysis that we do. We also need to open up debate about the values and standards by which any specific instance of writing might be recognised and in doing so open up debate about the functions of any instance of writing. The list of values nested in different academic traditions and outlined in Table 7.1 could be a useful starting point for considering the kinds of evaluative questions we are engaging with. This would involve reflecting on questions such as: Is this writing useful? beautiful? clear? playful ? serious? If so, which aspects of the writing and from whose perspective? Does it enable action – what kinds, under whose control? Does this writing reflect or enable participation and interaction – what kinds, under what conditions, and is it weakly or more strongly regulated? Is this phenomenon/object viewed as 'writing' or 'not writing' by whom and with what consequences? In what ways are the different dimensions to writing – linguistic forms, modes, materialities, technologies – shaping both what writers/producers construe as 'writing' as well as researcher-analysts' perspectives on these? These questions are too many and too large to be answered by individual researchers (or groups of researchers) but are rather questions that the field as a whole needs to address and to which researchers focusing on specific research projects can contribute.

THE QUESTION OF BOUNDARIES

A key challenge writing researchers face is the identification and definition of the boundaries of the phenomena being explored. Discussions in this book have illustrated a wide range of notions that are used to create and define boundaries for the purposes of research and analysis: these include boundaried notions related to the more obviously textual dimensions to writing, such as 'text', 'mode' and 'genre', as well as the more practice boundaried notions, such as 'event', 'role' and 'community'. More macro level boundaries include those around 'language', 'literacy' and 'writing'. We need such categories in order to focus in on particular instances and moments of writing but at the same time we need to be aware of how they may be: shaping producers' and reader-interactants' orientations to what producers are doing and why; shaping our (researcher/analysts') orientations and understandings as to what people are doing and why. I have pointed to some of the challenges around boundaries across the book; for example, for modes and writing, see Chapter 2; for literacy, see Chapter 4; for language, see Chapters 4 and 5; for events and practices, see Chapter 4; for genre see Chapters 3 and 5; for the nature of boundaries between producer and reader/respondent see Chapter 7.

Here I will simply reiterate some of the challenges we face in analysing writing as a phenomenon. Firstly what defines a 'text' formally in terms of its spatial organisation and design? The challenge is most easily illustrated with regard to some digital texts such as webpages – where does a 'text' begin and end? Secondly, what constitutes a text in terms of production, use and uptake? With regard to this last question I have suggested that notions such as 'genre chains', 'text histories' and 'text trajectories', as well as the use of more conventionally formalist or textual categories, such as argument, construed as trans-textual dimensions, may offer some way forward.

The question of boundary identification is, of course, as much an ideological as a methodological issue. And in this respect it's important to note that the evidence of the increasing amount and diversity of writing taking place, illustrated in this book, is not matched by evidence of an increasing acceptance of such diversity. Indeed, some writers would suggest that greater prescription is resulting from the increased diversity in the context of globalisation (Jenkins 2006; Blommaert 2005). This is most evident in gatekeepered or strongly regulated encounters where responses to, or uptake of, writing tend to be strongly centripetal. In a discussion around globalisation with specific regard to asylum seekers (see Chapter 5) Blommaert states:

> globalization phenomena [. . .] appear to trigger an emphasis on the global order of things. In the context of asylum application procedures, the imagination

of language, notably, is dominated by frames that refer to static and timeless national orders of things. So while asylum seekers belong to a truly global scale-level of events and processes, the treatment of their applications is brought down to a rigidly national scale: a very modernist response to post modern realities

(Blommaert 2010: 155)

What writing is and does in everyday practice is both being opened up and closed down, with the case of institutionally regulated writing being an example of the latter (and a centripetal pull) and writing in more weakly regulated spaces such as notebooks and some digital spaces where there is evidence of mixing and playing with semiotic resources (and evidence of a centrifugal pull), being examples of the former.

FUTURE RESEARCH

As with any area of communication, there is considerable scope for future research on writing. We live in a highly textually mediated world (Smith 2005) in which writing in all its forms plays a central part. We have available to us a wide range of methodological and theoretical tools for researching and analysing writing, many of which have been illustrated in this book. At the same time, any research on writing at this particular historical moment involves fundamental questions about what we mean by writing and we may have to start from some very different assumptions, the most obvious one being that the verbal is only one dimension. Acknowledging the multimodal dimension to writing does not cancel out the importance of the verbal dimension to writing but it does force us to consider exactly what is being produced and which aspects are being paid attention to, by producers and analysts, and why. There is evidence of an explosion of productive activity at this period in history in which writing plays a central role. Exactly what role it plays alongside or distinguished (in time or space) from other semiotic forms, such as still and moving images, colour, shape and sound, and exactly how writing travels around the world are questions that need considerable attention. This is an exciting time for writing research.

To close this book, it is worth considering some key questions we can ask – of ourselves and others – when engaging in the study of writing:

1. How am I construing writing – as a verbal heavy mode or a mixture of modes? And how does this influence my research and analysis?
2. What aspect am I focusing on – function, form content or a particular combination? And why?
3. What writing research traditions – or aspects of traditions – am I drawing on? And why?
4. Is my analysis oriented primarily towards the text and possible meanings that I can offer on the basis of textual analysis? And what frameworks can I use for analysing texts? And why choose one above another?
5. Is my analysis oriented towards making connections between key aspects of the text and how these enact and reflect larger social processes?

6. Is my primary interest in how one particular text seems to work, or am I interested in how clusters of text may together constitute a particular 'over-arching' text chain, trajectory, or action?
7. Am I interested in writing from the perspective mainly of production? What tools do I have to do this?
8. Am I interested in production and uptake? And what tools and frameworks can I use to do this?

The questions and answers will vary according to our/your specific interests. What is important is that we grapple explicitly and reflexively with such questions so that we can make clear (as far as possible) to ourselves and others the reasons for our decisions about the kind of research and analysis we are engaging in and why. It is my hope that this book will have convinced readers that writing is a fascinating topic of interest and will have provided some ideas, tools and questions for pursuing further writing research.

References

Abner, E. and S. Kierstead (2011), 'Text work as identity work for legal writers', electronic copy available at: http://ssrn.com/abstract=1878671 (accessed 5 December 2011).

Agha, A. (2003), 'The social life of cultural value', *Language and Communication*, 23: 231–73.

Akinnaso, F. N. (1982), 'On the differences between written and spoken language', *Language and Speech*, 25: 97–125.

Allington, D. and J. Swann (2009), 'Researching literary reading as social practice', in D. Allington and J. Swann (eds), *Literary Reading as Social Practice*, Special Issue of *Language and Literature*, 18: 3, 219–30.

Andrews, R. (2009), *Argumentation in Higher Education: Improving Practice through Theory and Research*, New York: Routledge.

Andrews, R. and A. Smith (2011), *Developing Writers. Teaching and Learning in the Digital Age*, Maidenhead: McGraw Hill/Open University Press.

Androutsopolous, J. (2011), 'From variation to heteroglossia in the study of computer-mediated discourse', in C. Thurlow and K. Mroczek (eds), *Digital Discourse: Language in the New Media*, Oxford: Oxford University Press, pp. 277–98.

Archer, A. (2006), 'Change as additive: harnessing students' multimodal semiotic resources in an engineering curriculum', in L. Thesen and V. Pletzen (eds), *Academic Literacy and the Languages of Change*, London: Continuum, pp. 130–51.

Austin, J. L. (1962), *How to Do Things with Words*, Cambridge, MA: Harvard University Press.

Baca, D. (2008), *Mestiz@ Scripts, Digital Migrations, and the Territories of Writing*, New York: Palgrave Macmillan.

Baca, D. and V. Villanueva (eds) (2010), *Rhetorics of the Americas: 3114 BCE to 2012 CE*, (Studies of the Americas Series), New York: Palgrave Macmillan.

Backhaus, P. (2005), 'Signs of multilingualism in Tokyo – a diachronic look at the linguistic landscape', *International Journal of the Sociology of Language*, 175: 6, 103–21.

Baker, C. (2010), *Sociolinguistics and Corpus Linguistics*, Edinburgh: Edinburgh University Press.

Bakhtin, M. [1935] (1981), 'Discourse in the novel', in M. Holquist (ed.), *The Dialogic Imagination. Four Essays by M. Bakhtin*, trans. C. Emerson and M. Holquist, Austin: University of Texas Press, pp. 259–422.

Bakhtin, M. (1986), 'The problem of speech genres', in C. Emerson and M. Holquist (eds), *Speech Genres and Other Late Essays*, trans. V. W. McGee, Austin: University of Texas Press, pp. 60–102.

Barber, K. (ed.) (2006), *Africa's Hidden Histories. Everyday Literacy and Making the Self*, Bloomington: Indiana University Press.

Baron, N. S. (2000), *From Alphabet to Email. How Written English Evolved and Where It's Heading*, London and New York: Routledge.

Baron, N. (2008), *Always On: Language in an Online and Mobile World*, New York: Oxford University Press.

Barthes, R. (1977), 'The death of the author', in S. Heath (ed.) *Image-Music-Text*, London: Fontana, pp. 142–8.

Barton, D. [1994] (2007), *Literacy. An Introduction to the Ecology of Written Language*, Oxford: Blackwell.

Barton, D. (2010), 'Vernacular writing on the web', in D. Barton and U. Papen (eds), *The Anthropology of Writing. Understanding Textually-Mediated Worlds*, London: Continuum, pp. 109–25.

Barton, D. and N. Hall (2000), 'Letter writing as a social practice', *Studies in Written Language and Literacy*, 9, Lancaster University/Manchester Metropolitan University.

Barton, D. and M. Hamilton (1998), *Local Literacies: Reading and Writing in One Community*, London: Routledge.

Barton, D. and M. Hamilton (2000), 'Literacy practices', in D. Barton, M. Hamilton and R. Ivanič (eds), *Situated Literacies*, London: Routledge, pp. 7–16.

Barton, D. and M. Hamilton (2005), 'Literacy, reification and the dynamics of social interaction', in D. Barton and K. Tusting (eds), *Beyond Communities of Practice. Language, Power and Social Context*, Cambridge: Cambridge Unviersity Press, pp. 1–35.

Barton, D. and Papen, U. (2010a), 'What is the anthropology of writing?', in D. Barton and U. Papen (eds), *The Anthropology of Writing. Understanding Textually-Mediated Worlds*, London: Continuum, pp. 30–1.

Barton, D. and U. Papen (eds) (2010b), *The Anthropology of Writing. Understanding Textually-Mediated Worlds*, London: Continuum.

Barton, D., Hamilton, M. and Ivanič, R. (eds) (2000), *Situated Literacies*, London: Routledge.

Basso, K. (1974), 'The ethnography of writing', in R. Baumann and J. Sherzer (eds), *Explorations in the Ethnography of Speaking*, Cambridge: Cambridge University Press, pp. 425–32.

Bate, J. (1998), *The Genius of Shakespeare*, London: Picador.

Baumann, R. anad C. Briggs (1990), 'Poetics and performance as critical perspectives on language and social life', *Annual Review of Anthropology*, 19: 59–88.

Bawarshi, A. (2010), 'The challenges and possibilities of taking up multiple discursive resources in U.S. composition', in B. Horner, M. Z. Lu and P. K. Matusda (eds), *Cross-Language Relations in Composition*, Carbondale: Southern Illinois University Press, pp. 196–203.

Baynham, M. (1995), *Literacy Practices*, London: Longman.

Bazerman, C. (1984), 'Evolution of the experimental report in physics: spectroscopic articles in physical review, 1893–1980, *Social Studies of Science*, 14: 2, 163–96.

Bazerman, C. (1997), 'The life of genre, the life in the classroom', in W. Bishop and H. Ostrum (eds), *Genre and Writing*, Portsmouth, NH: Boynton/Cook, pp. 19–26.

Bazerman, C. (2003), 'Intertextuality: how texts rely on other texts', in C. Bazerman and P. Prior (eds), *What Writing Does and How It Does It*, Mahwah, NJ: Lawrence Erlbaum, pp. 83–96.

Bazerman, C. and J. Paradis (eds) (1991), *Textual Dynamics of the Professions*, Madison: University of Wisconsin Press.

Bazerman, C. and P. Prior (eds) (2003), *What Writing Does and How it Does it. An Introduction to Analysing Texts and Textual Practices*, London/New Jersey: Lawrence Erlbaum.

Bazerman, C., A. Bonini and D. Figueiredo (2009), *Genre in a Changing World*. The WAC Clearinghouse wac.colostate.edu, Fort Collins, CO: Parlor Press.

Bell, A. (1991), *The Language of News Media*, Oxford: Blackwell.

Bell, A. (2007), 'Text, time and technology in news English', in. S. Goodman, D. Graddol and T. Lillis (eds), *Redesigning English*, London: Routledge, pp. 79–112.

Bennett, K. (2011), *Academic Writing in Portugal*, Coimbra: Universidade de Coimbra.

Beresford, D. (1987), *Ten Men Dead: the Story of the 1981 Hunger Strike*, New York: Atlantic Monthly Press.

Berkenkotter, C. and C. Hanganu-Bresch (2011), 'Lunatic asylum occult genres and the certification of madness in the 19th century', *Written Communication*, 28: 220–50.

Berlin, J. A. (1996), *Rhetorics, Poetics and Cultures: Refiguring College English Studies*, Urbana: NCTE.

Beroujon, A. (2010), 'Lawful and unlawful writings in Lyon in the seventeenth century', in D. Barton and U. Papen (eds), *The Anthropology of Writing. Understanding Textually-Mediated Worlds*, London: Continuum, pp. 190–213.

Besnier, N. (1988), 'The linguistic relationships of spoken and written Nukulaelae', *Language*, 64: 4, 707–36.

Besnier, N. (1995), *Literacy, Emotion and Authority: Reading and Writing on a Polynesian Atoll*, Cambridge: Cambridge University Press.

Bhabha, H. (1994), *The Location of Culture*, London: Routledge.

Biber, D. (1988), *Variation across Speech and Writing*, Cambridge: Cambridge University Press.

Black, R. (2005), 'Accent and affiliation: the literacy and composition practices of English language learners in an online fanfiction community', *International Reading Association*, 49, 2: 118–28.

Black, R. (2006), 'Language, culture and identity in online fanfiction', *E-learning*, 3: 2, 170–84.

Black, R. W. (2009), 'Online fanfiction, global identities, and imagination', *Research in the Teaching of English*, 43: 4, 397–425.

Blommaert, J. (2005), *Discourse: A Critical Introduction*, Cambridge: Cambridge University Press.

Blommaert, J. (2006), 'Ethnography as counter-hegemony: remarks on epistemology and method', *Working Papers in Urban Language and Literacies*, 34, London: Institute of Education.

Blommaert, J. (2008), *Grassroots Literacy*, London: Routledge.

Blommaert, J. (2010), *The Sociolinguistics of Globalization*, Cambridge: Cambridge University Press.

Blommaert, J. and D. Jie (2010), *Ethnographic Fieldwork: A Beginner's Guide*, Clevedon: Multilingual Matters.

Blommaert, J. and B. Rampton (2011), 'Language and superdiversity: a position paper', *Working Papers in Urban Language and Literacies*, 70. Available www.kcl.ac.uk/ldc (accessed 10 May 2012).

Bloomfield, L. (1933), *Language*, New York: Henry Holt.

Boas, F. (ed.) (1911), *Handbook of American Indian Languages*, Bureau of American Ethnology Bulletin 40.

Bourdieu, P. (1977), *Outline of a Theory of Practice*, Cambridge: Cambridge University Press.

Brandt, D. (2005), 'Writing for a living: literacy and the knowledge economy', *Written Communication*, 22: 166–97.

Brandt, D. (2009), 'When people write for pay', *Journal of Advanced Composition*, 29: 1(2), 165–97.

Brandt, D. and K. Clinton (2002), 'Limits of the local: expanding perspectives on literacy as a social practice', *Journal of Literacy Research*, 34: 3, 337–56.

Briggs, C. (1997), 'Introduction: from the ideal, the ordinary and the orderly to conflict and violence in pragmatic research', *Pragmatics*, 7: 4, 519–46.

Buckingham, D. (2007), *Beyond Technology: Children's Learning in the Age of Digital Media*, Cambridge: Polity Press.

Calvet, L. (2003) 'Reflections on the origins of sociolinguistics in Europe', in C. B. Paulston,

C. B. and G.R. Tucker (eds), *Sociolinguistics. The Essential Readings*, Oxford: Blackwell, pp. 17–25.

Cameron, D. (1992), *Feminism and Linguistic Theory*, 2nd edn, Basingstoke: Macmillan.

Cameron, D. [1995] (2012), *Verbal Hygiene*, London: Routledge.

Cameron, D. (2001), 'Verbal hygiene' in R. Mesthrie (ed.), *Concise Encyclopedia of Sociolinguistics*, Oxford/Amsterdam/New York: Elsevier, pp. 688–90.

Cameron, D. (2009), 'Sex/gender, language and the new biologism', *Applied Linguistics*, 31: 2, 173–92.

Cameron, L. (2010), *Metaphor and Reconciliation: The Discourse Dynamics of Empathy in Post-Conflict Conversations*, Routledge Studies in Linguistics, New York: Routledge.

Cameron, L. and D. Kulick (eds) (2006), *The Language and Sexuality Reader*, London: Routledge.

Campbell, J. (1992), 'Controlling voices: the legacy of English A at Radcliffe College 1893–1917', *College Composition and Communication*, 43: 4, 472–85.

Canagarajah, A. S. (2011), 'Codemeshing in academic writing: identifying teachable strategies of translanguaging', *The Modern Language Journal*, 95: iii, 401–16.

Candlin, C. (1989), 'Introduction', in N. Fairclough, *Language and Power*, London: Longman, pp. vi–x.

Carter, A, T. Lillis and S. Parkin (eds) (2009), *Why Writing Matters: Issues of Access and Identity in Writing Research and Pedagogy*, Amsterdam: Benjamins.

Castaño, C. (2008), *The Second Digital Divide and Young Women* (*La segunda brecha digital*), Madrid: Cátedra.

Chafe, W. (1982), 'Integration and involvement in speaking, writing and oral literature', in D. Tannen (ed.), *Spoken and Written Language: Exploring Orality and Literacy*, Norwood, NJ: Ablex, pp. 35–53.

Chase, G. (1988), 'Accommodation, resistance and the politics of student writing', *College Composition and Communication*, 39: 1, 13–22.

Chomsky, N. (1965), *Aspects of the Theory of Syntax*, Cambridge, MA: MIT Press.

Chouliaraki, L. and N. Fairclough (1999), *Discourse in Late Modernity. Rethinking Critical Discourse Analysis*, Edinburgh: Edinburgh University Press.

Coad, C. E. M. (1939), *How to Write, Think and Speak Correctly*, London: Oldhams Press Ltd.

Coffin, C. (2006), *Historical Discourse: The Language of Time, Cause and Evaluation*, London: Continuum.

Coffin, C., T. Lillis and K. O'Halloran (eds) (2010), *Applied Linguistics Methods. A Reader*, London: Routledge.

Collins, J. (1996), 'Socialization to text: structure and contradiction in schooled literacy', in M. Silverstein and G. Urban (eds), *Natural Histories of Discourse*, Chicago: University of Chicago Press, pp. 203–28.

Collins, J. and R. K. Blot (2003), *Literacy and Literacies: Texts, Power, and Identity*, Cambridge: Cambridge University Press.

Colloque de la casa de Velázquez (1981), *Livre et lecteur en Espagne et en France sous l'ancien régime*, Paris: Casa de Velázquez.

Connor, U. and R. Kaplan (eds) (1987), *Writing across Languages: Analysis of L2 Text*, Reading, MA: Addison-Wesley.

Connor, U., K. W. Davis and T. de Rycker (1995), 'Correctness and clarity in applying for overseas jobs: a cross-cultural analysis of US and Flemish applications', *Text*, 15: 4, 457–75.

Cook, G. (2001), *The Discourse of Advertising*, 2nd edn, London: Routledge.

Cook, G. (2010), 'Hearts and minds. Persuasive language in ancient and modern public debate', in J. Maybin and J. Swann (eds), *The Routledge Companion to English Language Studies*, Abingdon: Routledge, pp. 134–5.

Cook, G. (2011), 'In defence of genius', in J. Swann et al. (eds), *Creativity in Language and Literature*, Basingstoke: Palgrave Macmillan, pp. 290–303.

Cook-Gumperz, J. (ed.) (2006), *The Social Construction of Literacy*, 2nd edn, Cambridge: Cambridge University Press.

Corbett, E. P. J. and R. J. Connors (1999), *Classical Rhetoric for the Modern Student*, Cary, NC: Oxford University Press.

Coulmas, F. (ed.) (1996), *The Blackwell Encyclopaedia of Writing Systems*, Oxford: Blackwell.

Coulmas, F. (ed.) (1997), *The Handbook of Sociolinguistics*, Oxford: Blackwell.

Coulmas, F. (2005), *Sociolinguistics. The Study of Speakers' Choices*, Cambridge: Cambridge University Press.

Coupland, N. and A. Jaworski (eds) (2009), *The New Sociolinguistics Reader*, Basingstoke: Palgrave.

Coupland, N., S. Sarangi and C. Candlin (eds) (2001), *Sociolinguistics and Social Theory*, Essex: Pearson Educational Ltd.

Crowley, S. (1998), *Composition in the University. Historical and Polemical Essays*, Pittsburgh: University of Pittsburgh Press.

Curry, M. J. and T. Lillis (2010), 'Academic research networks: accessing resources for English-medium publishing', *English for Specific Purposes*, Special Issue on EAP in Europe, 29: 4, 281–95.

Cushman, E. (2010), 'The Cherokee Syllabary from script to print', *Ethnohistory*, 57: 4, 625–49.

Daoust, D. (1998), 'Language planning and language reform', in F. Coulmas (ed.), *The Handbook of Sociolinguistics*, Oxford: Blackwell, pp. 436–52.

Denis, J. and D. Pontille (2009), 'L'écologie informationnelle des lieux publics. Le cas de la signalétique du métro', in C. Licoppe (ed.), *L'évolution des cultures numériques, de la mutation du lien social a l'organisation du travail*, Paris: FYP, pp. 94–101.

Deumert, A. and S. O. Masinyana (2008), 'Mobile language choices – The use of English and isiXhosa in text messages (SMS)', *English World-Wide*, 29: 117–47.

Devitt, A. (2004), *Writing Genres*, Carbondale: Southern Illinois University Press.

Downer, S. R., J. G. Meara, A. C. da Costa and K. Sethuraman (2006), 'SMS text messaging improves outpatient attendance', *Australian Health Review*, 30: 3, 389–96.

Eagleton, T. (1983), *Literary Theory: An Introduction*, Oxford: Blackwell.

Eckert, P. and S. McConnell-Ginet (1992), 'Think practically and look locally: language and gender as community-based practice', *Annual Review of Anthropology*, 21: 461–90.

English, F. (2011), *Student Writing and Genre. Reconfiguring Academic Knowledge*, London: Continuum.

Fairclough, N. (1992), *Discourse and Social Change*, Oxford: Blackwell.

Fairclough, N. (2001), *Language and Power*, 2nd edn, Harlow: Pearson.

Fairclough, N. (2003), *Analysing Discourse*, London: Routledge.

Fairclough, N. (2006), *Language and Globalization*, London: Routledge.

Fasold, R. (1984), *The Sociolinguistics of Society*, Oxford: Basil Blackwell.

Fasold, R. (1990), *The Sociolinguistics of Language*, Oxford: Basil Blackwell.

Finnegan, R. (2002), *Communicating: The Multiple Modes of Human Interconnection*, London: Routledge.

Firth, J. R. [1959] (1968), *Selected Papers of J. R. Firth 1952–1959*, ed. Frank R. Palmer, London: Longman.

Fishman, J. (2010), *European Vernacular Literacy. A Sociolinguistic and Historical Introduction*, Clevedon: Multilingual Matters.

Flewitt, R. (2011), 'Bringing ethnography to a multimodal investigation of early literacy in a digital age', *Qualitative Research*, 11: 3, 293–310.

Fløttum, K., T. Dahl and T. Kinn (2006), *Academic Voices: Across Languages and Disciplines*, Amsterdam: John Benjamins.

Flower, L. (1994), *The Construction of Negotiated Meaning. A Social Cognitive Theory of Writing*, Carbondale and Edwardsville: Southern Illinois University Press.

Flower, L. and Hayes, J. R. (1981), 'A cognitive process theory of writing', *College Composition and Communication*, 32: 1, 365–87.

Foucault, M. (1972), *The Archaeology of Knowledge*, London: Tavistock Publications.

Foucault, M. (1973), *The Order of Things*, New York: Random House.

Fraenkel, B. (2001), 'La résistible ascension de l'écrit au travail', in A. Borzeix and B. Fraenkel (eds), *Langage et travail, communication, cognition, action*, Paris: CNRS editions, pp. 113–42.

Freadman, A. (2002), 'Uptake', in R. Coe, L. Lingard and T. Teslenko (eds), *The Rhetoric and Ideology of Genre: Strategies for Stability and Change*, Cresskill, NJ: Hampton Press, pp. 39–53.

Freedman A. and P. Medway (eds) (1994), *Genre in the New Rhetoric*, London: Taylor and Francis.

Frey, O. (1990), 'Beyond literary Darwinism: women's voices and critical discourse', *College English*, 52: 5, 507–26.

Gee, J. (2007), *Sociolinguistics and Literacies*, 3rd edn, London: Taylor and Francis.

Gee, J. P. (2004), *Situated Language and Learning: A Critique of Traditional Schooling*, New York: Routledge.

Giddens, A. (1979), *Central Problems in Social Theory: Action, Structure and Contradiction in Social Analysis*, Berkeley: University of California Press.

Gille, Z. (2000), 'Cognitive cartography in a European wasteland: multinational capital and Greens vie for village allegiance', in M. Burawoy, J. Blum, S. George, Z. Gille, T. Gowan, L. Haney, M. Klawiter, S. Lopez, S. O'Riain and M. Thayer, *Global Ethnography: Forces, Connections and Imaginations in a Postmodern World*, Berkeley: University of California Press, pp. 240–67.

Gillen, J. and N. Hall (2010), 'Edwardian postcards: illuminating ordinary writing', in D. Barton and U. Papen (eds), *The Anthropology of Writing. Understanding Textually-Mediated Worlds*, London: Continuum, pp. 169–89.

Goffman, E. (1971), *Relations in Public*, New York: Harper and Row.

Goodfellow, R. (2011), 'Literacy, literacies and the digital in higher education', *Teaching in Higher Education*, 16: 1, 131–44.

Goodman, S. (2006a), 'Word and image', in S. Goodman and K. O'Halloran (eds), *The Art of English: Literary Creativity*, Basingstoke: Palgrave Macmillan, pp. 244–98.

Goodman, S. (2006b), 'Literature and technology', in S. Goodman and K. O'Halloran (eds), *The Art of English: Literary Creativity*, Basingstoke: Palgrave Macmillan, pp. 299–363.

Goodman, S. and K. O'Halloran (eds) (2006c), *The Art of English: Literary Creativity*, Basingstoke: Palgrave Macmillan.

Goodman, S. (2007), 'Visual English', in S. Goodman, D. Graddol and T. Lillis (eds), *Redesigning English*, London: Routledge, pp. 13–159.

Goodman, S., T. Lillis, M. Maybin and N. Mercer (eds) (2003), *Language Literacy and Education: A Reader*, Stoke on Trent: Trentham Books.

Goodman, S., D. Graddol and T. Lillis (eds) [1996] (2007), *Redesigning English*, London: Routledge.

Goody, J. (1977), *The Domestication of the Savage Mind*, London: Cambridge University Press.

Goody, J. and I. Watt (1963), 'The consequences of literacy', *Comparative Studies in Society and History*, 5: 3, 304–45.

Graddol, D. (2007), 'English manuscripts: the emergence of a visual identity', in D. Graddol et al. (eds), *Redesigning English*, London: Routledge, pp. 161–204.

Gregory, E. and A. Williams (2003), 'Investigating family literacy histories and children's reading practices in London's East End', in S. Goodman et al. (eds), *Language Literacy and Education: A Reader*, Stoke on Trent: Trentham Books, pp. 103–22.

Gumperz, J. and D. Hymes (eds) (1972), *Directions in Sociolinguistics. The Ethnography of Communication*, Oxford: Basil Blackwell.

Gutierrez, K. D., P. Baquedano-Lopez and C. Tejeda (1999), 'Rethinking diversity: hybridity and hybrid language practices in the third space', *Mind, Culture and Activity*, 6: 4, 286–303.

Haas, C. (1995), *Writing Technology: Studies in the Materiality of Literacy*, London: Routledge.

Hall, E. T. (1959), *The Silent Language*, Garden City, New York: Doubleday.

Halliday, M. A. K. (1978), *Language as Social Semiotic: The Social Interpretation of Language and Meaning*, Sydney: Edward Arnold.

Halliday, M. A. K. (1993), *Writing Science. Literacy and Discursive Power*, Bristol, PA: Falmer Press.

Halliday, M. A. K. (1994), *An Introduction to Functional Grammar*, 2nd edn, London: Edward Arnold.

Halliday, M. A. K. and R. Hasan (1976), *Cohesion in English*, London: Longman.

Halliday, M. A. K. and R. Hasan (1985), *Language, Context, and Text: Aspects of Language in a Social Semiotic Perspective*, Geelong: Deakin University.

Hamilton, M. (2000), 'Expanding the New Literacy Studies: using photographs to explore literacy as social practice', in in D. Barton, M. Hamilton and R. Ivanič (eds), *Situated Literacies*, London: Routledge, pp. 16–34.

Hamilton, M. and D. Barton (2000), 'The International Adult Literacy Survey (IALS): what does it really measure?', *The International Review of Education* UNESCO 46: 5, 377–89.

Haraway, D. J. (1991), *Simians, Cyborgs, and Women*, New York: Routledge.

Harris, R. (1986), *The Origin of Writing*, London: Gerald Duckworth.

Harwood, N. (2006), '(In) appropriate personal pronoun use in political science: a qualitative study and a proposed heuristic for future research', *Written Communication*, 23: 4, 424–50.

Havelock, E. A. (1976), *Origins of Western Literacy*, Toronto: OISE.

Hayles, N. K. (1999), *How We Became Posthuman: Virtual Bodies in Cybernetics, Literature, and Informatics*, Chicago: University of Chicago Press.

Heath, S. B. (1983), *Ways with Words: Language, Life and Work in Communities*, Cambridge: Cambridge University Press.

Herring, S. C., I. Kouper, L. A. Scheidt and E. Wright (2004), 'Women and children last: the discursive construction of weblogs', available at http://blog.lib.umn.edu/blogosphere/women and children.html (accessed 30 June 2011).

Herring, S., L. A. Scheidt, E. Wright and S. Bonus (2005), 'Weblogs as a bridging genre', *Information, Technology and People*, 18: 2, 142–71.

Hessel, S. (2011), 'Indignez-vous, Indignaos, de Stéphane Hesserl, en formato PDF y en castellano', available at http://www.attacmadrid.org/wp/wp-content/uploads/Indignaos.pdf (accessed 31 Aug. 2011).

Hewings, A. and S. North (2010), 'Texts and practices', in J. Maybin and J. Swann (eds), *The Routledge Companion to English Language Studies*, Abingdon: Routledge, pp. 42–75.

Hinds, J. (1990), 'Inductive, deductive and quasi-inductive: expository writing in Japanese, Korean, Chinese and Thai', in U. Connor and A. M. Johns (eds), *Coherence on Writing: Research and Pedagogical Perspectives*, Alexandria, VA: TESOL, pp. 87–109.

Holland, D., W. Lachicotte, D. Skinner and C. Cain (1998), *Identity and Agency in Cultural Worlds*, Cambridge, MA: Harvard University Press.

Holmes, J. [1992] (2001), *An Introduction to Sociolinguistics*, 2nd edn, London: Longman.

Holmes, R. (2004), *Literacy. An Introduction*, Edinburgh: Edinburgh University Press.

hooks, b. (1988), *Talking Back: Thinking Feminist, Thinking Black*, Boston, MA: South End Press.

Horner, B. (1999), 'The birth of basic writing', in B. Horner and M. Zhan-Lu (eds), *Representing the Other: Basic Writers and the Teaching of Basic Writing*, Urbana: National Council of Teachers of English, pp. 3–29.

Horner, B. (2000), *Terms of Work for Composition: A Materialist Critique*, Albany: State University of New York Press.

Horner, B., M. Lu, J. J. Royster and J. Trimbur (2011), 'Language difference in writing: toward a translingual approach', *College English*, 62: 1, 303–21.

Horsman, J. (1990), *Something in my Mind besides the Everyday: Women and Literacy*, Toronto: Women's Press.

How, J. (2003), *Epistolary Spaces: English Letter Writing from the Foundations of the Post Office to Richardson's Clarissa*, Aldershot: Ashgate.

Huckin, T. (2003), 'Content analysis: what texts talk about', in C. Bazerman and P. Prior (eds), *What Writing Does and How it Does it*, Hillsdale, NJ: Lawrence Erlbaum, pp. 13–32.

Hudson, R. A. [1980] (1996), *Sociolinguistics*, 2nd edn, Cambridge: Cambridge University Press.

Hull, G. and M. E. Nelson (2005), 'Locating the semiotic power of multimodality', *Written Communication*, 22: 224–61.

Hyland, K. (1999), 'Disciplinary discourses: writer stance in research articles', in C. Candlin and K. Hyland (eds), *Writing: Text, Processes and Practices*, London: Longman, pp. 99–121.

Hyland, K. (2002), 'Authority and invisibility: authorial identity in academic writing', *Journal of Pragmatics*, 34: 1091–112.

Hymes, D. [1962] (1968), 'The ethnography of speaking', in J. A. Fishman (ed.), *The Ethnography of Communication*, The Hague: Mouton, pp. 99–138.

Hymes, D. (1971), 'Competence and performance in linguistic theory', in R. Huxley and E. Ingram (eds), *Language Acquisition: Models and Methods*, New York: Academic Press, pp. 3–28.

Hymes, D. (1972), 'Models of the interaction of language and social life', in J. Gumperz and D. Hymes (eds), *Directions in Sociolinguistics. The Ethnography of Communication*, Oxford: Basil Blackwell, pp. 35–71.

Hymes, D. [1973] (1996), 'Speech and language: on the origins and foundations of inequality among speakers', in D. Hymes, *Ethnography, Linguistics, Narrative Inequality. Towards an Understanding of Voice*, Abingdon: Taylor and Francis, pp. 25–62.

Hymes, D. (1974), *Foundations in Sociolinguistics: An Ethnographic Approach*, Philadelphia: University of Pennsylvania Press.

Ivanič, R. (1998), *Writing and Identity*, Amsterdam: John Benjamins.

Ivanič, R., R. Edwards, D. Barton, M. Martin-Jones, Z. Fowler, B. Hughes, G. Mannion, K. Miller, C. Satchwell and J. Smith (2009), *Improving Learning in College. Rethinking Literacies across the Curriculum*, London: Routledge.

Jakobson, R. (1960), 'Closing statement: linguistics and poetics', in. T. A. Sebeok (ed.), *Style in Language*, Cambridge, MA: MIT Press, pp. 350–77.

Janks, H. (2010), *Literacy and Power*, London: Routledge.

Jenkins, H. (2006), *Convergence Culture. Where Old and New Media Collide*, New York: New York University Press.

Jewitt, C. (ed.) (2009), *The Routledge Handbook of Multimodal Analysis*, London: Routledge.

Johnson, S. (2005), *Spelling Trouble? Language, Ideology and the Reform of German Orthography*, Bristol: Multilingual Matters.

Johnson, A. (2011), *A Brief History of Diaries: From Pepys to Blogs*, London: Hesperus Press Ltd.

Johnstone, B. (2000), *Qualitative Methods in Sociolinguistics*, New York: Sage.

Jones, J. (2008), 'Patterns of revision in online writing: a study of Wikipedia's featured articles', *Written Communication*, 25: 2, 262–89.

Jones, K. (2000), 'Becoming just another alphanumeric code: farmers' encounters with the literacy and discourse practices of agricultural bureaucracy at the livestock auction', in

D. Barton, M. Hamilton and R. Ivaniç (eds), *Situated Literacies*, London: Routledge, pp. 70–90.

Joseph, J. E. (2001), 'Saussurean tradition and sociolinguistics', in. R. Mesthrie (ed.), *Concise Encyclopedia of Sociolinguistics*, Oxford/Amsterdam/New York: Elsevier, pp. 73–80.

Juffermans, K. (2010), *Local Languaging. Literacy Products and Practices in Gambian Society*, PhD thesis, Tilburg University, Netherlands.

Kalman, J. (1999), *Writing on the Plaza*, Creskill, NJ: Hampton Press.

Kaplan, R. (1966), 'Cultural thought patterns in intercultural education', *Language Learning*, 16: 1, 1–20.

Kell, C. (1996), 'Moment by moment: context and crossings in the study of literacy in social practice', Unpublished PhD thesis.

Kell, C. (2010), 'Ethnographic studies and adult literacy policy in South Africa', in C. Coffin, T. Lillis and K. O'Halloran (eds), *Applied Linguistics Methods. A Reader*, London: Routledge, pp. 216–33.

Kiesling, S. F. (2011), *Linguistic Variation and Change*, Edinburgh: Edinburgh University Press.

Kinneavy, J. L. (1971), *A Theory of Discourse*, Englewood Cliffs, NJ: Prentice-Hall International.

Kirkup, G. (2010), 'Academic blogging: academic practice and academic identity', *London Review of Education*, 8: 1, 75–84.

Kress, G. (1996), 'Representational resources and the production of subjectivity: questions for the theoretical development of Critical Discourse Analysis in a multicultural society', in R. Caldas-Coulthard and M. Coulthard (eds), *Texts and Practices*, London: Routledge, pp. 15–31.

Kress, G. (2009), 'What is mode?', in C. Jewitt (ed.), *The Routledge Handbook of Multimodal Analysis*, London: Routledge, pp. 54–67.

Kress, G. (2010), *Multimodality: A Social Semiotic Approach to Contemporary Communication*, London: Routledge.

Kress, G. and T. van Leeuwen (1996), *Reading Images: The Grammar of Visual Design*, London: Routledge.

Kress, G., J. Ogborn and I. Martins (1998), 'A satellite view of language: some lessons from science classrooms', *Language Awareness*, 7: 2/3, 69–89.

Kress, G and T. van Leeuwen (2001), *Multimodal Discourse. The Modes and Media of Contemporary Discourse*, London: Arnold.

Kristeva, J. (ed.) (1986), 'Word, dialogue and novel', in Tori Moi (ed.), *The Kristeva Reader*, Oxford: Blackwell, pp. 34–61.

Kubota, R. (2010), 'Cross-cultural perspectives on writing: contrastive rhetoric', in N. H. Hornberger and S. L. McKay (eds), *Sociolinguistics and Language Education*, Bristol: Multilingual Matters, pp. 265–89.

Labov, W. (1966), *The Social Stratification of English in New York City*, Washington, DC: Centre for Applied Linguistics.

Labov, W. [1969] (1970), 'The logic of nonstandard English', in F. Williams (ed.), *Language and Poverty*, Chicago: Markham, pp. 153–89.

Labov, W. (1972), *Sociolinguistic Patterns*, Philadelphia: University of Pennsylvania Press.

Lakoff, G. and M. Johnson (1980), *Metaphors We Live By*, Chicago: University of Chicago Press.

Lam, W. S. E. (2000), 'Literacy and the design of the self: a case study of a teenager writing on the internet', *TESOL Quarterly*, 34: 457–82.

Laqueur, T. (1976), *Religion and Respectability: Sunday Schools and Working Class Culture, 1780–1850*, New Haven, CT: Yale University Press.

Latour, B. (1987), *Science in Action: How to Follow Scientists and Engineers through Society*, Milton Keynes: Open University Press.

Lea, M. R. and S. Jones (2011), 'Digital Literacies in Higher Education: Exploring Textual and Technological Practice', *Studies in Higher Education*, 36: 4, 377–93.

Lea, M. R. and B. Street (1998), 'Student writing in higher education: an academic literacies approach', *Studies in Higher Education*, 23: 2, 157–72.

Leander, K. and J. Loworn (2006), 'Literacy networks: following the circulation of texts, bodies and objects in the schooling and online gaming of one youth', *Cognition and Instruction*, 24: 3, 291–340.

Lee, C. K. M. (2007), 'Affordances and text-making practices in online instant messaging', *Written Communication*, 24: 3, 223–49.

Lemke, J. (1998), 'Multiplying meaning: visual and verbal semiotics in scientific text', in. J. R. Martin and R. Veel (eds), *Reading Science*, London: Routledge, pp. 87–113.

Lenhart, A., M. Madden, R. Rankin Macgill and A. Smith (2007), '1PEW internet project data memo', available online at Teens and Social Media http://www.inbox.com/homepage .aspx?tbid=80275&lng=en (accessed 25 Aug 2011).

Leont'ev, A. N. (1981), 'The problems of activity in psychology', in J. Wertsch, *The Concept of Activity in Soviet Psychology*, Armonk, NY: M. E. Sharpe, pp. 37–71.

Lewis, P. (2001), 'Missionaries and language', in R. Mesthrie (ed.), *Concise Encyclopedia of Sociolinguistics*, Oxford/Amsterdam/New York: Elsevier, pp. 509–12.

Lillis, T. (1996), 'Building on collective experience in developing bilingualism', *Multicultural Teaching*, 14: 3, 26–30.

Lillis, T. (2001), *Student Writing: Access, Regulation, Desire*, London: Routledge.

Lillis, T. (2003), 'An "academic literacies" approach to student writing in higher education: drawing on Bakhtin to move from "critique" to "design"', *Language and Education*, 17: 3, 192–207.

Lillis, T. (2006), 'Readers and writers', in S. Goodman and K. O'Halloran (eds), *The Art of English: Literary Creativity*, Basingstoke: Palgrave Macmillan, pp. 414–62.

Lillis, T. (2009), 'Bringing writers' voices to writing research: talk around texts', in A. Carter, T. Lillis and S. Parkin (eds) (2009), *Why Writing Matters: Issues of Access and Identity in Writing Research and Pedagogy*, Amsterdam: Benjamins, pp. 169–87.

Lillis, T. (2011), 'Legitimising dialogue as textual and ideological goal in academic writing for assessment and publication', *Arts and Humanities in Higher Education*, 10: 4, 401–32.

Lillis, T. (2012), 'Economies of signs in writing for academic publication: the case of English medium "national" journals', *Journal of Advanced Composition*, 695–722.

Lillis, T. and C. McKinney (2003), *Analysing Language in Context*, Stoke on Trent: Trentham Books

Lillis, T. and M. J. Curry (2010), *Academic Writing in a Global Context*, London: Routledge.

Lillis, T. and L. Rai (2011), 'A case study of a research-based collaboration around writing in social work', *Across the Disciplines*, 8: 3, available at http://wac.colostate.edu/atd/clil/ lillis-rai.cfm (accessed 28 Oct. 2011).

Lillis, T. and L. Rai (2012), 'Quelle relation entre l'écrit académique et l'écrit professionnel? Une étude de cas dans le domaine du travail social', *Pratiques*, 153/4: 51–70.

Lillis, T. and M. Scott (eds) (2007), 'New directions in academic literacies', Special Issue of *Journal of Applied Linguistics*, 4: 1.

Linell, P. (1998), *Approaching Dialogue*, Amsterdam: John Benjamins.

Lorca, F. (1933), *Teoría y juego del duende*, available at http://www.lainsignia.org/200i/ octubre/cul_068.htm (accessed 29 Feb. 2012).

Lorés-Sanz, R., P. Mur-Dueñas and E. Lafuente-Millán (eds) (2010), *Constructing Interpersonality. Multiple Perspectives on Written Academic Genres*, Newcastle: Cambridge Scholars Publishing.

Lu, M. (1994), 'Professing multiculturalism: the politics of style in the contact zone', *College Composition and Communication*, 45: 4, 442–58.

Lucas, C. (ed.) (2001), *The Sociolinguistics of Sign Languages*, Cambridge: Cambridge University Press.

Lunsford, A. and J. Ruszkiewicz (1999), *Everything's an Argument*, Boston/New York: Bedford/St Martins.

Lynam, E. W. (1969), *The Irish Character in Print: 1571–1923*, New York: Barnes and Noble. (First printed as Oxford University Press offprint 1924 in *Transactions of the Bibliographical Society*, 4th Series, Vol. IV, No. 4, March 1924.)

Lyons, M. (ed.) (2007), *Ordinary Writings, Personal Narratives: Writing Practices in 19th and 20th Century Europe*, Berne: Peter-Lang.

Malinowski, B. (1923), 'The problem of meaning in primitive languages', in C. K. Ogden and I. A. Richards (eds), *The Meaning of Meaning*, London: Routledge and Kegan Paul, pp. 146–52.

Malinowski, B. (1935), *Coral Gardens and Their Magic,* vol. 2, London: Allen and Unwin.

Mallon, T. (1984), *A Book of One's Own: People and Their Diaries*, New York: Ticknor and Fields.

Marsh, J., G. Brooks, J. Hughes, L. Ritchie, S. Roberts and K. Wright (2005), *Digital Beginnings: Young Children's Use of Popular Culture, Media and New Technologies*, Report of the 'Young Children's Use of Popular Culture, Media and New Technologies' Study, funded by BBC Worldwide and the Esmée Fairbairn Foundation.

Martin, J. (1984), 'Language, register, and genre', in F. Christie (ed.), *Children Writing: Reader*, Geelong: Deakin University Press, pp. 21–9.

Martin, J. (2010), 'Language, register and genre', in C. Coffin, K. O'Halloran and T. Lillis (eds), *Applied Linguistics Methods. A Reader*, London: Routledge, pp. 12–32.

Matthiessen, C. and M. A. K. Halliday (1997), *Systemic Functional Grammar: A First Step into the Theory*, Sydney: Macquarie University.

Maybin, J. (2006), *Children's Voices. Talk, Knowledge and Identity*, Basingstoke: Palgrave Macmillan.

Maybin, J. (2011), 'Intimate strangers', in J. Swann, R. Pope and R. Carter (eds), *Creativity in Language and Literature*, Basingstoke: Palgrave Macmillan, pp. 129–40.

Maybin, J. and J. Swann (eds) (2010), *The Routledge Companion to English Language Studies*, Abingdon: Routledge.

Mbodj-Pouye, A. (2010), 'Keeping a notebook in rural Mali: a practice in the making', in D. Barton and U. Papen (eds), *The Anthropology of Writing. Understanding Textually-Mediated Worlds*, London: Continuum, pp. 126–44.

Mbodj-Pouye, A. and C. van den Avenne (2007), 'C'est bambara et français mélangés. Analyser des écrits plurilingues a partir du cas de cahiers villageois recueillis au Mali', *Langage et société*, 120: 99–127.

Menezes de Souza, L. M. (2003), 'Literacy and dreamspace: multimodal texts in a Brazilian indigenous community', in. S. Goodman et al. (eds), *Language Literacy and Education: A Reader*, Stoke on Trent: Trentham Books, pp. 221–30.

Mesthrie, R. (2001a), 'Sociolinguistic variation', in R. Mesthrie (ed.), *Concise Encyclopedia of Sociolinguistics*, Oxford/ Amsterdam/New York: Elsevier, pp. 377–89.

Mesthrie, R. (ed.) (2001b), *Concise Encyclopedia of Sociolinguistics*, Oxford/ Amsterdam/New York: Elsevier.

Mesthrie, R., J. Swann, A. Deumert and W. L. Leap (2009), *Introducing Sociolinguistics*, Edinburgh: Edinburgh University Press.

Meyerhoff, M. (2006), *Introducing Sociolinguistics*, London: Routledge/Taylor and Francis.

Meyerhoff, M. and E. Schleef (eds) (2010), *The Routledge Sociolinguistics Reader*, London: Routledge.

Michaels, S. (1981), '"Sharing time": children's narrative styles and differential access to literacy', *Language in Society*, 10: 336–56.

Mignolo, W. D. (1996), 'Linguistic maps, literary geographies, and cultural landscapes: languages, languaging and (trans)nationalism', *Modern Language Quarterly*, 57: 2, 181–96.

Miller, C. (1984), 'Genre as social action', *Quarterly Journal of Speech*, 70: 2, 151–67.

Miller, C. (2001), 'Speech and writing', in R. Mesthrie (ed.), *Concise Encyclopedia of Sociolinguistics*, Oxford/ Amsterdam/New York: Elsevier, pp. 270–6.

Miller, C. and D. Shepherd (2004), 'Blogging as social action: a genre analysis of the weblog: http://blog.lib.umn.edu/blogosphere/ blogging_as_social_action_a_genre_analysis_of_the_weblog.html (accessed 18 Aug. 2011).

Milroy, L. (1987), *Language and Social Networks*, 2nd edn, Oxford: Basil Blackwell.

Milroy, L. and M. Gordon (2003), *Sociolinguistics: Method and Interpretation*, Oxford: Blackwell.

Moje, E. B. and A. Luke (2009), 'Literacy and identity: examining the metaphors in history and contemporary research', *Reading Research Quarterly*, 44: 4, 415–37.

Moll, L., C. Amanti, D. Neff and N. Gonzalez (1992), 'Funds of knowledge for teaching: using a qualitative approach to connect homes and classrooms', *Theory into Practice*, 31: 2, 132–41.

Møller, J. S. and J. N. Jørgensen (2009), 'From language to languaging: changing relations between humans and linguistic features', *Acta Linguistica Hafniensia*, 41: 143–66.

Moon, R. (2007), 'Sinclair, lexicography, and the Cobuild Project. The application of theory', *International Journal of Corpus Linguistics*, 12: 2, 159–81.

Moore, R. E. (2003), 'From genericide to viral marketing: on "brand"', *Language and Communication*, 23: 331–57.

Moore, T. (2010), 'The "processes" of learning: on the use of Halliday's transitivity in academic skills advising', in C. Coffin, T. Lillis and K. O'Halloran (eds), *Applied Linguistics Methods. A Reader*, London: Routledge, pp. 52–71.

Moss, G. (2001), 'On literacy and the social organisation of knowledge inside and outside school', *Language and Education*, 15: 2 and 3, 146–61.

Mugglestone, L. C. (2001), 'Academies: dictionaries and standards', in R. Mesthrie (ed.), *Concise Encyclopedia of Sociolinguistics*, Oxford/Amsterdam/New York: Elsevier, pp. 615–16.

Nabi, R. (forthcoming), *'Hidden Literacies': Case Studies of Literacy and Numeracy Practices in Pakistan*.

Negra, D. (ed.) (2006), *The Irish in Us: Irishness, Performativity and Popular Culture*, Durham, NC: Duke University Press.

Nomdo, G. (2006), 'Identity, power and discourse: the socio-political self-representations of successful "black students"', in L. Thesen and E. van Pletzen (eds), *Academic Literacy and the Languages of Change*, London: Continuum, pp. 180–206.

Norton, B. (2000), *Identity and Language Learning: Gender, Ethnicity and Educational Change*, London: Longman.

Nye, A. (1990), *Words of Power*, New York/London: Routledge.

Ochs, E. (1979), 'Transcription as theory', in E. Ochs and B. B. Schieffelin (eds), *Developmental Pragmatics*, New York: Academic Press, pp. 43–72.

O'Halloran, K. (2009), 'Historical changes in the semiotic landscape. From calculation to computation', in C. Jewitt (ed.), *The Routledge Handbook of Multimodal Analysis*, London: Routledge, pp. 98–113.

Olson, D. (1977), 'From utterance to text: the bias of language in speech and writing', *Harvard Educational Review*, 47: 3, 267–333.

Olson, D. (1994), *The World on Paper*, Cambridge: Cambridge University Press.

Olson, D. [1996] (2003), 'Literate mentalities: literacy, consciousness of language and modes of thought', in S. Goodman et al. (eds), *Language Literacy and Education: A Reader*, Stoke on Trent: Trentham Books, pp. 67–76.

Ong, W. (1982), *Orality and Literacy: The Technologizing of the World*, London: Routledge.

Orbach, B. Y. (2002), 'The law and economics of creativity at the workplace: Discussion Paper 356', Harvard Law School, John M. Olin Center for Law, Economics and Business, available at http://lsr.nellco.org/harvard_olin/356 (accessed 17 June 2009)

Ormerod, F. and R. Ivanič (2002), 'Materiality in children's meaning-making practices', *Visual Communication*, 1: 1, 65–91.

Pahl, K. and J. Rowsell (2010), *Artifactual Literacy: Every Object Tells a Story*, New York: Teachers College Press.

Papen, U. (2005), *Adult Literacy as Social Practice: More Than Skills*, London: Routledge.

Papen, U. (2007), *Literacy and Globalization: Reading and Writing in Times of Social and Cultural Change*, London: Routledge.

Papen, U. (2010), 'Writing in healthcare contexts: patients, power and medical knowledge', in D. Barton and U. Papen (eds), *The Anthropology of Writing. Understanding Textually-Mediated Worlds*, London: Continuum, pp. 145–68.

Papen, U. (2012), 'Commercial discourses, gentrification and citizens' protest: the linguistic landscape of Prenzlauer Berg, Berlin', *Journal of Sociolinguistics,* 16: 1, 56–80.

Papen, U. and K. Tusting (2008), 'Creativity in everyday literacy practices: the contribution of an ethnographic approach', *Literacy and Numeracy Studies*, 16: 1, 5–25.

Paulston, C. B. and G. R. Tucker (eds) (2003), *Sociolinguistics. The Essential Readings*, Oxford: Blackwell.

Pelli, D. G. and C. Bigelow (2009a), 'A writing revolution', available at http://seedmagazine.com/content/article/a_writing_revolution/ (accessed 20 Nov. 2011).

Pelli, D. G. and C. Bigelow (2009b), 'Sources online supplement for "A Writing Revolution"', *Seed magazine*, available at http://seedmagazine.com/supplementary/a_writing_revolution/pelli_bigelow_sources.pdf (accessed 20 Nov. 2011).

Petraglia, J. (ed.) (1995), *Reconceiving Writing, Rethinking Writing Instruction*, Mahwah, NJ: Lawrence Erlbaum.

Pietikäinen, S. and H. Kelly-Holmes (2011), 'The local political economy of languages in a Sámi tourism destination: authenticity and mobility in the labelling of souvenirs, *Journal of Sociolinguistics*, 15: 3, 323–46.

Pontille, D. (2010), 'Updating a biomedical database: writing, reading and invisible contribution', in D. Barton and U. Papen (eds), *The Anthropology of Writing*, London: Continuum, pp. 47–66.

Pope, R. (2003), 'Re-writing texts, re-constructing the subject: work as play on the critical-creative interface', in T. Agathocleous and A. Dean (eds), *Teaching Literature: A Companion*, Basingstoke: Palgrave Macmillan, pp. 105–24.

Pope, R. (2004), *Creativity Theory, History, Practice*, London/New York: Routledge.

Pratt, C. and C. Pratt (1995), 'Comparative content analysis of food and nutrition advertisements, *Ebony, Essence* and *Ladies' Home Journal*', *Journal of Nutrition Education*, 27: 1, 11–18.

Prensky, M. (2001), 'Digital natives, digital immigrants', *On the Horizon*, NCB University Press, 9: 5, available at http://www.marcprensky.com/writing/Prensky%20-%20Digital%20Natives,%20Digital%20Immigrants%20-%20Part21.pdf (accessed 20 Jan. 2011).

Prinsloo, M. and M. Breier (eds) (1996), *The Social Uses of Literacy*, Cape Town and Amsterdam: Sached Books and John Benjamin.

Prior, P. (1998), *Writing/Disciplinarity*, Mahwah, NJ: Lawrence Erlbaum.

Quispe-Agnoli, R. (2010), 'Spanish scripts colonize the image: Inca visual rhetorics', in D. Baca and V. Villanueva (eds), *Rhetorics of the Americas: 3114 BCE to 2012 CE*, (Studies of the Americas Series), New York: Palgrave Macmillan, pp. 41–61.

Rai, L. (2004), 'Exploring literacy in social work education: a social practices approach to student writing', *Social Work Education*, 23: 2, 149–62.

Rampton, B. (1995), *Crossing: Language and Ethnicity among Adolescents*, London: Longman.

Rampton, B. (1998), 'Speech community', in J. Verschueren, J. O. Östman, J. Blommaert and C. Bulcarn (eds), *Handbook of Pragmatics*, Amsterdam: John Benjamins, pp. 1–30.

Rampton, B. (2007), 'Neo-Hymesian linguistic ethnography in the United Kingdom', *Journal of Sociolinguistics*, 11: 5, 584–607.

Rampton, B. (2010), 'Linguistic ethnography, interactional sociolinguistics and the study of identities', in C. Coffin et al. (eds), *Applied Linguistics Methods. A Reader*, London: Routledge, pp. 234–50.

Rampton, B., K. Tusting, J. Maybin, R. Barwell, A. Creese and V. Lytra (2004), 'UK linguistic ethnography: a discussion paper', retrieved 14 December 2007, from http://www.lancs.ac.uk/fss/organisations/lingethn/documents/

Rasmussen, B. B. (2010), '"Attended with great inconveniences": slave literacy and the 1740 South Carolina Negro Act', *Publications of Modern Language Association*, 125: 1, 201–3.

Reddy, M. J. (1979), 'The conduit metaphor – a case of conflict in our language about language', in A. Orrtony (ed.), *Metaphor and Thought*, Cambridge: Cambridge University Press, pp. 284–310.

Reuter, Y. and D. Lahanier-Reuter (2007), 'Presentation of a few concepts for analyzing writing in relation to academic disciplines', *L1 Educational Studies in Language and Literature*, 7: 5.

Richardson, W. (2006), *Blogs, Wikis, Podcasts and Other Powerful Web Tools for Classrooms*, Thousand Oaks, CA: Corwin Press.

Richardson, E. (2003), *African American Literacies*, London: Routledge.

Richardson, W. (2006), *Blogs, Wikis, Podcasts and Other Powerful Webtools for Classrooms*, Thousand Oaks, CA: Crown Press/Sage.

Roberts, C. (1997), 'Transcribing talk: issues of representation', *TESOL Quarterly*, 31: 1, 167–72.

Roberts, C. and B. Street (1997), 'Spoken and written language', in F. Coulmas (ed.), *The Handbook of Sociolinguistics*, Oxford: Blackwell, pp. 168–86.

Robinson-Pant, A. (2001), *Why Eat Green Cucumber at the Time of Dying? Exploring the Link between Women's Literacy and Development*, Hamburg: UNESCO Institute for Education.

Rockhill, K. (1994), 'Gender, language and the politics of literacy', in J. Maybin (ed.), *Language and Literacy in Social Practice*, Bristol: Multilingual Matters, pp. 233–51.

Romaine, S. (2000), *Language in Society. An Introduction to Sociolinguistics*, Oxford: Oxford University Press.

Rowsell, J. and K. Pahl (2007), 'Sedimented identities in texts: instances of practice', *Reading Research Quarterly*, 42: 3, 388–401.

Russell, D. (1997), 'Rethinking genre in school and society: an activity theory analysis', *Written Communication*, 14: 504–54.

Sarangi, S. and C. Candlin (eds) (2000), *Sociolinguistics and Social Theory*, Harlow: Pearson Educational Limited.

Saussaure, F. de [1916] (1959), *Course in General Linguistics*, ed. C. Bally and A. Sechehaye, trans. W. Baskin, New York: McGraw Hill.

Saxena, M. (1991), 'Literacies among Panjabis in Southall', in M. Hamilton, D. Barton and R. Ivanič (eds), *Worlds of Literacy*, Clevedon: Multilingual Matters, pp. 185–214.

Schiller, A. (2008), *Aspects of Cohesion in Web Site Translation: A Translator's Perspective*, (unpublished PhD thesis), Dublin: Dublin City University.

Scollon, R. and S. B. K. Scollon (1981), *Narrative, Literacy and Face in Interethnic Communication*, Norwood, NJ: Ablex.

Scollon, R. and S. Scollon (2003), *Discourses in Place. Language in the Material World*, London: Routledge.

Scott, M. (forthcoming), '"Error" or ghost text? Reading, ethnopoetics, and knowledge making', in L. Thesen and L. Cooper (eds), *Risk, Writing Research and Knowledge Making*, Bristol: Multilingual Matters.

Scribner, S. and M. Cole (1981), *The Psychology of Literacy*, Cambridge, MA: Harvard University Press.

Sebba, M. (2001), 'Orthography', in R. Mesthrie (ed.), *Concise Encyclopedia of Sociolinguistics*, Oxford/Amsterdam/New York: Elsevier, pp. 669–72.

Sebba, M. (2007), *Spelling and Society*, Cambridge: Cambridge University Press.

Sebba, M. (2009), 'Sociolinguistic approaches to writing systems research, *Writing Systems Research*, 1: 1, 35–49.

Sebba, M., S. Mahootian and C. Jonsson (2012), *Language Mixing and Code-Switching in Writing. Approaches to Mixed-Language Written Discourse*, London: Routledge.

Shannon, C. E. and W. Weaver (1949), *A Mathematical Model of Communication*, Urbana: University of Illinois Press.

Shelley, P. B. (1821), *A Defence of Poetry*, available at http://www.gutenberg.org/ebooks/5428 (accessed 2 Sept. 2012).

Shi, L. (2002), 'How western-trained Chinese TESOL professionals publish in their home environment', *TESOL Quarterly*, 36: 4, 625–34.

Shklovsky, V. [1925] (1990), *Theory of Prose*, trans. B. Sher, Urbana: Dalkey Archive Press, Illinois State University.

Shohamy, E. and D. Gorter (eds) (2009), *Linguistic Landscape. Expanding the Scenery*, London/New York: Routledge.

Short, M. (1996), *Exploring the Language of Poems, Plays and Prose*, London: Longman.

Shuy, R. W. (2003), 'A brief history of American sociolinguistics 1949–1989', in C. B. Paulston and G. R. Tucker (eds), *Sociolinguistics. The Essential Readings*, Oxford: Blackwell, pp. 4–16.

Silverstein, M. (1998), 'Contemporary transformations of local linguistic communities', *Annual Review of Anthropology*, 27: 401–26.

Silverstein, M. and G. Urban (eds) (1996), *Natural Histories of Discourse*, Chicago: University of Chicago Press.

Sinor, J. (2002), *The Extraordinary Work of Ordinary Writing*, Iowa City: University of Iowa Press.

Skutnabb-Kangas, T. (2000), *Linguistic Genocide in Education – or Worldwide Diversity and Human Rights?*, Mahwah, NJ: Lawrence Erlbaum,.

Smart, G. (2006), *Writing the Economy: Activity, Genre and Technology in the World of Banking*, London: Equinox.

Smith. D. (2005), *Institutional Ethnography*, New York/Oxford: Altamira Press.

Smitherman, G. (2000), *Talkin That Talk. Language Culture and Education in African America*, London/New York: Routledge.

Sousa Santos, B. (1994), *Pela mão de Alice: o social eo político na pós-modernidade*, Porto: Edico'es Afrontamento.

Spellmeyer, K. (1989), 'A common ground: The essay in the academy', *College English* 51(3): 262–76.

Spender, D. (1989), *The Writing or the Sex or Why You Don't Have to Read Women's Writing to Know It's No Good*, Athene Series, Oxford/Amsterdam/New York: Elsevier.

Stein, P. (2008), *Multimodal Pedagogies in Diverse Classrooms: Rights, Representations and Resources*, London: Routledge.

Stockwell, P. (2002), *Sociolinguistics. A Resource Book for Students*, London: Routledge.

Street, B. (1984), *Literacy in Theory and Practice*, Cambridge: Cambridge University Press.

Street, B. (1995), *Social Literacies*, London: Longman.

Street, B. (2001a), 'Introduction', in B. Street (ed.), *Literacy and Development. Ethnographic Perspectives*, London: Routledge, pp. 1–17.

Street, B. (ed.) (2001b), *Literacy and Development. Ethnographic Perspectives*, London: Routledge.

Street, B. (2003), 'The implications of "New Literacy Studies" for literacy education', in S. Goodman et al. (eds), *Language Literacy and Education: A Reader*, Stoke on Trent: Trentham Books, pp. 77–88.

Street, B. (2010), 'Adopting an ethnographic perspective in research and pedagogy', in C. Coffin et al. (eds), *Applied Linguistics Methods. A Reader*, London: Routledge, pp. 201–15.

Street, B. and C. Leung (2010), Sociolinguistics, language teaching and New Literacy Studies', in N. H. Hornberger and S. L. McKay (eds), *Sociolinguistics and Language Education*, Bristol: Multilingual Matters, pp. 290–316.

Stubbs, M. (1980), *Language and Literacy. The Sociolinguistics of Reading and Writing*, London: Routledge and Kegan Paul.

Swales, J. (1990), *Genre Analysis*, Cambridge: Cambridge University Press.

Swales, J. (2004), *Research Genres: Explorations and Applications*, Cambridge: Cambridge University Press.

Swales, J. (2009), 'Worlds of genre – metaphors of genre', in C. Bazerman et al. (eds), *Genre in a Changing World*. The WAC Clearinghouse wac.colostate.edu, Fort Collins, CO: Parlor Press, pp. 3–16.

Swann, J. and D. Allington (2009), 'Reading groups and the language of literary texts: a case study in social reading', in D. Allington and J. Swann (eds), *Literary Reading as Social Practice*. Special Issue of *Language and Literature*, 18: 3, 247–64.

Swann, J., A. Deumert, T. Lillis and R. Mesthrie (2004), *A Dictionary of Sociolinguistics*, Edinburgh: Edinburgh University Press.

Swann, J., R. Pope and R. Carter (eds) (2011), *Creativity in Language and Literature*, Basingstoke: Palgrave Macmillan.

Tagg, C. (2011), 'Wot did he say or could u not c him 4 dust? Written and spoken creativity in text messaging', in C. M. L. Ho, K. T. Anderson and A. P. Leong (eds), *Transforming Literacies and Language: Multimodality and Literacy in the New Media Age*, London: Continuum, pp. 223–36.

Tannen, D. (2005), *Conversational Style. Analyzing Talk Among Friends*, 2nd edn, Oxford: Oxford University Press.

Taylor, G. and T. Chen (1991), 'Linguistic, cultural, and subcultural issues', *Applied Linguistics*, 12: 319–36.

Texier, P., P. Guillaume, J. Parkington, J-P. Rigauda, C. Poggenpoel, C. Miller, C. Tribolod, C. Cartwright, A. Coudenneau, R. Klein, T. Steele and C. Vernai (2009), 'A Howiesons Poort tradition of engraving ostrich eggshell containers dated to 60,000 years ago at Diepkloof Rock Shelter, South Africa', *Proceedings of the National Academy of Sciences of the USA (PNAS)*. available at http://www.pnas.org/content/early/2010/02/17/0913047107.full.pdf+html (accessed Sept. 2010).

Thesen, L. and E. van Pletzen (eds) (2006), *Academic Literacy and the Languages of Change*, London: Continuum.

Thesen, L. and L. Cooper (eds) (forthcoming), *Risk, Writing Research and Knowledge Making*, Bristol: Multilingual Matters.

Threadgold, T. (2001), 'Genre', in R. Mesthrie (ed.), *Concise Encyclopedia of Sociolinguistics*, Oxford/Amsterdam/New York: Elsevier, pp. 235–9.

Toulmin, S. (1958), *The Uses of Argument*, Cambridge: Cambridge University Press.

Trousdale, G. (2010), *An Introduction to English Sociolinguistics*, Edinburgh: Edinburgh University Press.

Trudgill, P. [1974, 1983, 1995] (2002), *Sociolinguistics: An Introduction to Language and Society*, Harmondsworth: Penguin.

Trudgill, P. and J. Cheshire (1998a), *The Sociolinguistics Reader: Vol. 1. Multilingualism and Variation*, London: Edward Arnold.

Trudgill, P. and J. Cheshire (1998b), *The Sociolinguistics Reader: Vol. 2. Gender and Discourse*, London: Edward Arnold.

Turner, J. (2011), *Language in the Academy. Cultural Reflexivity and Intercultural Dynamics*, Bristol: Multilingual Matters.

UNESCO (2006), *Education for All. Literacy for Life*, UNESCO: Paris.

UNESCO (2011), Factsheets, available at http://www.uis.unesco.org/FactSheets/Documents/FS16-2011-Literacy-EN.pdf (accessed 18 Nov. 2011).

van Eemeren, F. H. and Grootendorst, R. (1984), *Speech Acts in Argumentative Discussions*, Dordrecht: Foris.

Velasco, P. (2011), *NO nos representan. El manifiesto de los indignados en 25 propuestas*, Madrid: Ediciones Planeta.

Vertovec, S. (2007), 'Super-diversity and its implications', *Ethnic and Racial Studies*, 29: 6, 1024–54.

Vold Lexander, K. (2011), 'Texting and African language literacy', *New Media and Society*, 13: 3, 427–43.

Wales, K. (2001), *A Dictionary of Stylistics*, 2nd edn, London: Longman.

Wallerstein, I. (1991), *Geopolitics and Geoculture*, Cambridge: Cambridge University Press.

Walsh, L. (2009), 'Marking territory: legislated genres, stakeholder beliefs and the possibilities for common ground in the Mexican wolf blue range reintroduction project', *Written Communication*, 26: 2, 115–53.

Weedon, C. (1987), *Feminist Practice and Poststructuralist Theory*, Oxford: Basil Blackwell.

Weinrich, U., W. Labov and M. Herzog (1968), 'Empirical foundations for a theory of change', in W. Lehman and Y. Malkiel (eds), *Directions for Historical Linguistics*, Austin: University of Texas Press, pp. 95–188.

Wenger, E. (1998), *Communities of Practice*, Cambridge: Cambridge University Press.

Williams, B. Y. (2009), *Shimmering Literacies: Popular Culture and Reading and Writing Online*, New York: Peter Lang.

Williams, E. (2006), *Bridges and Barriers: Language in African Education and Development*, Manchester: St Jerome.

Williams, V. and G. J. White (1988), *Adult Education and Social Purpose: History of the Workers' Educational Association, Eastern District, 1913–88*, Brighton: Graham-Cameron Illustration.

Wilson, A. (2000), 'There's no escape from third-space theory – borderland discourse and the in-between literacies of prison', in D. Barton, M. Hamilton and R. Ivanič (eds), *Situated Literacies*, London: Routledge, pp. 54–69.

Wilson, A. (2003), 'Researching in the third space; locating, claiming and valuing the research domain', in S. Goodman et al. (eds), *Language Literacy and Education: A Reader*, Stoke on Trent: Trentham Books, pp. 293–307.

Wilson, A. (2010), 'Reading the signs: prison officers' mindful diagnosis of potential self-harm and suicide', in M. Büscher, D. Goodwin and J. Mesman (eds), *Ethnographies of Diagnostic Work: Dimensions of Transformative Practice*, Basingstoke: Palgrave Macmillan, pp. 17–34.

Young, V. A. (2007), *Your Average Nigga: Performing Race, Literacy, and Masculinity*, Detroit: Wayne State University Press.

Index